CONTEMPORARY REVIEWS OF ROMANTIC POETRY

Contemporary Reviews of Romantic Poetry

EDITED BY

JOHN WAIN

Essay Index Reprint Series

 BOOKS FOR LIBRARIES PRESS
FREEPORT, NEW YORK

First published 1953 by George G. Harrap & Co. Ltd.
as part of the Life, Literature, and Thought Library

Reprinted 1969 by arrangement

INTERNATIONAL STANDARD BOOK NUMBER:
0-8369-0033-2

LIBRARY OF CONGRESS CATALOG CARD NUMBER:
75-76920

PRINTED IN THE UNITED STATES OF AMERICA
BY
NEW WORLD BOOK MANUFACTURING CO., INC.
HALLANDALE, FLORIDA 33009

FOREWORD

THIS series aims at presenting in an attractive form English texts which have not only intrinsic merit as literature, but which are also valuable as manifestations of the spirit of the age in which they were written. The plan was inspired by the desire to break away from the usual annotated edition of English classics and to provide a series of books illustrating some of the chief developments in English civilization since the Middle Ages. Each volume will have a substantial introduction, which will relate the author to the main currents of contemporary life and thought, and which will be an important part of the book. Notes, where given, will be brief, stimulating, and designed to encourage the spirit of research in the student. It is believed that these books will be of especial value to students in universities and the upper forms of schools, and that they will also appeal very much to the general reader.

VIVIAN DE SOLA PINTO

General Editor,
Life, Literature
And Thought Library

PREFACE

THE intention governing the selection of the texts included in this book has been to provide supplementary reading in the period 1800–30, for the student who is familiar with the best-known poets and critics of the time, but not with the body of anonymous criticism that accompanied their work. For this reason, essays from the pens of such well-known figures as Hazlitt, De Quincey, and Lamb have, with two exceptions, been excluded, as the tastes and methods of these writers can be studied elsewhere. The selection has, furthermore, been confined to two Reviews, the *Edinburgh* and the *Quarterly*, and one magazine, *Blackwood's*; to do this is to risk fostering the absurd impression that there were no others of importance, but to open the volume to all the periodical literature of these years would have resulted in an atmosphere of unreality; a collection of star turns, giving no impression of what periodical criticism was really *like*.

In view of the audience for which the book is intended, a good deal of space has been given to well-known extracts; after some hesitation, I have even reprinted essays which have appeared in such valuable anthologies as Brimley Johnson's *Famous Reviews* and Professor Nichol Smith's *Jeffrey's Literary Criticism*, since neither of these books is as widely read as it deserves.

J.W.

CONTENTS

INTRODUCTION

WHAT IS A CRITIC?

OF all forms of the literary art, Criticism is the least self-sufficient, the easiest to retard, to discourage, to snuff out altogether. And there is a simple reason why this should be so. For criticism, unlike poetry or fiction, is not its own reward. The exercise of the creative imagination, though arduous, is in itself so rich an experience that, come what may, its devotees will practise it; there will always be some one composing a lyric poem or constructing a serious novel, even in an age when these things bring their authors no reward—or only the inverted rewards of poverty and loneliness, the twin campaign medals that glitter on the lapel of the serious author. The artist is an artist even though there is no one to welcome his work. But the critic, on the other hand, cannot be said to *be* a critic, in the full meaning of the word, until his work has reached an audience. For, by the very nature of his function, he is out to persuade; he stands in the market-place where ideas are bought and sold, shouting, tub-thumping, waving his samples in the air, trying by every means in his power to influence the taste of his audience and to lead it in the direction he sincerely feels to be the right one. He is perpetually attacking and defending; denouncing one author for his false glitter, extolling another whose sterling qualities have not yet found proper recognition; all the time striving to create an atmosphere which will be favourable to the kind of work he admires. And the greatest critics have done no less than this. Nearly every major movement in English literature has been ushered in, and accompanied, by the tireless critic with his formidable array of reasons and justifications. We need only think what the Augustan age owed to Dryden, Dennis, and Dr Johnson; what the Romantics owed to Coleridge, Lamb, and Hazlitt;

what 'modern' poetry owes to the critics who have hacked a
path for it through the jungles of timidity and prejudice.

It is here that the critic differs from the scholar. The scholar
is not concerned with contemporary taste. He does not want
to persuade anyone: he prefers to present his evidence and step
aside. It is true that the labours of the scholar have often pro-
foundly influenced the course of literary taste, but on investiga-
tion one usually finds that in these cases the critic has been at
work, stepping in to act as middleman between the scholar and
the reading public. Familiarity with the latest work of the pure
scholars is thus an important part of the critic's duty. Neverthe-
less, the two functions are quite distinct. The scholar does not
measure the degree of success or failure of his work by the
effect it has had on public taste. He has his own standards of
excellence, and, like the artist, cares less for popular acclaim
than for the regard of a few fellow-craftsmen.

Criticism, then, is marked off by important differences from
other kinds of literary work. Not that it is less arduous; good
criticism is notoriously rarer even than good poetry. But it is
more tied to a practical purpose. Like the banker, the doctor,
or the engineer, but unlike the poet or novelist, the critic can
look back at the end of his career and judge pretty accurately
whether he has succeeded or failed. If he has won an appre-
ciable section of the public to his way of thinking—if it is
easier to write, and publish, the kind of work he admires, than
when he began—then he has succeeded. If not, he has failed.
I do not, of course, mean to present a picture of the critic as a
mere publicity agent. It is common knowledge that the kind of
critic who reaches a vast audience, and whose name is a house-
hold word, is nearly always quite negligible as an influence on
opinion. The late James Agate, a great master of the art of
making criticism acceptable to the readers of the *Daily Express*,
cannot be said to have affected twentieth-century literary taste
in the slightest degree; yet that same taste was revolutionized
by a handful of writers who were read by tens where Agate
was read by hundreds of thousands. The critic diminishes in
stature as he approaches the advertising copy-writer.

These considerations lead us to the first major fact about

literary criticism. It is an art that depends on favourable cir-
cumstances for its very existence. No one is going to write
criticism for the good of his own soul; he writes it to influence
others, and also, let it be remembered, to earn a living. If there
is no prospect of attaining these two objects, then the critic
will not write at all. Hence, in part, the very remarkable diver-
gences in the standard of criticism between one age and the
next. For example, the eighteenth century, though it produced
many fine critics, did not, on the whole, enjoy a generally high
standard of criticism. Some of its most celebrated works, such
as Joseph Warton's *Essay on the Genius and Writings of Pope*, are
poor performances when considered as products of the most
brilliant age our civilization has known. The nineteenth cen-
tury, on the other hand, though as an epoch it was more con-
fused, less cultivated, not so leisurely, enjoyed a very high
standard of criticism. It produced no critic greater than John-
son, and not many of the stature of Burke or Addison, but it
was an age in which tolerably competent criticism was exceed-
ingly plentiful. New works, in particular, were better handled,
for that specialized branch of criticism which now came to be
called 'reviewing' had taken a great stride forward. During
the eighteenth century, magazines were for the most part
owned and directed by booksellers (a good example being the
Gentleman's Magazine of Edward Cave, which kept Johnson
from starving outright during his early London years); and the
bookseller, a semi-piratical figure who had not yet developed
into his respectable modern counterpart, the publisher, saw
to it that reviewing was governed by a simple principle; his
own books were praised to the skies ('puffed' was the word),
and those of his rivals plentifully smirched with mud. Then,
quite suddenly, the situation was completely transformed. A
new book, if it seemed to merit the attention, could be made
the subject of a long article from one of the most able pens in
the kingdom.

And the reason for this improvement was a very common-
place and mundane one. It had become possible to earn hand-
some sums of money by the practice of reviewing and criticism
generally. New periodicals had arisen which took literature

seriously. The career of a Hazlitt or a De Quincey, not to mention that of a Croker or a Gifford, had become possible.

THE 'GREAT REVIEWS'

As the eighteenth century ebbed away, periodical writing seemed to be dying with it. The two chief publications were, not to put too fine a point on it, corpses left over from the age of Johnson. There was the Whig *Monthly Review* (1749–1845), to which, in its heyday, Goldsmith had contributed; and the Tory *Critical Review* (1756–1817), first edited by Tobias Smollett. Of more recent origin, there was the *British Critic* (1793–1843), which purveyed an extremely dull line in orthodoxy, with regard both to Church and State (it is usually held to be the target aimed at in Edward Copleston's *Advice to a Young Reviewer*) and the savagely satirical *Anti-Jacobin, or, Weekly Examiner* (1797–98), designed by a group of young Tories to support the government and its system of taxation, which it did largely by the negative, but exhilarating, method of bitter attacks on its opponents. This magazine, though short-lived and devoted mainly to ephemeral topics, has an importance for the historian of literature because of its policy of including parodies of those poets who expressed Radical sympathies; but neither it nor its feeble offspring the *Anti-Jacobin Review and Magazine* could be said to have been any use to the struggling art of literary criticism.

The cobwebs, in fact, were enticingly thick; and in the second year of the new century a group of remarkable young men, talking and laughing together in an Edinburgh garret, decided that it was time to sweep them away. There was the clever and ambitious young clergyman Sydney Smith, who had been rescued from the (to him) unbearable *ennui* of a country parish by the offer of a post as private tutor to the squire's son; they had been bound for Weimar when the outbreak of war caused them to choose the University of Edinburgh as the best available spring from which the young man, Michael Hicks Beach, could drink the draught of learning. There was the

young Scottish lawyer, Francis Jeffrey, waiting for some briefs
to turn up, and meanwhile enduring "slow, obscure, and
philosophical starvation"; he it was who provided the garret
in Buccleugh Place where the idea was born. There was Henry
Brougham, the future Lord Chancellor, but at the moment as
briefless and obscure as Jeffrey. Their ages were thirty-one,
twenty-nine, and twenty-three respectively; and when they
were joined by their friends Allen (aged thirty-two), Brown
(twenty-four), and Francis Horner (also twenty-four), the new
broom began to bristle at once. Constable, wiliest of pub-
lishers—he was known as "the Crafty"—was buttonholed
without delay. Smith wrote him a letter in which he made the
perhaps unconsciously amusing suggestion that the criticism
which the proposed Review was to dispense was such as would
gain from being delivered at a safe distance.

> This town, I am convinced, is preferable to all others for such an under-
> taking, from the abundance of literary men it contains, and from the
> freedom which at this distance they can exercise towards the wits of the
> south.

But it was not only a literary purpose that was to be served
by the Review. For, during the first twenty years of its life, it
was to see the writing of the blackest chapter in the history of
England. The weary tale has been told often enough: a parlia-
ment to a fantastic degree unrepresentative; wave upon wave of
legislation designed to help those enriched by a long and bitter
war to keep their money and help it breed; an administration
in which all the powers of reaction and short-sightedness were
massed so as to buttress and magnify one another. (A few years
later Bagehot was asking incredulously whether such a man as
Lord Eldon had ever really existed.) The reason, evidently,
was not simply a moral one. The nation had not suddenly
become inhumanly greedy and heartless. It was simply one of
those periods—they are to be found in the history of every
nation—when the governing intelligence lags behind the pro-
gress of events, continuing to apply the methods and standards
which worked fairly enough half a century earlier. The Revolu-
tion of 1688 had laid down principles of government that
had worked well enough until the sudden creation of a huge

landless proletariat. Then, with dramatic swiftness, it went out of date: it was framed for an age in which most Englishmen had what could be described as a stake in the land. The industrial worker of the early nineteenth century was, literally, an outlaw: the law had been made at a time when he did not exist. And so, during the long time-lag before the law could be altered, he had no rights, no justice, and no protection. Even in the twentieth century we can still shudder at the mention of "Peterloo," the day in 1819 when a crowd which had gathered to listen to a Radical orator was 'dispersed' by a yeomanry regiment. It says much for the restraint of the English character—"our habit," as the late George Orwell put it, "of not killing one another"—that even this, the most notorious act of repressive violence in modern English history, left only nine dead and four hundred and eighteen wounded. But it was enough. Murder has worn a mask like Castlereagh in the minds of Englishmen ever since.

What is more to our immediate purpose is the immense weight of intolerance that smothered the freedom of the individual to speak his mind. It is the first lesson of practical politics that the opponents of reform find a useful weapon in any danger that threatens their country from outside. Already in the 1790's, Pitt had been forced to abandon many of his cherished projects for reform by the excited bawling of those to whom the French Revolution seemed a disease that might be catching. And English literature is full of echoes of the struggle that raged, for a quarter of a century, between the Radicals (who were not afraid to defend what seemed to them the good features even of the dreaded Revolution) and the purple-faced shoot-the-lot Anti-Jacobins. The vindictiveness engendered by panic reached a fresh height during the hungry, chaotic years that followed Waterloo, but the administration had been in an ugly mood for some years: in 1810 Sir Francis Burdett was committed to the Tower for having suggested that Roman Catholics might be allowed to hold commissions in the armed forces. "Writers who propounded doctrines adverse to monarchy and aristocracy, were proscribed and punished without mercy," commented Macaulay in a retrospect of this period.

"It was hardly safe for a republican to avow his political creed over his beefsteak and his bottle of port at a chophouse." Worse, it was by those who professed to honour the memory of Burke that the howl against reform was raised and kept up; as if Burke had not denounced, again and again, the folly of an inflexible yard-stick or "system," such as they now erected in his name; as if Burke's arguments against the French Revolution could be applied without modification to quash any suggestion of change or adjustment. Most literary historians have contrived somehow to minimize the extent to which the work of the great Romantic poets is saturated in politics; but the same tactics would certainly not work when applied to the periodical criticism of the time. Its political tint is too obvious. In an age when the mere suspicion of a Radical or Jacobin flavour was felt to mark an author as the enemy of his nation, his class, his religion, and his profession, literary criticism took on a note of urgency. A Croker or a Lockhart went to work on a batch of Radical poets with the eager grimness of a bomb disposal squad working against time. "Party," said Croker, "is much the strongest passion of an Englishman's mind. Friendship, love, even avarice, give way before it."

It is therefore to the credit of the *Edinburgh Review* that its voice was raised on behalf of reform and tolerance, and against xenophobia, from the beginning. Its editors could not, indeed, have failed to respond to the desperate state of affairs that prevailed in the very city of its title, where, amid the horrors of the Old Town, crime and pestilence went unchecked: where the Resurrectionists, typified by the nightmare figures of Burke and Hare, suffocated their victims for the sake of the market price of corpses, while at intervals such calamities as the cholera epidemic of 1832, by thinning the ranks of the poor, seriously interfered with the supply of cheap labour. When Sydney Smith published his collected writings in 1839, he added a Preface in which he surveyed the part played by the Review in bringing about a happier state of affairs.

"To appreciate the value of the *Edinburgh Review*," he wrote,

the state of England at the period when that journal began should be had in remembrance. The Catholics were not emancipated—the

B

Corporation and Test Acts were unrepealed—the Game Laws were horribly oppressive—Steel Traps and Spring Guns were set all over the country—Prisoners tried for their Lives could have no Counsel—Lord Eldon and the Court of Chancery pressed heavily upon mankind—Libel was punished by the most cruel and vindictive imprisonments—the principles of Political Economy were little understood—the Laws of Debt and Conspiracy were upon the worst possible footing—the enormous wickedness of the Slave Trade was tolerated—a thousand evils were in existence, which the talents of good and able men have since lessened or removed; and these effects have been not a little assisted by the honest boldness of the *Edinburgh Review*.

It was this "honest boldness" that led, after nearly seven years, to that split among the Review's contributors from which emerged its great rival, the *Quarterly*. Originally the policy of the Review had been one of political neutrality, and its increasing partisanship seems to have been due largely to the influence of Jeffrey, who rapidly became recognized as editor-in-chief. Sydney Smith, with the assistance of Horner, had supervised the publication of the first issue—the atmosphere of genteel amateurism which prevailed at the beginning of the enterprise meant that there was, officially, no editor in the modern sense—but the immediate success of the Review made it imperative that a more methodical, and professional, method be adopted, and Jeffrey was formally appointed as editor just after the publication of the second number. He held the post until 1829, when he was succeeded by Macvey Napier, a man about whom the most interesting known fact is that he had changed his name (why?) from Napier Macvey.

Jeffrey, despite a warning from Francis Horner, continued to impose a reforming, Whiggish colour on the Review. 'Colour' is an apt word, for the very hues of the cover—the famous 'blue and buff'—were the colours adopted by the followers of Charles James Fox. As time went on it became less and less easy for a sincere Tory to be associated with the publication; yet its great prestige was tempting both to readers and writers. Finally, in the issue for February 1809, Jeffrey wrote an article entitled "Don Cevallos and the French Usurpation in Spain," which, it seems, was felt by his non-Whig associates to be the last straw. (It is hard to see why; in fact a glance at this article is the quickest way for a modern reader to assure himself of the eagerness with which heresies were sniffed out and denounced). The *Edinburgh's* challenge to the *status quo* had reached a point at which an answer must be found.

The prime mover in this answer was Scott, who by 1806 had written ten articles for Jeffrey. He now approached John Murray on the possibility of a rival review. As it happened, Murray was already no stranger to the suggestion. One day early in 1808, the diplomatist Stratford Canning, cousin of the better-known George, was walking down Pall Mall when the idea occurred to him of a Tory counterpart to the *Edinburgh*. He proposed it to his cousin, who referred him to William Gifford; whom he accordingly sought out and introduced to Murray. The credit, therefore, for the original conception of the *Quarterly Review* goes to Stratford Canning; who received a complimentary copy of the first issue (March 12, 1809) together with a letter from Murray in which the Review is described as "a work which owes its birth to your obliging countenence and introduction of me to Mr Gifford."

Nevertheless, the prime mover—we must repeat—was Scott, with whom conservatism was not merely an intellectual conviction, but the breath of his being. His collection *The Minstrelsy of the Scottish Border*, published in 1802, gave him his first taste of literary success; and the impulse that led him to soak himself in English and Scottish tradition was matched by, if it were not identical with, the impulse to lock the wheels of change in practical affairs. That his deepest instincts were engaged in the struggle against any kind of reform is obvious from the violence with which he expressed himself on political matters. In a letter to Southey in 1807 he summed up his objection to Catholic Emancipation with the remark,

> If a gentleman chooses to walk about with a couple of pounds of gunpowder in his pocket, if I give him the shelter of my roof, I may at least be permitted to exclude him from the seat next to the fire.

And there is Lockhart's famous anecdote (Life, cap. xv):

> . . . he regarded with special jealousy certain schemes of innovation with respect to the courts of law and the administration of justice, which were set on foot by the Crown officers for Scotland. At a debate

of the Faculty of Advocates on some of these propositions, he made a speech much longer than any he had ever before delivered in that assembly; and several who heard it have assured me that it had a flow and energy of eloquence for which those who knew him best had been quite unprepared. When the meeting broke up, he walked across *the Mound*, on his way to Castle Street, between Mr Jeffrey and another of his reforming friends, who complimented him on the rhetorical powers he had been displaying, and would willingly have treated the subject-matter of the discussion playfully. But his feelings had been moved to an extent far beyond their apprehension: he exclaimed, "No, no—'tis no laughing matter; little by little, whatever your wishes may be, you will destroy and undermine, until nothing of what makes Scotland Scotland shall remain." And so saying, he turned round to conceal his agitation—but not until Mr Jeffrey saw tears gushing down his cheek—resting his head until he recovered himself on the wall of the Mound.

In view of the enormous celebrity that Scott was later to attain, his position in 1808 strikes us as one of comparative obscurity. Still a commoner—he was not created baronet until 1820—and with his triumphant emergence as a best-selling novelist still some years distant, he was no more than on the threshold of his resplendent and tragic career. Yet the esteem in which he was held by publishers is revealed by several anecdotes dating from about this time. It seemed a matter of course, for example, that he should be offered the editorship of the *Quarterly*; and on his declining, it was understood by every one concerned that his active support was a positive necessity if the Review were to succeed. When an editor was finally appointed, William Gifford being chosen as the obvious second best, Scott's letter of advice to him was of prime importance in determining the nature and policy of the Review (see Appendix I).

It must have seemed to most loyal Tories that Murray, having failed to secure Scott as editor, was doing well in getting the services of Gifford. For Gifford had been trained in a tough school; he had been editor of the *Anti-Jacobin* during its short and savage career, and his subsequent literary work was all of a nature either critical or satiric. He had published two satires, the *Baviad* (1794) and the *Maeviad* (1795), aimed at the now completely forgotten 'Della Cruscan' school of poets; he had

translated the satires of Juvenal (1802) into an English style
that matched the originals at any rate in bad-temperedness; and
he was later to produce capable editions of Ben Jonson (1816)
and Ford (1827), and to add to his *Juvenal* a version of the fiery
and crabbed satires of Persius (1821). Seldom has any man of
letters been so widely and venomously disliked; but Gifford
was, as the saying goes, old enough and ugly enough to look
after himself. A fair example of his habitual tone of concen-
trated hostility would be his reply to the *Critical Review*, which
had launched an attack (2nd series, vol. xxxvi) on his *Juvenal*.
His answer took the form of a pamphlet, *An Examination of the
Strictures of the Critical Reviewers on the Translation of Juvenal*,
published in the following year. In it he describes how, as a
boy, it was one of his duties to help cultivate a cabbage-patch,
and how he seized the opportunity this gave him to study the
habits of insects and animals. In particular there was one toad
he came to know well.

> This toad, then, who had taken up his residence under a hollow stone
> in a hedge of blind nettles, I used to watch for hours together. It was
> a lazy, lumpish animal, that squatted on its belly, and perked up its
> hideous head with two glazed eyes, precisely like a Critical Reviewer.
> In this posture, perfectly satisfied with itself, it would remain as if it
> were a part of the stone that sheltered it, till the cheerful buzzing of
> some winged insect provoked it to give signs of life. The dead glaze
> of its eyes then brightened into a vivid lustre, and it awkwardly shuffled
> to the entrance of its cell, and opened its detestable mouth to snap the
> passing fly or honey-bee. Since I have remarked the manners of the
> Critical Reviewers, these passages of my youth have often occurred to
> me.

As might be expected, Gifford's editorial hand was a heavy
one. He did little actual writing for the Review; his chief con-
tribution was an examination of Weber's edition of Ford
(December 1811) in which he declares that "we know not
where the warmest of his [Weber's] friends will seek either
palliation or excuse." But he never scrupled to alter his con-
tributors' work—sometimes, it seems, to an outrageous extent.
Southey was particularly incensed at this ceaseless tampering.
Once, when he was slating Pope's translation of Homer,
Gifford inserted a sentence, "praising the translation," as

Southey complained to Herbert Hill, "in a manner which gives a lie to all that follows." And this despite the fact that Southey was obviously, next to Scott, the *Quarterly's* most valued contributor; so much so that Gifford described him as "the sheet-anchor of the Review."

At least once, however, Gifford made an addition to an article that must have been an easy one for the author to forgive. When Scott reviewed his own *Tales of My Landlord* (*Quarterly Review*, January 1817), the tone he adopted towards the anonymous author was rather stiff. Venturing to attribute the book to the same pen as *Waverley*, *Guy Mannering*, and *The Antiquary*, he sternly draws attention to certain faults in all these books (chiefly "the total want of interest felt by the reader in the character of the hero"), and advises the author to rid himself of them if he wishes to keep his hold on the public. Then, quite suddenly, the review ends on a note of generous, even enthusiastic, praise. Clearly, the editorial pencil has been at work; but this time blamelessly.

Gifford edited the *Quarterly* until 1824. Then, after an interval of two years during which the editor was Sir John Taylor Coleridge, the post was filled by John Gibson Lockhart, whose closer acquaintance we must make in a moment. He, too, had a long reign, retiring in 1853 in favour of Whitwell Elwin, a scholarly Norfolk clergyman of extremely conservative literary tastes. But by 1853 the great days of the *Quarterly*, or at any rate its great *literary* days, were over.

What was its effect during the years of its prime? How did it use its great power? Less wisely, on the whole, than the *Edinburgh*. The personal characters of Gifford and Lockhart, coupled with the fact that almost every writer of genius was in the opposite political camp and had therefore to be raked with shot whenever he published anything, made the *Quarterly* a vehicle of monotonously expressed reaction. It is always scolding. Mr R. B. Clark, the biographer of Gifford, has summed up the literary situation in this way:

Samuel Rogers, Lamb, Leigh Hunt, Wordsworth, Coleridge, Hazlitt, Shelley, Keats, and Landor all felt in the *Quarterly* an enemy they had to fight against; and all despised, in a greater or less degree, its editor.

The only Quarterly Reviewer who can be counted on to be fair, and to refrain from personalities, is Scott himself, whose chief motive in reviewing seems to have been to help his fellow-authors. He actually returned to the pages of the *Edinburgh* in June 1818 to review, favourably, one of the novels of Charles Maturin—a struggling hack with a streak of genius to whom he had already lent money.

But, Scott apart, the Quarterly Reviewers were a costive tribe; and, as we have seen, this can be accounted for on personal as well as political grounds. The characters of the men who ran it contained, too often, a streak of the bully. John Wilson Croker, never the editor but an influential contributor for forty years, is a good example. Croker was nine years old when the French Revolution broke out, and appears to have passed the rest of his life in a state of trembling expectation that an exactly parallel sequence of events would happen in England; so that in 1832 he was quite convinced that the immediate future held, first, revolution, and then a military despotism bringing with it a much more repressive version of the *status quo*. His constant effort was to resist change of any kind, the more vehemently if that change appeared to threaten the comfort, wealth, or prestige of the *parvenu* landed aristocracy, who, in his eyes, were the backbone of England. Croker was everywhere respected (he founded the Athanæum Club, an achievement that must represent the dizziest pinnacle of respectability) but nowhere liked; and he was the object of two of the most devastating attacks in English literature. In September 1821 Macaulay, reviewing his edition of Boswell in the *Edinburgh*, gave him the most thorough pounding in the history of reviewing; and seventeen years later came Disraeli's *Coningsby* with its portrait of Croker as Mr Rigby, the brutal party hack who is also a finicking pedant. No man of letters has ever been dismissed with such utter finality; yet in his day he set the political tone of the *Quarterly*, and his articles were often submitted, in the proof stage, for the approval of the Tory front bench.

A somewhat similar figure among the *Quarterly* men, though with less of a genius for making himself disliked, was John Gibson Lockhart. But before making Lockhart's acquaintance it will be necessary to glance at another event of considerable importance to English literature: the rise of "Maga."

THE MAGAZINES

It is unfortunately true that the difference between a Review and a Magazine is, like many other useful distinctions, becoming more and more blurred: the late, and mourned, *Horizon* bore on its cover the words "A Review of Literature and Art," but was consistently described in editorials as "this magazine," which in fact it was. In the early nineteenth century there was no such difficulty. A Review was entirely critical, its purpose being to subject the events, intellectual and otherwise, of each quarter to a responsible and grave examination. A Magazine, on the other hand, was so called because it contained a medley of various kinds of writing; the name itself was intended to suggest the wide and even startling variety of the Quarter-master's store. Not only criticism, but fiction, announcements, recipes—in short anything that might be expected to interest any potential reader—could find a home in its columns. To the Edinburgh publisher William Blackwood, therefore, when he wished to enter the lists with a periodical publication, it seemed the natural thing to launch, not a Review—for the two great rivals had between them divided the market—but a Magazine. In this way he hoped to strike a blow at once for his political principles, which were Tory, and for his trade, which was constantly threatened by the acumen of Constable.

Blackwood's was thus, in a sense, a part of the protest called forth by the success of the *Edinburgh*, but it does not really invite comparison with the *Quarterly*. The excellence and usefulness of the Magazine were quite different from those of the Review; *Blackwood's* was important for its criticism, but its distinctive contribution to English literature lay in its willingness to publish fiction, verse, and other imaginative material. Its stories, collected now and then in the familiar volumes of *Tales from Blackwood's*, helped to create the tradition which made the Magazines, in the next half-century, so important as the cradle of Victorian fiction. Not that *Blackwood's* itself could be credited with a particularly dazzling record in its dealings with fiction; most of the *Tales* have the essential stuffiness of competent journey-work, though the story of *The Iron Shroud* is said to have given Poe the hint for *The Pit and the Pendulum*. However, the tradition was a valuable one, and it was continued to give at least the possibility of a vehicle for good fiction all through the century; in 1900 the magazine accepted Conrad's *Lord Jim* for serial publication.

Blackwood's venture got away to a bad start; as *The Edinburgh Monthly Magazine* it was so poor in quality, and so poorly received, that Blackwood was driven to dismiss the two incompetents who were in charge of it. In dramatic contrast he handed it over to two of the most brilliant and restless minds of his day. Both John Wilson and John Gibson Lockhart had been educated at Oxford; subsequently Lockhart had travelled and generally put himself to the trouble of seriously investigating European literature, both by personal acquaintanceships—he had met Goethe at Weimar—and by diligent reading. Wilson, for his part, had settled down to live as a country gentleman on the shores of Lake Windermere, but the failure of his private fortune had driven him to Edinburgh to read for the Bar. His connexion with *Blackwood's* thus adds one more to the list of young lawyers who found in periodical writing their true profession.

Closely associated with these two men in their work, though widely different in temperament and background, was James Hogg, the "Ettrick Shepherd." Hogg, after a long period of neglect during which his name was chiefly associated with a few naïve pieces of verse in the anthologies ("That's the way for Billy and me"), has recently been rediscovered as the author of a great masterpiece, the *Confessions of a Justified Sinner*; and it is with this book that his name is linked in the mind of the modern reader. But in his own day the work that did most for his reputation was the series of conversations known as *Noctes Ambrosianæ*. These slabs of reported talk, in which the Ettrick Shepherd is built up into a picturesque character who dispenses sound if rather gritty wisdom on a large variety of topics, literary and otherwise, will still bear reading, though the reader's enjoyment will depend to some extent on the strength of his appetite for dialect in written form; if he shares the modern dislike of it, he should be warned that much of the *Noctes* consists of passages like this:

> Tuts—What's the use o' reviewin? Naething like a skreed o' extracts into a magazeen taken in the kintra. When I fa' on, tooth and nail, on an article about some new work, oh, Mr North, but I'm wud when I see the cretur that's undertaken to review't, settin himsel wi' clenched teeth to compose a philosophic creeticism, about the genius o' an author that every man kens as well as his ain face in the glass. . . .

At all events the *Noctes* were a popular feature of "Maga," as its editors called it. They are usually held to have been suggested by William Maginn, a picturesque character (he is the original of Captain Shandon in Thackeray's *Pendennis*) who, after a mixed career, joined the staff of the magazine in 1819. However, the point is debatable, for the series did not begin until 1822, and in 1819 Wilson and Lockhart had already begun a run of similar dialogues under the title "Christopher in the Tent," in which the foundations of the *Noctes* were laid. But even if Maginn suggested the *Noctes*, even though Hogg provided, in actual conversation, much of the material they contained, the actual writing of the series was mainly the work of Wilson. In the geniality and range of the conversations, and in the rough and ready skill with which the characters are delineated and distinguished, are the marks of Wilson's very real ability. The method, a kind of realistic fantasy involving both actual and imaginary figures, is half-way between fiction and the technique of such a writer as Boswell or Eckermann. The Ettrick Shepherd appears *in propria persona*, Wilson as "Christopher North"; the other chief character, "Timothy Tickler," has not been certainly identified, but it is thought that he may represent a real person—to be precise, an uncle of Wilson's named Sym, who was an Edinburgh lawyer. From time to time other figures make fleeting appearances, of whom some are imaginary and some (such as "The English Opium Eater") drawn from living models.

The nature of the *Noctes* as a literary form was worth a

moment's consideration, for it goes far to illuminate the
methods of Wilson and of "Maga" generally. Hogg used to
complain that Wilson had chosen to introduce him into the
conversations so as to be able, without actually committing
a punishable form of libel or misrepresentation, to pass off
his own provocative and opinionated remarks as those of some
one else. And there was a germ of truth in the grumble. For,
by comparison with the honest intransigence of the Reviews,
Blackwood's indulged in what seems to us a fantastic degree of
mystification in order to shuffle off the responsibility for the
virulent attacks it was fond of making. Famous from the begin-
ning for the extreme violence of its polemic writing and the
bitterly personal note of its attacks, "Maga" put up a smoke-
screen behind which "knavery's plain face was never seen."
Wilson, who was evidently handicapped by a very unstable
temperament, would sometimes behave in a way that was
almost idiotic in its maliciousness; while Lockhart's bitter gibing
earned him the nickname of "the Scorpion," and a reputation
which, in his more sober years as editor of the *Quarterly*, he
would gladly have lived down. Between them they used every
device to throw dust in the reader's eyes. The same opinion
would be expressed under two different names, though actually
from the same pen, in order to give it the appearance of addi-
tional support. Conversely, two pen-names would fight it out,
expressing violently contradictory views; again from the same
pen. Each of the two guiding spirits had a sheaf of pseudo-
nyms, and on very little provocation the whole stage army
would march. They would even play tricks with the names of
living people, as when they took it into their heads to credit
a number of clever verse contributions to a certain Glasgow
dentist, thus providing him with the reputation of a wit. (With
the realism and canniness of his race, the object of their joke
was able to turn it to his own advantage by accepting a dinner
given in his honour by a literary society in Liverpool.)

Coupled with this high-spirited irresponsibility was an
almost hysterical fear of exposure. For instance, Wilson had
rather let himself go over the *Noctes Ambrosianæ* dialogue
for September 1825. Every one whose name crops up in the

conversation is ridiculed to some extent; Wordsworth is pelted with extravagant abuse, Scott and Lord Brougham are lightly brushed with satire, B. W. Procter is described as "a slight, slim poetaster amuck among the great English bards"; but the most vigorous abuse is reserved for a certain Richard Martin, M.P. for Galway, who had carried through Parliament a Bill for the prevention of cruelty to animals. Once this had become law, it appears, Martin had exerted himself to the full in seeing that it was enforced, by reporting instances of cruelty many times a week to the police offices. This earned him the polite attentions of the ambrosial talkers.

> Confound all cruelty to animals!—but I much question the efficacy of law to protect the inferior creation against the human. Let that protection be found in the moral indignation of the people. That Irish jackass, Martin, throws an air of ridicule over the whole matter by his insufferable idiotism. I hope to see his skull, thick as it is, cracked one of these days, etc. etc.

When Martin retaliated by threatening legal proceedings, Wilson was at once thrown into an agony of terror. If the law began to sift the matter, his authorship of that particular dialogue would be established in public, and Wordsworth, Scott, and the rest would see who had attacked them. It was an unthinkable violation of the first principle of "Maga." When Blackwood passed on the information to him (for it was typical of their policy that there was no *editor*: no one was officially in charge of the magazine, so that Blackwood could protest that his young men were to blame and they could pass the responsibility back), Wilson wrote in reply:

> On reading your enclosures I was seized with a trembling and shivering fit, and was deadly sick for some hours. . . . To own that article is for a thousand reasons impossible. It would involve me in lies abhorrent to my nature. I would rather die this evening.

Eventually they smoothed the matter over. This kind of thing should be borne in mind when considering Wilson's dealings with Wordsworth (see p. 54).

Lockhart, unlike Wilson, is remembered chiefly for writings that did not appear in the pages of periodicals, but in more permanent form. His biography of his father-in-law, Sir Walter

Scott, is of course an acknowledged classic, and the earlier life of Burns is not far beneath it. He also wrote novels, which I have not read, though one of them, *Adam Blair* (1821) was described by George Saintsbury as "a wonderful little book."

As the *Edinburgh* called forth the *Quarterly*, so *Blackwood's* produced its own antidote, as the dock is said to grow near the nettle. This was the brilliant and short-lived *London Magazine*. Its dates are given as 1820 to 1829, but it was only a really important power in English literature during the lifetime of its first editor, John Scott—and Scott died in February 1821. Liberal in politics, 'romantic' in literature, the *London* was ideally placed to collect and present the most advanced writing of its day: Hazlitt's *Table Talk*, Lamb's *Essays of Elia*, and work by Carlyle, Landor, De Quincey, and John Clare all appeared sooner or later in its pages, and so did the work of such lesser, but notable, figures as Thomas Hood, B. W. Procter, George Darley, and H. F. Cary, the translator of Dante.

The tragic death of this magazine followed, not quickly but inevitably, on that of its editor. John Scott, who had not been personally attacked by *Blackwood's*, nevertheless felt it his duty to speak out against the ruffianly methods of its writers. This he did in the issues of his magazine for May, November, and December 1820, and January 1821. Beginning with calm, even good-natured, remonstrance, he gradually warmed up to the round accusation of "duplicity and treachery as mean and grovelling as their scurrility has been foul and venomous." He made an especial attack on Lockhart, and, during the long and involved correspondence that followed, matters ultimately reached the point at which a duel became necessary. The man who actually provoked the challenge from Scott was not Lockhart himself but a friend of his living in London, by name C. H. Christie, who had somehow managed to take the quarrel on himself. The duellists met at night near Chalk Farm; it was the age when serious duelling was declining into a series of gestures, and Christie fired his pistol into the air to avoid harming his adversary. Scott, in the darkness, did not realize this, and fired in good earnest, but missed. They fired once more, and this time Christie's second insisted that, in self-defence, he should aim seriously. As a result Scott received fatal injuries. The long literary wrangle had at last claimed the life of a man.

GENERAL REFLECTIONS: CRITICISM THEN AND NOW

If, after reading the criticism reprinted in this book, we try to come to some conclusion regarding the work of the Reviewers, I think we shall find that we shall place it, at all events, higher than it would have been placed fifty years ago. The nineteenth century adopted a curious attitude towards the Romantic poets who lived during its early years. After a certain amount of initial opposition, they were quickly canonized as the saints of English literature; the four major 'influences,' as examination papers call them, on English poetry from 1830 to 1910, were undoubtedly Keats, Shelley, Coleridge, and Wordsworth. Transmitted through Beddoes, through Tennyson, through Rossetti, through Arnold, through Francis Thompson, they reached the twentieth century unimpaired; until the rise of the detested 'moderns,' English poetry had ears for nothing else. Across the Channel Baudelaire, Rimbaud, and Mallarmé were enlarging the boundaries of their art, so that France became the leader of European poetry in the early twentieth century as decisively as Italy had been in the late sixteenth. And still English literary taste slumbered on, unable to break the hypnotic spell of the great lyric poets of a century before. It is an astonishing spectacle.

Now it is not to be wondered at that the reputation of the Reviewers, during this long period, should have sunk to a very low point. These were the men who had dared to criticize the sacred poets. They had said that a poem of Wordsworth's would "never do." They had declared themselves unable to follow what Shelley was getting at. Instead of worshipping the ground that Keats walked on, they had sniffed at him as a promising young apprentice who had still to master his art. Further, as the Reviewers receded in time, fewer and fewer people remembered what they had actually said, and a distorted version of their work became current.

It was equally natural that when, at last, the long overdue reaction came, the Reviewers should have been rediscovered with delight, and hailed as great allies. When the Romantic poets began to be seriously questioned, and occasionally attacked outright, the hostile criticisms of their own contemporaries were read with eager approval. They were even exaggerated, since, if you wished to attack Keats, and turned up the *Edinburgh* to see what Jeffrey had said about him, it was no use quoting the generous praises you found there. No, you selected the bitter medicine, and left the jam.

Now that the excitement has died away, it should be possible for us to reach a middle position. As a first move towards this, we might isolate the fundamental idea on which both these views were based. This idea, which is also the one put forward in most short histories of English literature, might be briefly stated as follows:

"The Reviewers were above all conservative. In an age when literary ideas, like all others, were changing rapidly, they preferred to remain stationary. Most of them were politically reactionary, and associated all new ventures in literature with the Jacobin and Radical movements; at all events they applied to the nascent literature of the nineteenth century the inflexible standards of the eighteenth, and so could not hope to succeed."

But the truth is seldom as simple as that. To begin with, this view is obviously generated, fundamentally, by the Victorian notion of automatic and beneficent progress. They took Darwin to mean that even the Almighty was a believer in this progress. Hence to resist progress (*i.e.*, to resist the evolution of one age from another) was both foolish and sinful. They did not believe, as we nowadays have been forced to believe, that a worse age can evolve from a better. To the literary men of that time, the Reviewers were trying to hinder a healthy and natural process—the process by which the Victorians themselves had been made—and it was this picture that they bequeathed to the textbooks of our own day.

Secondly, it is not true that the Reviewers were applying the standards of the eighteenth century. They did not swallow the new age whole, but they belonged to it unmistakably. They differed among themselves, of course—for it is another part of the libel to suggest that the Reviewers were all of one stamp—but they can all be found somewhere along the line that stretches from Gifford, who really does resemble the Victorian conception of the stubborn reactionary critic, to Jeffrey, who went out of his way more than once to declare that the poetry of his own time was better than that of the eighteenth century. John Wilson was a convinced Romantic: Lockhart, though his taste was more restrained, was thoroughly contemporary in his attitude; Scott was himself one of the great writers of the Romantic epoch; James Hogg was another; and it was from these, quite as much as from the Crokers and Giffords, that the body of anonymous critics took their cue. And in any case, the sheer quantity of critical writing offered to the public was enough to guard against a narrow dictatorship.

The nineteenth century, materially the most peaceful in English history, was essentially an age of discussion; there were many topics waiting to be thrashed out, and many readers willing to learn what was being "thought and said in the world." Accordingly, a large and formidable array of reviews and magazines quickly grew up to surround, and at times to challenge, the handful of pacemakers. The most interesting of these are the ones which explored some particular avenue, or expressed some set of convictions, which were felt to be neglected elsewhere. The *Retrospective Review*, founded in 1820 by Henry Southern, comes to mind as the most outstanding of these specialized periodicals: in format and general organization it resembled the other reviews, save that the works discussed were not newly published, but singled out from among the past achievements of English literature, and, in this way, brought to notice with a freshness and immediacy of interest that did much to stimulate the renewed study of the past. "The design of this review of past literature," wrote Southern in his Preface to the first volume, had its origin in the decisively modern direction of the reading of the present day; it is an attempt to recall the public from an exclusive attention to new books, by making the merit of old ones the subject of critical discussion.

Though, as its date indicates, the *Retrospective* followed, rather than set, the fashion for a revived attention to Elizabethan and seventeenth-century literature, there is no doubt that its provision of "criticism upon, analyses of, and extracts from curious, valuable, and scarce old books," made it an influence in its day. It was discontinued after 1828, but reappeared during 1853 and 1854. Another review with intense, though limited, preoccupations was James Mill's *Westminster Review* of 1824, the organ of the 'philosophical radicals.' Mill, who was evidently a believer in beginning as he meant to go on, attacked the *Edinburgh* in the second number and the *Quarterly* in the fourth, providing in each case a spirited analysis; but the major names associated with the *Westminster* are those of his son John Stuart Mill and 'George Eliot.' The latter was taken on by John Chapman as assistant editor when the review, sunk by early difficulties, was refloated in October 1851 as the *Westminster and Foreign Quarterly Review*.

The monthlies, too, continued to flourish. 1814 saw the founding of Henry Colburn's *New Monthly Magazine and Universal Register*; after a rather lukewarm start, it gained considerably in interest after the appointment of the poet Thomas Campbell as editor in 1820, when the title was changed to the *New Monthly Magazine and Literary Journal*. Campbell himself contributed both prose and verse, including at least one piece of permanent value, his remarkable poem *The Last Man*. As far as poetry was concerned, however, the highest point was easily reached by the ill-fated *Liberal*. This magazine, which was described as being published "occasionally," and which actually survived for four issues, appeared in circumstances which have made it famous in English literature, for no fewer than four great celebrities were involved in its production: Thomas Love Peacock, who first suggested the founding of a new magazine to Shelley in 1818; Shelley himself, who was engaged in pushing it forward at the time of his death in 1822;

C

Leigh Hunt, who travelled to Italy to undertake the editor-
ship; and Byron, who offered Hunt the doubtful blessing of his
hospitality. Since Shelley was dead before the magazine
appeared, it was Byron who actually provided the most striking
contributions, including his *Vision of Judgment*, which graced the
opening pages of the first issue. The four numbers carried
other specimens of his work, together with a good deal of
Hunt's, and some of Shelley's unpublished remains. The im-
mortality of *The Liberal* is therefore in safe hands.

Other magazines appeared in profusion, a signal illustration
of the appetite shown by English readers for this kind of fare.
Some, like *Knight's Quarterly Magazine* (1823-24) and *Sharpe's
London Magazine* (1829), collapsed after struggling through a
few issues; others were more robust. *The Metropolitan*, a
monthly devoted to fiction and notices of new books, stayed
the course from 1831 to 1857, with Captain Marryat as editor
for three years (1832-35); *Tait's Edinburgh Magazine*, a northern
counterpart to the *Westminster Review*, lived from 1832 to 1864.
The list is bewildering; some cast their net wide (*Chambers's
London Journal of History, Literature, Poetry, Biography, and
Adventure*, 1841-43), others appealed to a special taste (*The
Christian Lady's Magazine*, 1834-49; *The Gardener's Magazine*,
1826-43). But of course we cannot survey the whole field
without straying from our chosen plot of English literature,
and we had better conclude by naming one more magazine,
Moxon's *Englishman's Magazine* of 1831, which carried contri-
butions from Lamb, Leigh Hunt, Tennyson, Hood, John
Clare, and A. H. Hallam.

As if this were not enough, a large number of weekly papers
carried literary notices, sometimes of a high standard. Leigh
Hunt's famous *Examiner* was, of course, the best of these; in
his *Autobiography*, Hunt tells us that when he joined with his
brother John to launch it, he took his cue from Jonathan Swift,
who had also been concerned in a paper named *The Examiner*,
and whose "wit and fine writing . . . I proposed to myself to
emulate." The paper lived on until 1881, but its effective inter-
est in literature may be said to have ceased when the Hunt
brothers, unhappily quarrelling in the process, gave up the

joint editorship in 1825; Leigh returned to England after the
episode of *The Liberal* to find that John regarded him as having
forfeited any claim to a share in the publication. Like the
Liberal, the *Examiner* is too well known, as the chairman puts
it, "to need any introduction"; it defended Shelley and Keats,
attacked the Prince Regent, and generally progressed for thirty
years in an atmosphere of continual explosions, prosecutions,
and generous indignations.

It had its imitators, of which two deserve mention. John
Scott, whose tragic death we have already recounted, edited
The Champion (1814-24), and one William Jerdan, who seems
to have been a remarkable character, founded in 1817 his
Literary Gazette, which continued till 1862 to provide a weekly
supply of

> original essays on polite literature, the arts and sciences, a review of
> new publications, poetry; criticisms of fine arts, the drama, etc.; bio-
> graphy, correspondence of distinguished persons, anecdotes, *jeux d'esprit*,
> proceedings of literary societies, and literary intelligence.

Far from sinking under the weight of this programme, the
Gazette really did provide a degree of what would now be
called 'coverage' which foreshadowed the august *Times
Literary Supplement* of to-day.

And so to our summary. Quite apart from the excellence and
vigour of many of their criticisms, the function of the Reviews
and Magazines, in relation to English literature in the pre-
Victorian nineteenth century, was twofold. First, they served,
moulded, and to some extent called into being, the new reading
public; secondly, they helped to maintain the essential lines of
communication between criticism and original writing.

To amplify these two points in turn: when an author sits
down to write a book, he nearly always has a clear mental
picture of the kind of reader to whom the book is addressed.
It may seem at first sight that the poet is an exception to this
rule, but in reality he bears it out, for he is talking, not to him-
self, as his enemies assert, but to the small number of people
who resemble him in taste and outlook: and these are clearly
defined in his mind. For all other kinds of writing the fact is
self-evident: even a book which is aimed at a public of only a

few thousand is aimed clearly and consciously at a definite *type* of reader; while the professional author of fiction, who wrings a living out of the circulating libraries, has to judge with great accuracy the exact tastes (or perhaps a better word would be 'reflexes') of his potential public. When literature becomes a commercial undertaking it has to carry out its own market research. It follows that an author's work cannot be fully understood without some enquiry into the kind of public for whom it was intended; 'Who was going to read this? To what kind of person was it meant to appeal?' become the important preliminary questions. The art of literary history thus pivots largely on the attempt to define this public in each successive age, and to sort out, in any given period, how many different publics existed side by side, and to which one each individual work was directed.

Now it so happened that the Reviews made their appearance at a crucial moment in the growth of the English reading public. The eighteenth century had seen the first of that series of cataclysmic changes that were to lead, ultimately, to the splintered literary world of our own day. At the beginning of the century, literature, it is quite obvious, is firmly anchored to the tastes and moods of the aristocracy. Successful men of letters, such as Pope and Swift, are received on equal terms into the extreme upper reaches of the governing class. This in itself represents a triumph to which many men and many historical factors contributed, though the largest personal contribution was probably made by Dryden. Go back two hundred years, and one finds that the typical Elizabethan poet is a fawning sycophant, or (at best) a professional trying to look like an amateur. (See J. W. Saunders, "The Stigma of Print: A Note on the Social Bases of Tudor Poetry," *Essays in Criticism*, vol. i, no. 2, Oxford, 1951.) When Dryden claimed that Restoration playwrights, as compared with Elizabethans, had the advantage of being able to introduce gentlemen into their work and make them credible from first-hand observation, he was not being snobbish, but simply stating a fact. The catalogues of proper names in Pope's poems are there to emphasize the same point. This is metropolitan, courtly, aristocratic poetry, intended to circulate among a tiny group of readers, most of whom knew each other at least by sight. Provincials and tradesmen could go round to the side door. The parallel is, of course, with the Roman society of Horace—literature is produced by and for the metropolitan *beau monde*, who naturally encourage in it qualities of brilliance and finish rather than depth or grandeur. (That Pope's work has, in fact, both depth and grandeur is simply because a great poet can work against the grain at the same time as with it.)

This is the situation as the eighteenth century opens. Come forward half a lifetime or so, look into the poems of a man like Cowper or Akenside, and the immensity of the change becomes apparent. This is poetry addressed to much humbler people—less great in the world's eye, more retiring, less appreciative of brilliance, more of sensibility and gravity. The typical reader of English poetry, from being a witty and hard-bitten courtier or statesman, has become a country parson. Gone are the lists of proper names and the endless stream of personalities, for insult and compliment have both lost their point. These people do not know one another personally; they tend to run true to type, but they are not all gathered in one place. The reading public has, in a word, become much more difficult to control. In Pope's day 'the opinion of the Town' meant a great deal; a glance at the tangled story of his quarrels reveals that it was not necessary to *publish* any adverse criticism of his work to make an enemy of him: he would often bear a grudge against a man for something he had *said*. Quite rightly, for an author's reputation could be made or broken in such conversation; and this sheds a light on why eighteenth-century literary criticism did not, as we noticed at the beginning, keep pace with the general brilliance of the age. It did not need to. But by 1750 all that is changed, and will change more rapidly as the century lengthens out. Before the nineteenth century appears, communications have improved; there are half-a-dozen big cities in the British Isles instead of the traditional two, London and Bristol, and the stranglehold of the metropolis is relaxed. The next move, obviously, was to produce a body of criticism that could be both printed and circulated impartially, so that the reader who lived in the country could unpack it with his parcel of new books—and learn what to order in the next parcel. The point need not be laboured. That it was the Scots who seized on this opportunity, and cornered the market before London was alive to the new developments was, of course, only be be expected.

The second point is even simpler. A literature, as Matthew Arnold patiently explained, is not the creation of a few individual men of genius, who arise one after another by a kind of divine accident. It is created by a civilization; and criticism is an essential part of that civilization. Thus the critic is not merely riding on the back of the artist; he is "sent with broom before, To sweep the dust behind the door." He creates, as we have already seen, the atmosphere in which literature flourishes. But for this to be accomplished it is necessary that the gap between criticism and original writing should be kept narrow. The two must interact and be constantly aware of one another. The Reviewers understood this, and were, I think it must be said, brilliantly successful in their efforts to bring it about. The task of endless correlation that had formerly been carried out in the coffee-houses was now passed on to them. The three or four leading periodicals bore the main weight of responsibility, and any loose ends were gathered up by the profusion of lesser ones with which, as time went on, they became surrounded.

The parallel, in many respects, is with soil husbandry. If a piece of land is in danger of being eroded and washed away by rain, the best remedy is to plant trees and other vegetation, which will bind the earth with their roots and give it a resistant firmness. The Reviews and Magazines, some resembling sturdy oaks, others exotic shrubs, with here and there a patch of dead wood, at least prevented English literary taste from becoming a dust-bowl. They created a relatively solid and homogeneous body of taste which made the production of a vigorous literature not, indeed, easy—it is never easy—but possible.

The stages whereby that solid structure was broken down, the successive uprootings and fellings which destroyed that plantation, would be too long and too melancholy a task to

trace. It is hardly necessary to point out that the 'reading
public' of to-day simply does not exist. There are, instead,
several distinct publics who never read the same books and
remain almost completely unaware of each other. For this we
must thank the disastrous division of the population into 'high-
brow' and 'lowbrow'—a division which did not just happen by
chance, but which was, as Aldous Huxley pointed out long ago,
deliberately engineered in an elaborate sociological campaign
by powerful interests. For the modern world abounds in
people who, consciously or unconsciously, are the enemies of
discrimination.

It is probably too late to remedy this state of affairs, since,
whatever the immediate future is like, it will, manifestly, not
be a time in which the virtues that make for good criticism
are highly valued. At such a time it may be profitable to turn
to the criticism which directed our literary taste in a more for-
tunate age and which shows those qualities in which our own
time would be admitted, even by its warmest partisans, to be
lacking. Some specimens of that criticism I now invite the
reader to consider.

THE ART OF REVIEWING

From *Advice to a Young Reviewer, with a Specimen of the Art* [by Edward Copleston]. Oxford, sold by J. Parker and J. Cooke; and by F. C. and J. Rivington, St Paul's Church Yard, London, 1807.

It has been idly said, that a Reviewer acts in a judicial capacity, and that his conduct should be regulated by the same rules by which the Judge of a civil court is governed: that he should rid himself of every bias; be patient, cautious, sedate, and rigidly impartial; that he should not seek to shew off himself, and should check every disposition to enter into the case as a partizan.

Such is the language of superficial thinkers; but in reality there is no analogy between the two cases. A Judge is promoted to that office by the authority of the state; a Reviewer by his own. The former is independent of controul, and may therefore freely follow the dictates of his own conscience: the latter depends for his very bread upon the breath of public opinion: the great law of self-preservation therefore points out to him a very different line of action. Besides, as we have already observed, if he ceases to please, he is no longer read, and consequently is no longer useful. In a court of justice, too, the part of amusing the bystanders rests with the counsel: in the case of criticism, if the Reviewer himself does not undertake it, who will? Instead of vainly aspiring therefore to the gravity of a magistrate, I would advise him, when he sits down to write, to place himself in the imaginary situation of a cross-examining pleader. He may comment, in a vein of agreeable irony, upon the profession, the manner of life, the look, dress, or even the name of the witness he is examining: when he has raised a contemptuous opinion of him in the minds of the court, he may proceed to draw answers from him capable of a ludicrous turn, and he may carve and garble these to his own liking. This mode of proceeding you will find most practicable in Poetry, where the boldness of the image, or the delicacy of thought for which the reader's mind was prepared in the original, will easily be made to appear extravagant or affected, if judiciously singled out, and detached from the group to which it belongs. Again, since much depends upon the rhythm and the terseness of expression, both of which are sometimes destroyed by dropping a single word, or transposing a phrase, I have known much advantage arise from not quoting in the form of a literal extract, but giving a brief summary in prose of the contents of a poetical passage; and interlarding your own language with occasional phrases of the Poem, marked with inverted commas. These, and a thousand other little expedients, by which the arts of quizzing and banter flourish, practice will soon teach you. If it should be necessary to transcribe a dull passage, not very fertile in topics of humour and raillery, you may introduce it as a "favourable specimen of the Author's manner."

[*The 'Specimen' follows: a comically hostile analysis of Milton's "L'Allegro."*]

The 'Apologia' of *Blackwood's*: Preface to vol. xix, January 1826

The world has acknowledged that the appearance of our Magazine was indeed an era in the history of criticism. For some months, indeed, here too we were assailed by the most frantic falsehoods. Dunces whom we had most mercifully knocked on the head, or rather killed in a moment by scientifically putting the well-sharpened point of our pen into their spinal marrow, were buried by their friends with all the pomp of martyrs. Their blood, it was said, would lie heavy on our heads—ay, heavy as their works on our shelves. And the Sanctum, within No. 17, Prince's Street, it was prophesied, would be haunted by their ghosts. The few spectres that ventured thither, O'Doherty tumbled neck and heels into the Balaam-Box, where they were laid as effectually as in the Red

Sea. At such enormities as these the public could not but simper, and the names of the slain were soon wiped as effectually from the memories of all mankind, as chalk-writings on the walls of houses by the sponges of the police. "Mention the names of the gentlemen whom you blame us for having murdered," and the answer uniformly was, "Their names, Christopher?—Why, we have forgotten their names." "Hold your tongue, then; for a murder, without the Christian and surname of the defunct, is not worth mentioning before ears polite." But our humanity in all this was most exemplary—for our murders were all metaphorical—and we had merely driven a number of our fellow-creatures from the folly, shame, and exposure of a life of literary prostitution, into the necessity of gaining an honest livelihood in compting-houses, upon wharfs, and in agriculture.

There was another class of writers (we mention no names) who had long been prodigiously overrated by themselves and their party. Merit they had, and we allowed it; but not one of them all was a Phoenix or a Phenomenon of any sort, and we took the liberty of speaking of them as if they were mere men, of various sizes, some with wigs and some without wigs, and all comprehended within the Bills of Mortality. This, too, gave offence, as it was meant to do. A man hates to be undeified—to be reduced to the ranks of humanity. These persons were bitter against us, but it would not do. They felt it henceforth to be up-hill work, and accepted their proper level as we laid it down. Nay, by and by, they absolutely grew into contributors (rejected ones of course) and inundated the Blue-Parlour with articles that could have lighted all the cigars in Edinburgh. What has become of most of these distinguished literary characters now, we have sometimes puzzled ourselves in conjecturing but we would fain hope that they have died in the course of nature of a good old age.

But the living literature of England, thank God, is of a glorious spirit. Scott, Byron, Wordsworth, Southey, Coleridge, and others are men to stand undiminished—undwindled by the side of the giants of the olden time. They too had, one and all of them, been insulted equally by the abuse and by the panegyric of pigmies. Praise was absolutely doled out to these illustrious writers, with the most stately eleemosynary airs, by critics in the last stage of mental famine and starvation. The prating coxcombs did not bend their little insignificant knees before the image which they pretended and presumed to idolize, but they strutted up in self-worship, with an old stump of a pen behind their ears, and laid their small articles of oblation on the shrine—articles that never could be made to take fire, but evaporated in a stink of smoke most offensive to Apollo. Then, like savages, they grew angry with their gods, if their invocations were not heard, and positively abused the very objects of their former idolatry; forgetting, however, that, in their cases, they could not pull down what they had not set up, and that nature guarded the sons and daughters of genius. True it is, that the worst and basest passions alternately tore the hearts of critics in their abject superstitions; and that their works are a perfect chaos of unshaped thought and feeling, presenting a wonderful and melancholy contrast with those ordered creations that had provoked their spleen, their envy, or their admiration. Out of the hands, or rather the paws, of such worthless worshippers, we took the office of Priest to the Muses. We hailed the sunrise of genius with very different strains. We inspired men with that spirit in which alone genius can be known, felt, or seen. We attended the car of its triumphs, to clear the way, and to swell the hymn. Without enthusiasm—without something of the same transport that seizes on the poet's soul—what signify the imperfect sympathies of the critic? The due expression of delight awaked in sincere hearts by the glories of genius must be eloquent. That delight does not speak in short, measured, precise, analytical sentences, nor yet in the long-winded ambulatory parade of paragraphs circuitously approaching, against all nature and all art, to a catastrophical climax. But thoughts that breathe, and words that burn, break from the critic's lips who is worthy of his bard; and his prose panegyric is, in body and soul, itself a poem.

It is thus we have ever spoken, and ever will speak, of the Magnates of Parnassus. Yet should any one—even of them—

be led astray, not "by the light from heaven," but by the coruscations of his own clouded and tempestuous genius, it is well known how we have ever stood affected towards the glorious but dangerous delinquent. Remember how we bearded Byron in his Den—ay, at a time when all the puny whipsters stood aloof trembling, and feared to breathe a whisper, lest the Childe should grasp them in his ire, flog, flay, and anatomize. *We alone* met him hand to hand, and in the Open Ring of Europe, challenged the mighty wrestler to try a fall. Much was said of our presumption, and more, as usual, of our personality— that weary watchword of the weak and wicked—and the trembling cowards cried, "Shame, shame, to abuse Byron!" But Byron thought otherwise. He knew that his match was before him; and although Byron feared no man's face, yet we know he respected our bearing on that occasion.

Nor let it be said that, either on this or any other occasion, the moral Satyrists in this Magazine ever wished to remain unknown. How, indeed, could they wish for what they well knew was impossible? All the world has all along known the names of the gentlemen who have uttered our winged words. Nor did it ever, for one single moment, enter into the head of any one of them to wish—not to scorn concealment. To gentlemen, too, they at all times acted like gentlemen; but was it ever dreamt by the wildest visionary that they were to consider as such the scum of the earth? "If I but knew who was my slanderer," was at one time the ludicrous skraigh of the convicted Cockney. Why did he not ask? and what would he have got by asking? Shame and confusion of face—unanswerable argument and cruel chastisement. For before one word would have been deigned to the sinner, he must have eaten—and the bitter roll is yet ready for him—all the lies he had told for the last twenty years, and must either have choked or been kicked —no pleasing alternative. But why thus bastinado the Specimens—they are but stuffed skins.

But there is yet another class of writers, of our conduct respecting whom, permit us to say a very few words. We mean youthful aspirants after literary fame. Let them show either taste, or feeling, or genius—much or little—and have they not

all found us their friends? They are overlooked by the world—
What is that to us? If they have any lustre, they are soon
discerned by us, be they glow-worms or stars, and their
place pointed out in heaven or on earth. Perhaps they are so
very unfashionable, that their volumes never get farther than
the servants' hall. What is that to us, if the volumes have any
merit? Show us either promise or performance, and without
any appearance of patronage, which is the mere triumph of
pride over humility, we address the writer in terms of friendly
encouragement and inspiriting commendation. We have the
pure satisfaction of knowing that we have been of substantial
service to several persons of merit in this way: and without
wishing to misrepresent the character of any one of our Con-
temporaries, we simply ask, which of them have treated unob-
trusive and modest merit with half the kindness of that bloody-
minded hobgoblin—*Blackwood's Magazine*.

With some two or three writers of more than ordinary
genius, or talent, or taste, we alone have dealt either with com-
mon sense or common feeling. We may mention three—
Keats, Shelley, Procter. Keats possessed from nature some
"fine powers," and that was the very expression we used in the
first critique that ever mentioned his name. We saw, however
with mixed feelings of pity, sorrow, indignation, and con-
tempt, that he was on the road to ruin. He was a Cockney, and
Cockneys claimed him for their own. Never was there a young
man so encrusted with conceit. He added new treasures to his
mother-tongue—and what is worse, he outhunted Hunt in a
species of emasculated pruriency, that, although invented in
Little Britain, looks as if it were the product of some imagina-
tive Eunuch's muse within the melancholy inspiration of the
Haram. Besides, we know that the godless gang were flattering
him into bad citizenship, and wheedling him out of his Chris-
tian faith. In truth, they themselves broke the boy's heart,
and blasted all his prospects. We tried to save him by whole-
some and severe discipline—they drove him to poverty, expa-
triation, and death. Then they howled out murder against,
first the *Quarterly Review*, and then this Magazine. Heartless
slaves! Did not John Hunt himself, even Prince John,

publish, for the sake of filthy lucre, Byron's cutting sarcasms on poor Keats, after he was in his grave? Nay, did he not publish Byron's outrageous merriment on this very charge of murder? —an instance of heartless effrontery unparalleled since the Age of Bronze?

We remember—we believe it was in John Scott's abuse of us—having it particularly bandied against us as a heinous crime that we had ventured to hint that Keats was an apothecary, and been jocose on his pestle and mortar. A sad offence! These people must be quite new in the world of wit. We thought all these common-places of quizzing were perfectly understood, and of course harmless. From long prescription in this style of writing, a lawyer is a rogue—a physician kills his patients—a parson has a round paunch—an alderman guttles and guzzles—an attorney is an arrant knave—and so on. What man of the least sense in these eminent professions, takes offence at these threadbare jests? Some of our jesters, it appears, could not resist the revival of the union of poetry and pharmacy in John Keats, as they had existed in Apollo, and made sorry jokes thereupon. But for the spirit of exaggeration which has attended everything connected with our Magazine, this never would have been considered as an offence. It was set down as a most grievous one by the same party who were calling Dr Phillpotts (one of the most accomplished men in England) a foul-mouthed parson, and cracking jokes on Wordsworth for being a stampmaster—Wordsworth, who, independently of his unequalled genius, is by birth, education, character, and independence, precisely the man best fitted to hold in any country an office of trust and responsibility, and of such moderate emoluments as suits and satisfies the wishes of a Poet and Philosopher.

Percy Bysshe Shelley was a man of far superior powers to Keats. He had many of the faculties of a great poet. He was, however, we verily believe it now, scarcely in his right mind. His errors in private life had been great, but not *prodigious*, as the *Quarterly Review* represented them; and they brought evils along with them with which Shelley bore with fortitude and patience. He had many noble qualities; and thus gifted, thus erring, and thus outcast, we spoke of him with kindness and with praise. He felt, and gratefully acknowledged both; and was proud to know, that some of the articles in our work on his poetry, were written by a poet whose genius he admired and imitated. How did the Cockneys swallow our praises of Shelley?—As wormwood. For envy and jealousy are the corroding and cancerous passions which are for ever gnawing at a Cockney's heart.

Procter we once loved to praise, and our praises did much for him, as he must know, now that his popularity has departed from him. Most cordially will we praise him again, whenever he shall produce a poem worthy of himself—of his taste and his genius. But Mr Procter forgot altogether the measure of his powers—wrote on in opposition to the advice of his wisest friends—and sunk every additional poem deeper and deeper into the mire of mannerism—selected classical subjects of which he knew nothing, and less than nothing, committing flagrant falsehoods in sincerest truth—till, ere his shoes were old, he dozed the public *usque ad nauseam*—got set down for a bore—was teased, tolerated, defended, damned, and forgotten.

So much for our critical character; and we have merely furnished a few slight hints for the world at large to ruminate upon. But that is but part, and a very small part too, of our general character. Were we to enlarge upon that, we should have to write till next Christmas. Are there any of our readers old enough to recollect or to have forgotten the Chaldee Number? We then laid before mankind a list of intended articles. They stared, quaked, gabbled, or were dumb. "All Fudge!" exclaimed many wiseacres, with brains of their own as the barren summit of Benevis. "Why do you tell?" said other nincompoops; "other editors will forestall you." What say ye now, ye miserables? Essays on all imaginable subjects under the sun—letters to, from, for, and against almost every party, profession, and individual in the British Empire—sketches of character, so multiform and multitudinous, as to give an extended idea of the inexhaustible varieties of human nature—inquiries into a thousand subjects, the very existence of which had never been previously suspected—advices to

people under every possible coincidence of circumstances—
memoirs of men in the moon—disquisitions on the drama, epic,
lyrical, didactic, and even pastoral poetry, here, there, and
everywhere, on continent and isle, all over the face of the
habitable globe—songs, epigrams, satires, elegies, epithalamia,
epicedia—and God knows what: out they all came, helter-
skelter, head-over-heels, and leap-frog, to the endless amaze-
ment of the wide-mouthed world. For upwards of eight years,
has this inexplicable system prevailed; and with the true
vires-acquirit-eundo spirit, the Magazine is now more pregnant
and productive than ever—boiling over like a Geyser, scalding
all natural philosophers that approach without wisdom or
warning; but diffusing a flowery warmth over every region,
it overflows and astonishing [*sic*] the natives with unexpected
and almost untoiled-for harvest.

True it is, and most happy are we to be able to say it, that
other periodicals are spouting away very respectably, in imita-
tion of Maga. Long may they spout. But who taught the
art of well-digging? who *fanged* the wells when dug? Chris-
topher North. And however unwilling we are at all times to
allude, even distantly, to our own name, we are much mistaken
if posterity, nay, not posterity—but our grateful coevals or con-
temporaries, will not place our names in juxtaposition with
those of Smeaton, Arkwright, and Watt.

As for our literary articles, knowing by whom they are
written, and by what men they are valued, we leave them freely
to be criticised by any petty *littérateur* that pleases. In our poli-
tics, we have been Tory through thick and thin, through good
report and evil report; or as Mr Montgomery well expressed it,
come wind, come sun; come fire, come flood. Honouring and
venerating the churches established under divine Providence
in these islands, we have to the utmost of our power supported
their interests—not from any idle or obstinate bigotry, but
because we conscientiously look upon them as the main stay of
the constitution of England, as the bulwarks of the Protestant
faith, as tending in the highest degree to promote Christianity,
i.e. virtue and happiness. Finally, believing that a kingly
government, checked and balanced by a proud aristocracy, and

a due mixture of a popular representation, is the only one fit for these kingdoms (we meddle not with what may be fit under other circumstances in other lands or ages) we have always inculcated the maxim of honouring the King, and all put in authority under him, with the honours they deserve. *Their* enemies, Whig, Jacobin, Radical, Deist, Demagogue, or whatever other title they take, are *our* enemies, and with them we have no truce. Caring little for the newfangled and weathercock doctrines every day broached around us, and knowing, by long experience, that we have thriven under the old notions, we hold to them with a tenacity, which to some may appear obstinate, but which, as yet, we have seen no reason to repent. Intimately convinced that this country is a great instrument in the hands of God, we hope that it will not be turned to evil, and to the utmost of our ability shall resist all machinations for that purpose. And loving that country with a more than filial love, attached to all its interests, rejoicing in its prosperity, grieved to the soul in its adversity, delighted to see it victorious in war, still more delighted to see it tranquil at home, and honoured abroad during peace, we shall never cease to advocate the cause of those whose excursions we firmly believe have promoted, and will promote, its happiness or its glory. Of the effect of our work in diffusing a healthy and manly tone throughout the empire, and of creating a proper spirit of courage and patriotism, it would be vanity to speak. It has had its effect, and we are satisfied.

A Modern Comment

(Howard Nemerov in *The Hudson Review*, New York, vol. i, No. 3, Autumn 1948)

The received opinion about reviewing [books of information and criticism], if I may generalize from contemporary practice, seems to be that the reviewer who *knows more* than the author, requires the book merely as a stimulus and as a means of directing his attention to the area of discourse under survey, whereupon his qualifications by some miraculous means far exceed

D

those of the author; his function then, still according to con-
temporary practice, is to inform the public and the author of
those things the author did which he should not have done,
of those things he did not do which he should have done, and of
those things which he did and did badly—the reviewer plays
the trump of that small learning he can add to the author's large
learning and takes the trick; or, as in the parable of the flea and
the elephant, he sits in the author's ear and says to him, "We
sure shook that bridge." Having done these things the re-
viewer, if he doesn't much like the book, is at liberty to make a
nasty remark about its thesis if any (whereupon the rules of the
game allow the sentence, "Space does not permit me to go into
my reasons," etc., or one of its many recognized variants) and
then—something that is hardly licensed except in a review—
to denigrate The Style, that is, to make use of the wonderful
and meaningless conception, left over from a school of polite
editorial prose and inherited for some reason by criticism in-
stead of by schools of business English, that Good Writing
is Good Writing no matter what. Then the reviewer may go
home, having in a manner *written* the book by symbolically
triumphing over it.

WORDSWORTH

It was not to be expected that either the personality or the poetry of this superb, overbearing, crotchety, independent, and egocentric figure would be to the taste of the Reviewers. And, in any case, Wordsworth had some hard things to say about critics. Sometimes he was merely sarcastic, as when he called Adam Smith "the worst critic, David Hume not excepted, that Scotland, a soil to which this sort of weed seems natural, has produced"; sometimes he burrowed at the very foundations on which the Reviewers had planted their work, as in the famous passage in his "Essay, Supplementary to the Preface," where he discusses the qualifications of the ideal critic; for he, this ideal, will be found "among those and those only, who, never having suffered their youthful love of poetry to remit much of its force, have applied to the consideration of the laws of this art the best power of their understandings." But, Wordsworth goes on, this class contains the worst as well as the best critics, for—and this is the stinging sentence:

> For to be mistaught is worse than to be untaught; and no perverseness equals that which is supported by systems, no errors are so difficult to root out as those which the understanding has pledged its credit to uphold.

This is indeed to lay one's finger on the one weak spot that causes most of what is below standard in the Reviews. Of necessity, a man who is continually criticizing new books cannot pause every few minutes to formulate his principles of criticism anew; he has his permanent standards and applies them, flexibly if he is a good critic, mechanically if a bad, but apply them he must. In this way Wordsworth does more than complain about his treatment; he makes damaging criticisms of his critics. An allied point, which he often made, was that his poetry, with its bareness, its silences, and its bleak repose, was necessarily unintelligible to worldlings. With characteristic egoism he went so far as to apply this truth not merely to his own, but to all great poetry. "It is an awful truth," he wrote to Lady Beaumont in 1807,

> that there neither is, nor can be, any genuine enjoyment of poetry among nineteen out of twenty of those persons who live, or wish to live, in the broad light of the world—among those who either are, or are striving to make themselves, people of consideration in society.

One has the feeling that the "nineteen out of twenty" is a concession to enable Lady Beaumont, who was certainly a person of "consideration in society," to get out of the way of the steam-roller.

The elusiveness, the determined non-popularity of Wordsworth's poetry, is so important in any estimate of his contemporary reception that we must dwell on it a little longer. All attempts to sell Wordsworth to the common run of readers have failed; the reason for this is partly that the wrong methods have been adopted (such as the selection of his most vapid poems to be rammed down the throats of school-children), but chiefly that, as Hazlitt insisted, Wordsworth is essentially a poet for the few.

> The vulgar do not read them [*i.e.*, his works]; the learned, who see all through books, do not understand them, the great despise, the fashionable may ridicule them: but the author has created himself an interest in the heart of the retired and lonely student of nature, which can never die.

Now it is certainly true that, while none of the Reviewers could be described as a "retired and lonely student of nature," the one among them who came nearest to it was Wilson, who wrote of Wordsworth in terms of high praise; and the furthest removed from it was Jeffrey, who was, on the whole, contemptuous of Wordsworth's aims and achievements. Jeffrey was a thorough worldling; his good qualities, as well as his deficiencies, were those of a man who has mixed much in society and its practical concerns—who has lived, as Wordsworth put it, "in the broad light of the world." Consequently he was never able to get beyond his original distaste for the uncouth surface of Wordsworth's poems. He simply did not understand how any grown man could write in a style so primitive, not to say prattling and vapid. From time to time he used Burns or Crabbe as a stick to beat Wordsworth with; let him follow these models if he wished for simplicity and naturalness!

These gentlemen [*i.e.*, "the new school of poetry"] are outrageous for simplicity; and we beg leave to recommend to them the simplicity of Burns. He has copied the spoken language of passion and affection, with infinitely more fidelity than they have ever done, on all occasions which properly admitted of such adaptations: but he has not rejected the help of elevated language and habitual associations; nor debased his composition by an affectation of babyish interjections, and all the puling expletives of an old nursery-maid's vocabulary. They may look long enough in his nervous and manly lines, before they find any "Good lacks!"—"Dear hearts!"—or "As a body may say," in them; or any stuff about dancing daffodils and sister Emmelines. Let them think, with what infinite contempt the powerful mind of Burns would have perused the story of Alice Fell and her duffle cloak—of Andrew Jones and the half-crown—or of Little Dan without breeches, and his thievish grandfather. (*Edinburgh Review*, January 1809).

This is good criticism, for, although wrong-headed, it is trenchant enough to make us pause and search our minds for the answer. Jeffrey's practical common-sense has suggested a typically rough-and-ready course of action. You want simplicity?—very well! read Burns and Crabbe: they are simple; and they are universally admired; and they will teach you not to overdo it. In fact, of course, both the earthly knowingness and humorous extravagance of Burns's familiar style, and the harsh creaking of Crabbe's grim narratives, would have failed dismally to cope with Wordsworth's subject matter; but Jeffrey was not of a sufficiently literary turn of mind to appreciate such points. And if we seek an antidote to this overdose of common sense, it can be found in (of all places) the *Quarterly* for October 1814, in which Lamb reminded his readers that poetry on the subject of childhood is not necessarily childish, and cautioned them against critics who treated the solemn mystery of childhood with less than its due reverence.

Wilson did better than Jeffrey, although even here his extraordinary inconsistency produced some strange results. In 1816, Wordsworth had published his *Letter to a Friend of Burns*, in which he had vigorously attacked Jeffrey. Wilson, who was at this time on good terms with Jeffrey, published in the *Edinburgh Monthly Magazine* for June 1817 (for it had not yet become *Blackwood's*) an article entitled, "Observations on Mr Wordsworth's Letter to a Friend of Burns," in which the attack was harshly answered in kind. In October 1817 he answered his own criticisms in a "Vindication of Mr Wordsworth's Letter," also in *Blackwood's* and also anonymous. This article, part of which is given below, contains some of Wilson's best Wordsworthian criticism. But it was followed, in the next issue, by another violent attack on Wordsworth: and, incredible as it seems, this third article, too, has been traced to the pen of Wilson. The tradition of anonymous reviewing has sheltered some strange growths.

Nevertheless, Wilson's praise of Wordsworth far outweighs his abuse, even measuring by quantity, and certainly in quality; if there was the notorious attack on the poet in *Noctes Ambrosianæ*, September 21, 1825, there were the complimentary articles in "Maga" for July and December 1818 and August 1822.

The *Quarterly*, it will surprise no one to learn, carried very little criticism of Wordsworth. Only Lamb's review of the *Excursion* seems worth saving, and even this, as the accompanying letter shows, had suffered at the hands of Gifford.

Jeffrey: digression in review of Crabbe's *Poems*; *Edinburgh Review*, April 1808

Mr Crabbe exhibits the common people of England pretty much as they are, and as they must appear to every one who will take the trouble of examining into their condition; at the same time that he renders his sketches in a very high degree interesting and beautiful—by selecting what is most fit for description—by grouping them into such forms as must catch the attention or awake the memory—and by scattering over the whole such traits of moral sensibility, of sarcasm, and of deep reflection, as every one must feel to be natural, and own to be powerful. The gentlemen of the new school, on the other hand,

scarcely ever condescend to take their subjects from any des-
cription of persons at all known to the common inhabitants
of the world; but invent for themselves certain whimsical
and unheard-of beings, to whom they impute some fantastical
combination of feelings, and then labour to excite our sym-
pathy for them, either by placing them in incredible situations,
or by some strained and exaggerated moralisation of a vague
and tragical description. Mr Crabbe, in short, shows us some-
thing which we have all seen, or may see, in real life; and draws
from it such feelings and such reflections as every human being
must acknowledge that it is calculated to excite. He delights
us by the truth, and vivid and picturesque beauty of his repre-
sentations, and by the force and pathos of the sensations with
which we feel that they are connected. Mr Wordsworth and
his associates, on the other hand, introduce us to beings whose
existence was not previously suspected by the acutest observers
of nature; and excite an interest for them—where they do
excite any interest—more by an eloquent and refined analysis
of their own capricious feelings, than by any obvious or intelli-
gible ground of sympathy in their situation.

Those who are acquainted with the *Lyrical Ballads*, or the
more recent publications of Mr Wordsworth, will scarcely deny
the justice of this representation; but in order to vindicate it to
such as do not enjoy that advantage, we must beg leave to make
a few hasty references to the former, and by far the least excep-
tional of those productions.

A village schoolmaster, for instance, is a pretty common
poetical character. Goldsmith has drawn him inimitably; so
has Shenstone, with the slight change of sex; and Mr Crabbe,
in two passages, has followed their footsteps. Now, Mr Words-
worth has a village schoolmaster also—a personage who makes
no small figure in three or four of his poems. But by what
traits is this worthy old gentleman delineated by the new poet?
No pedantry—no innocent vanity of learning—no mixture of
indulgence with the pride of power, and of poverty with the
consciousness of rare acquirements. Every feature which
belongs to the situation, or marks the character in common
apprehension, is scornfully discarded by Mr Wordsworth;

who represents his grey-haired rustic pedagogue as a sort of
half crazy, sentimental person, overrun with fine feelings, con-
stitutional merriment, and a most humorous melancholy. Here
are the two stanzas in which this consistent and intelligible
character is portrayed. The diction is at least as new as the
conception.

> The sighs which Matthew heav'd were sighs
>   Of one tir'd out with *fun and madness*;
> The tears which came to Matthew's eyes
>   Were tears of light—*the oil of gladness.*
>
> Yet sometimes, when the secret cup
>   Of still and serious thought went round,
> He seem'd as if *he drank it up,*
>   He felt with spirit so profound.
> Thou *soul* of God's best *earthly mould, etc.*

A frail damsel again is a character common enough in all
poems; and one upon which many fine and pathetic lines have
been expended. Mr Wordsworth has written more than three
hundred on the subject: but, instead of new images of tender-
ness, or delicate representation of intelligible feelings, he has
contrived to tell us nothing whatever of the unfortunate fair
one, but that her name is Martha Ray; and that she goes up to
the top of a hill, in a red cloak, and cries "O misery!" All the
rest of the poem is filled with a description of an old thorn and
a pond, and of the silly stories which the neighbouring women
told about them.

The sports of childhood, and the untimely death of promis-
ing youth, is also a common topic for poetry. Mr Wordsworth
has made some blank verse about it; but, instead of the delight-
ful and picturesque sketches with which so many authors of
moderate talent have presented us on this inviting subject, all
that he is pleased to communicate of *his* rustic child, is, that he
used to amuse himself with shouting to the owls, and hearing
them answer. To make amends for this brevity, the process of
his mimicry is most accurately described.

> With fingers interwoven, both hands
> Press'd closely palm to palm, and to his mouth
> Uplifted, he, as through an instrument,
> Blew mimic hootings to the silent owls,
> That they might answer him.

This is all we hear of him; and for the sake of this one accomplishment, we are told, that the author has frequently stood mute, and gazed on his grave for half an hour together!

Love, and the fantasies of lovers, have afforded an ample theme to poets of all ages. Mr Wordsworth, however, has thought fit to compose a piece, illustrating this copious subject by one single thought. A lover trots away to see his mistress one fine evening, gazing all the way on the moon; when he comes to her door,

> O mercy! to myself I cried,
> If Lucy should be dead.

And there the poem ends!

Now, we leave it to any reader of common candour and discernment to say, whether these representations of character and sentiment are drawn from that eternal and universal standard of truth and nature, which every one is knowing enough to recognize, and no one great enough to depart from with impunity; or whether they are not formed, as we have ventured to allege, upon certain fantastic and affected peculiarities in the mind or fancy of the author, into which it is most improbable that many of his readers will enter, and which cannot, in some cases, be comprehended without much effort and explanation. Instead of multiplying instances, of these wide and wilful aberrations from ordinary nature, it may be more satisfactory to produce the author's own admission of the narrowness of the plan upon which he writes, and of the very extraordinary circumstances which he himself sometimes thinks it necessary for his readers to keep in view, if they would wish to understand the beauty or propriety of his delineations.

A pathetic tale of guilt or superstition may be told, we are apt to fancy, by the poet himself, in his general character of poet, with full as much effect as by any other person. An old nurse, at any rate, or a monk or parish clerk, is always at hand to give grace to such a narration. None of these, however, would satisfy Mr Wordsworth. He has written a long poem of this sort, in which he thinks it indispensably necessary to apprise the reader, that he has endeavoured to represent the language and sentiments of a particular character—of which character he adds . . .

> . . . the reader will have a general notion, if he has ever known a man, *a captain of a small trading vessel,* for example, who, being *past the middle age of life,* has retired upon an *annuity,* or *small independent income,* to some *village* or country town to which he was not a *native,* or in which he has not been accustomed to live!

Now, we must be permitted to doubt, whether, among all the readers of Mr Wordsworth (few or many), there is a single individual who has had the happiness of knowing a person of this very peculiar description; or who is capable of forming any sort of conjecture of the particular disposition and turn of thinking which such a combination of attributes would be apt to produce. To us, we will confess, the *annonce* appears as ludicrous and absurd as it would be in the author of an ode or an epic to say,

> Of this piece the reader will necessarily form a very erroneous judgment, unless he is apprised, that it was written by a pale man in a green coat—sitting cross-legged on an oaken stool—with a scratch on his nose, and a spelling dictionary on the table.

Wilson: digression on Wordsworth in review of Crabbe's *Tales of the Hall*; *Blackwood's,* July 1819

Wordsworth, on the other hand, is a man of high intellect and profound sensibility, meditating in solitude on the phenomena of human nature. He sometimes seems to our imagination like a man contemplating from the shore the terrors of the sea, not surely with apathy, but with a solemn and almost impassioned sense of the awful mysteries of Providence. This seeming self-abstraction from the turmoil of life gives to his highest poetry a still and religious character that is truly sublime— though, at the same time, it oftens leads to a sort of mysticism, and carries the poet out of those sympathies which are engendered in human hearts by a sense of our common imperfections. Perhaps it would not be wrong to say, that his creed is sometimes too austere, and that it deals, almost unmercifully, with misguided sensibilities and perverted passions. Such, at least, is a feeling that occasionally steals upon us from the loftiest passages of the *Excursion*, in which the poet, desirous of soaring to heaven, forgets that he is a frail child of earth, and would in vain free his human nature from those essential passions, which, in the pride of intellect, he seems unduly to despise!

But the sentiment which we have now very imperfectly expressed, refers almost entirely to the higher morals of the *Excursion*, and has little or no respect to that poetry of Wordsworth in which he has painted the character and life of certain classes of the English People. True, that he stands to a certain degree aloof from the subjects of his description, but he ever looks on them all with tenderness and benignity. Their cares and anxieties are indeed not his own, and therefore, in painting them, he does not, like Burns, identify himself with the creatures of his poetry. But, at the same time, he graciously and humanely descends into the lowliest walks of life—and knowing that humanity is sacred, he views its spirit with reverence. Though far above the beings whose nature he delineates, he yet comes down in his wisdom to their humble level, and strives to cherish that spirit

> Which gives to all the same intent,
> When life is pure and innocent.

The natural disposition of his mind inclines him to dwell rather on the mild, gentle, and benignant affections, than on the more agitating passions. Indeed, in almost all cases, the passions of his agents subside into affections—and a feeling of tranquility and repose is breathed from his saddest pictures of human sorrow. It seems to be part of his creed, that neither vice nor misery should be allowed in the representations of the poet, to stand prominently and permanently forward, and that poetry should give a true but a beautiful reflection of life. Certain it is, that all the poets of this age, or perhaps any age, Wordsworth holds the most cheering and consolatory faith— and that we at all times rise from his poetry, not only with an abatement of those fears and perplexities which the dark aspect of the world often flings over our hearts, but almost with a scorn of the impotence of grief, and certainly with a confiding trust in the perfect goodness of the Deity. We would appeal, for the truth of these remarks, to all who have studied the Two Books of the *Excursion*, entitled, "The Church-Yard among the Mountains." There, in narrating the history of the humble dead, Wordsworth does not fear to speak of their frailties, their terrors and their woes. It is indeed beautifully characteristic of the benignant wisdom of the man, that when he undertakes the task of laying open the hearts of his fellow mortals, he prefers the dead to the living, because he is willing that erring humanity should enjoy the privilege of the grave, and that his own soul should be filled with that charity which is breathed from the silence of the house of God. It is needless to say with what profound pathos the poet speaks of life thus surrounded with the images of death—how more beautiful beauty rises from the grave—how more quietly innocence seems there to slumber—and how awful is the rest of guilt.

Two Critics on "The White Doe of Rylstone"

Jeffrey: *Edinburgh Review*, October 1815

The White Doe of Rylstone; or the Fate of the Nortons: a Poem by WILLIAM WORDSWORTH. 4to. pp. 162. London 1815.

This, we think, has the merit of being the very worst poem we ever saw imprinted in a quarto volume; and though it was scarcely to be expected, we confess, that Mr Wordsworth, with all his ambition, should so soon have attained to that distinction, the wonder may perhaps be diminished, when we state, that it seems to us to consist of a happy union of all the faults, without any of the beauties, which belong to his school of poetry. It is just such a work, in short, as some wicked enemy of that school might be supposed to have devised, on purpose to make it ridiculous; and when we first took it up, we could not help fancying that some ill-natured critic had taken this harsh method of instructing Mr Wordsworth, by example, in the nature of those errors, against which our precepts had been so

often directed in vain. We had gone far, however, till we felt
intimately, that nothing in the nature of a joke could be so in-
supportably dull—and that this must be the work of one who
honestly believed it to be a pattern of pathetic simplicity, and
gave it out as such to the admiration of all intelligent readers.
In this point of view, the work may be regarded as curious at
least, if not in some degree interesting; and, at all events, it must
be instructive to be made aware of the excesses into which
superior understandings may be betrayed, by long self-indul-
gence, and the strange extravagances into which they may run,
when under the influence of that intoxication which is pro-
duced by unrestrained admiration of themselves. This poetical
intoxication, indeed, to pursue the figure a little further, seems
capable of assuming as many forms as the vulgar one which
arises from wine; and it appears to require as delicate a manage-
ment to make a man a good poet by the help of the one, as to
make him a good companion by the means of the other. In both
cases, a little mistake as to the dose or the quality of the inspir-
ing fluid may make him absolutely outrageous, or lull him over
into the most profound stupidity, instead of brightening up the
hidden stores of genius: And truly we are concerned to say,
that Mr Wordsworth seems hitherto to have been unlucky in
the choice of his liquor—or of his bottle holder. In some of his
odes and ethic exhortations, he was exposed to the public
in a state of incoherent rapture and glorious delirium, to which
we think we have seen a parallel among the humbler lovers of
jollity. In the Lyrical Ballads, he was exhibited, on the whole,
in a vein of very pretty deliration; but in the poem before us,
he appears in a state of low and maudlin imbecility, which
would not have misbecome Master Silence himself, in the close
of a social day. Whether this unhappy result is to be ascribed
to any adulteration of his Castalian cups, or to the unlucky
choice of his company over them, we cannot presume to say.
It may be, that he has dashed his Hippocrene with too large
an infusion of lake water, or assisted its operation too exclu-
sively by the study of the ancient historical ballads of 'the
north countrie.' That there are palpable imitations of the style
and manner of those venerable compositions in the work

before us, is indeed undeniable; but it unfortunately happens, that while the hobbling versification, the mean diction, and flat stupidity of these models are very exactly copied, and even improved upon, in this imitation, their rude energy, manly simplicity, and occasional felicity of expression, have totally disappeared; and, instead of them, a large allowance of the author's own metaphysical sensibility, and mystical wordiness, is forced into an unnatural combination with the borrowed beauties which have just been mentioned.

The story of the poem, though not capable of furnishing out matter for a quarto volume, might yet have made an interesting ballad; and, in the hands of Mr Scott, or Lord Byron, would probably have supplied many images to be loved, and descriptions to be remembered. The incidents arise out of the short-lived Catholic insurrection of the Northern counties, in the reign of Elizabeth, which was supposed to be connected with the project of marrying the Queen of Scots to the Duke of Norfolk, and terminated in the ruin of the Earls of Northumberland and Westmorland, by whom it was chiefly abetted. Among the victims of this rash enterprise was Richard Norton of Rylstone, who comes to the array with a splendid banner, at the head of eight tall sons, but against the will and advice of a ninth, who, though he refused to join the host, yet follows unarmed in its rear, out of anxiety for the fate of his family; and, when the father and his gallant progeny are made prisoners, and led to execution, at York, recovers the fatal banner, and is slain by a party of the Queen's horse near Bolton priory, in which place he had been ordered to deposit it by the dying voice of his father. The stately halls and pleasant bowers of Rylstone are wasted and fall into desolation; while the heroic daughter, and only survivor of the house, is sheltered among its faithful retainers, and wanders about for many years in its neighbourhood, accompanied by a beautiful white doe, which had formerly been a pet in the family; and continues, long after the death of this sad survivor, to repair every Sunday to the churchyard of Bolton priory, and there to feed and wander among their graves, to the wonder and delight of the rustic congregation that came there to worship.

This, we think, is a pretty subject for a ballad; and, in the author's better day, might have made a lyrical one of considerable interest: Let us see, however, how he deals with it since he has bethought him of publishing in quarto.

[*Destructive analysis of the poem follows.*]

Wilson in *Blackwood's*, July 1818; from "Essays on the Lake School of Poetry," No. 1

If Byron be altogether unlike Scott, Wordsworth is yet more unlike Byron. With all the great and essential faculties of the Poet, he possesses the calm and self-commanding powers of the Philosopher. He looks over human life with a steady and serene eye; he listens with a fine ear "to the still sad music of humanity." His faith is unshaken in the prevalence of virtue over vice, and of unhappiness over misery; and in the existence of a heavenly law operating on earth, and, in spite of transitory defects, always visibly triumphant in the grand field of human warfare. Hence he looks over the world of life, and man, with a sublime benignity; and hence, delighting in all the gracious dispensations of God, his great mind can wholly deliver itself up to the love of a flower budding in the field, or of a child asleep in its cradle; nor, in doing so, feels that Poetry can be said to stoop or to descend, much less to be degraded, when she embodies, in words of music, the purest and most delightful fancies and affections of the human heart. This love of the nature to which he belongs, and which is in him the fruit of wisdom and experience, gives to all his Poetry a very peculiar, a very endearing, and, at the same time, a very lofty character. His Poetry is little coloured by the artificial distinctions of society. In his delineations of passion or character, he is not so much guided by the varieties produced by customs, institutions, professions, or modes of life, as by those great elementary laws of our nature which are unchangeable and the same; and therefore the pathos and the truth of his most felicitous Poetry are more profound than of any other, not unlike the most touching and beautiful passages in the Sacred Page. The same spirit of love, and benignity, and etherial purity, which breathes over all his pictures of the virtues and the happiness of man, pervades those too of external nature. Indeed, all the Poets of the age—and none can dispute that they must likewise be the best Critics—have given up to him the palm in that Poetry which commences with the forms, and hues, and odours, and sounds, of the material world. He has brightened the earth we inhabit to our eyes; he has made it more musical to our ears; he has rendered it more creative to our imaginations.

We are well aware, that what we have now written of Wordsworth is not the opinion entertained of his genius in Scotland, where, we believe, his Poetry is scarcely known, except by the extracts from it, in the *Edinburgh Review*. But in England his reputation is high—indeed, among many of the very best judges, the highest of all our living Poets; and it is our intention, in this and some other articles, to give our readers an opportunity of judging for themselves, whether he is or is not a great Poet. This they will best be enabled to do by fair and full critiques on all his principal Poems, and by full and copious quotations from them, selected in an admiring but impartial spirit. We purpose to enter, after this has been done, at some length into the peculiarities of his system and of his genius, which we humbly conceive we have studied with more care, and, we fear not to say, with more knowledge and to better purpose, than any writer in the *Edinburgh Review*. Indeed, the general conviction of those whose opinions are good for any thing on the subject of Poetry is, that, however excellent many of the detached remarks on particular passages may be, scarcely one syllable of truth—that is, of knowledge—has ever appeared in the *Edinburgh Review* on the general principles of Wordsworth's Poetry, or, as it has been somewhat vaguely, and not very philosophically, called, the Lake School of Poetry. We quarrel with no critic for his mere critical opinions; and in the disquisitions which, ere long, we shall enter into on this subject, we shall discuss all disputed points with perfect amenity, and even amity, towards those who, *toto cælo*,

dissent from our views. There is by far too much wrangling
and jangling in our periodical criticism. Every critic, now-a-
days, raises his bristles, as if he were afraid of being thought too
tame and good-natured. There is a want of genial feeling in
professional judges of Poetry; and this want is not always sup-
plied by a deep knowledge of the laws. For our own parts,
we intend at all times to write of great living Poets in the same
spirit of love and reverence with which it is natural to regard
the dead and the sanctified; and this is the only spirit in which
a critic can write of his contemporaries without frequent dog-
matism, presumption, and injustice.

We shall now direct the attention of our readers to the
White Doe of Rylstone, a poem which exhibits in perfection
many of Wordsworth's peculiar beauties, and, it may be, some
of his peculiar defects. It is in itself a whole; and on that
account we prefer beginning with it, in place of the Lyrical
Ballads, or the subsequent "Poems" of the author, which con-
tain specimens of so many different styles; and still more, in
place of the *Excursion*, which, though a great work in itself, is
but a portion of a still greater one, and will afford subject-
matter for more than one long article.

[*Here follows the usual conducted tour through the poem, accompanied
by substantial quotations.*]

It will be soon seen, by those who have not read this Poem,
that in it Mr Wordsworth has aimed at awakening the feelings
and affections through the medium of the imagination. There
are many readers of Poetry who imperiously demand strong
passion and violent excitement, and who can perceive little
merit in any composition which does not administer to that
kind of enjoyment. Such persons will probably consider this
Poem feeble and uninteresting, as they will do numerous pro-
ductions that have, nevertheless, established themselves in the
literature of our country. But it is owing to a defect of imagina-
tion that the beauty, apparent and delightful to others, shines
not upon them. All those magical touches, by which a true
Poet awakens endless trains of thought in an imaginative mind,
are not felt at all by persons of such character. It is wonderful
what influence a delicate tune, or shade, or tone, may have

E

over the poetical visions of a poetical reader. In poetry, as in painting, gentle lineaments, and sober colouring, and chastened composition, often affect and delight the mind of capable judges more than even the most empassioned efforts of the art. But, to the vulgar—and even to minds of more power than delicacy or refinement—such delineations carry with them no charm—no authority. Many persons, in some things not only able but enlightened, would look with untouched souls on the pictures of Raphael—and turn, undelighted, from the countenance and the eyes of beings more lovely than human life—to the rapturous contemplation of mere earthly beauty. If we do not greatly err, the Poem we have now been analyzing possesses much of the former characters, and will afford great delight on every perusal—new and gentle beauties stealing and breathing from it like fragrance from perennial flowers.

Indeed, the tradition on which the Poem is founded must, to an unimaginative mind, appear childish and insignificant; but to purer spirits, beautifully adapted to the purposes of Poetry. The creature, with whose image so many mournful and sublime associations are connected, is by nature one of the loveliest—wildest—of the lower orders of creation. All our ordinary associations with it are poetical. It is not the first time that a great Poet has made this fair animal the friend of his human innocence. During the happy days of the Lady Emily we can figure to ourselves nothing more beautiful than her and her mute favourite gliding together through the woods and groves of Rylstone-hall; and when utter desolation comes over that Paradise, and the orphan is left alone on the hopeless earth, a more awful bond of connexion is then felt to subsist between the forlorn lady and the innocent companion of her days of blessedness. We willingly attribute something like human reason and human love to that fair creature of the woods —and feel the deep pathos implied in such communion between a human soul in its sorrow with an inferior nature, that seems elevated by its being made the object of tender affection to a being above itself. A ring, a lock of hair, a picture, a written word of love, would be cherished with holy passion, by a solitary heart that mourned over their former possessor.

To the Lady Emily nothing remained of all she had loved on earth—nothing but the play-mate of herself and youthful brothers—the object which the dead had loved in their happiness, and which, with a holy instinct, forsook the wild life to which it had returned, when the melancholy face of its protector once more shone among the woods.

Of Emily herself little need be said. From the first moment she is felt to be orphaned—all her former happiness is to us like a dream—all that is real with her is sorrow. In one day she becomes utterly desolate. But there is no agony, no convulsion, no despair; profound sadness, settled grief, the everlasting calm of melancholy, and the perfect stillness of resignation. All her looks, words, movements, are gentle, feminine, subdued. Throughout all the Poem an image of an angelical being seems to have lived in the Poet's soul—and without effort, he gives it to us in angelical beauty.

The character and situation of Francis, the eldest brother, are finely conceived, and coloured in the same calm and serene style of painting. He is felt to be a hero, though throughout branded with the name of coward. It required some courage in a Poet to describe a character so purely passive. There is, we think, a solemnity, and piety, and devotion, in the character that becomes truly awful, linked, as they are, throughout, with the last extremities of human suffering and calamity.

But we must conclude—and we do so with perfect confidence, that many who never have read this Poem, and not a few who may have read extracts from it with foolish and unbecoming levity, will feel and acknowledge, from the specimens we have now given, that the *White Doe of Rylstone* is a tale written with singularly beautiful simplicity of language, and with a power and pathos that have not been often excelled in English Poetry.

Lamb on *The Excursion*: *Quarterly Review*, October 1814

The causes which have prevented the poetry of Mr Words-worth from attaining its full share of popularity are to be found in the boldness and originality of his genius. The times are past when a poet could securely follow the direction of his own mind into whatever tracts it might lead. A writer, who would be popular, must timidly coast the shore of prescribed senti-ment and sympathy. He must have just as much more of the imaginative faculty than his readers, as will serve to keep their apprehensions from stagnating, but not so much as to alarm their jealousy. He must not think or feel too deeply.

If he has had the fortune to be bred in the midst of the most magnificent objects of creation, he must not have given away his heart to them; or if he have, he must conceal his love, or not carry his expressions of it beyond that point of rapture, which the occasional tourist thinks it not overstepping decorum to betray, or the limit which that gentlemanly spy upon Nature, the picturesque traveller, has vouchsafed to countenance. He must do this, or be content to be thought an enthusiast.

If from living among simple mountaineers, from a daily intercourse with them, not upon the footing of a patron, but in the character of an equal, he has detected, or imagines that he has detected, through the cloudy medium of their unlettered discourse, thought and apprehensions not vulgar; traits of patience and constancy, love unwearied, and heroic endurance, not unfit (as he may judge) to be made the subject of verse, he will be deemed a man of perverted genius by the philan-thropist who, conceiving of the peasantry of his country only as objects of pecuniary sympathy, starts at finding them ele-vated to a level of humanity with himself, having their own loves, enmities, cravings, aspirations, etc., as much beyond his faculty to believe, as his beneficence to supply.

If from a familiar observation of the ways of children, and much more from a retrospect of his own mind when a child, he has gathered more reverential notions of that state than fall to the lot of ordinary observers, and, escaping from the dis-

sonant wranglings of men, has tuned his lyre, though but for
occasional harmonies, to the milder utterance of that soft age,
—his verses shall be censured as infantile by critics who con-
found poetry 'having children for its subject' with poetry that
is 'childish,' and who, having themselves, perhaps, never been
children, never having possessed the tenderness and docility
of that age, know not what the soul of a child is—how appre-
hensive! how imaginative! how religious!

We have touched upon some of the causes which we con-
ceive to have been unfriendly to the author's former poems.
We think they do not apply in the same force to the one before
us. There is in it more of uniform elevation, a wider scope of
subject, less of manner, and it contains none of those starts and
imperfect shapings which in some of this author's smaller
pieces offended the weak, and gave scandal to the perverse.
It must indeed be approached with seriousness. It has in it
much of that quality which "draws the devout, deterring the
profane." Those who hate the *Paradise Lost* will not love this
poem. The steps of the great master are discernible in it; not in
direct imitations or injurious parody, but in the following of
the spirit, in free homage and generous subjection.

One objection it is impossible not to foresee. It will be asked,
why put such eloquent discourse in the mouth of a pedlar? It
might be answered that Mr Wordsworth's plan required a char-
acter in humble life to be the organ of his philosophy. It was
in harmony with the system and scenery of his poem. We read
Piers Plowman's Creed, and the lowness of the teacher seems
to add a simple dignity to the doctrine. Besides, the poet has
bestowed an unusual share of education upon him. Is it too
much to suppose that the author, at some early period of his
life, may himself have known such a person, a man endowed
with sentiments above his situation, another Burns; and that
the dignified strains which he has attributed to the Wanderer
may be no more than recollections of his conversation, height-
ened only by the amplification natural to poetry, or the lustre
which imagination flings back upon the objects and companions
of our youth? After all, if there should be found readers will-
ing to admire the poem, who yet feel scandalized at a *name*, we

would advise them, wherever it occurs, to substitute silently the word *Palmer*, or *Pilgrim*, or any less offensive designation, which shall connect the notion of sobriety in heart and manners with the experience and privileges which a wayfaring life confers.

From Lamb's Letter to Wordsworth, December 1814

DEAR WORDSWORTH,

I told you my Review was a very imperfect one. But what you will see in the *Quarterly* is a spurious one which Mr Baviad Gifford has palm'd upon it for mine. I never felt more vexd in my life than when I read it. I cannot give you an idea of what he has done to it out of spite at me because he once sufferd me to be called a lunatic in his Thing. The *language* he has alterd throughout. Whatever inadequateness it had to its subject, it was in point of composition the prettiest piece of prose I ever writ, and so my sister (to whom alone I read the MS.) said. That charm if it had any is all gone: more than a third of the substance is cut away, and that not all from one place, but *passim*, so as to make utter nonsense. Every warm expression is changed for a nasty cold one. . . . I assure you my complaints are founded. I know how sore a word alterd makes one, but indeed of this Review the whole complexion is gone. I regret only that I did not keep a copy. I am sure you would have been pleased with it, because I have been feeding my fancy for some months with the notion of pleasing you. Its imperfection or inadequateness in size and method I knew, but for the *writing part* of it, I was fully satisfied. I hoped it would make more than atonement. Ten or twelve distinct passages come to my mind, which are gone, and what is left is of course the worse for their having been there, the eyes are pulld out and the bleeding sockets are left. I read it at Arch's shop with my face burning with vexation secretly, with just such a feeling as if it had been a review written against myself, making false quotations from me. But I am ashamed to say so much about a short piece. How are *you* served! and the labors of years turn'd into contempt by scoundrels.

. But I could not but protest against your taking that thing as mine. Every *pretty* expression, (I know there were many) every warm expression, there was nothing else, is vulgarised and frozen—but if they catch me in their camps again let them spitchcock me. They had a right to do it, as no name appears to it, and Mr Shoemaker Gifford I suppose never wa[i]ved a right he had since he commencd author. God confound him and all caitiffs.

C.L.

(Letters, ed. Lucas, vol. ii, p. 148)

Jeffrey: in *Edinburgh Review*, November 1814

The Excursion; being a Portion of the Recluse, a Poem. By WILLIAM WORDSWORTH. 4to. Pp. 447. London, 1814.

THIS will never do! It bears no doubt the stamp of the author's heart and fancy: but unfortunately not half so visibly as that of his peculiar system. His former poems were intended to recommend that system, and to bespeak favour for it by their individual merit; but this, we suspect, must be recommended by the system—and can only expect to succeed where it has been previously established. It is longer, weaker, and tamer, than any of Mr Wordsworth's other productions; with less boldness of originality, and less even of that extreme simplicity and lowliness of tone which wavered so prettily, in the Lyrical Ballads, between silliness and pathos. We have imitations of Cowper, and even of Milton here; engrafted on the natural drawl of the Lakers—and all diluted into harmony by that profuse and irrepressible wordiness which deluges all the blank verse of this school of poetry, and lubricates and weakens the whole structure of their style.

Though it fairly fills four hundred and twenty good quarto pages, without note, vignette, or any sort of extraneous assistance, it is stated in the title—with something of an imprudent candour—to be but "a portion" of a larger work; and in the preface, where an attempt is rather unsuccessfully made to explain the whole design, it is still more rashly disclosed, that it is but "*a part of the second part*, of a *long* and laborious work" —which is to consist of three parts!

What Mr Wordsworth's ideas of length are, we have no means of accurately judging: but we cannot help suspecting that they are liberal to a degree that will alarm the weakness of most modern readers. As far as we can gather from the preface, the entire poem—or one of them (for we really are not sure whether there is to be one or two)—is of a biographical nature; and is to contain the history of the author's mind, and of the origin and progress of his poetical powers, up to the period when they were sufficiently matured to qualify him for the great work on which he has been so long employed. Now, the quarto before us contains an account of one of his youthful rambles in the vales of Cumberland, and occupies precisely the period of three days! So that, by the use of a very powerful *calculus*, some estimate may be formed of the probable extent of the entire biography.

This small specimen, however, and the statements with which it is prefaced, have been sufficient to set our minds at rest in one particular. The case of Mr Wordsworth, we perceive, is now manifestly hopeless, and we give up as altogether incurable, and beyond the power of criticism. We cannot, indeed, altogether omit taking precautions now and then against the spreading of the malady; but for himself, though we shall watch the progress of his symptoms as a matter of professional curiosity and instruction, we really think it right not to harass him any longer with nauseous remedies—but rather to throw in cordials and lenitives, and wait in patience for the natural termination of the disorder. In order to justify this desertion of our patient, however, it is proper to state why we despair of the success of a more active practice.

A man who has been for twenty years at work on such matter as is now before us, and who comes complacently forward with a whole quarto of it, after all the admonitions he has received, cannot reasonably be expected to "change his hand, or check his pride," upon the suggestion of far weightier monitors than we can pretend to be. Inveterate habit must now have given a kind of sanctity to the errors of early taste; and the very powers of which we lament the perversion, have probably become incapable of any other application. The very quantity, too, that he has written, and is at this moment working up for publication upon the old pattern, makes it almost hopeless to look for any change of it. All this is so much capital already sunk in the concern; which must be sacrificed if that be abandoned: and no man likes to give up for lost the time and talent and labour which he has embodied in any permanent production. We were not previously aware of these obstacles to Mr Wordsworth's conversion; and, considering the peculiarities of his former writings merely as the result of certain wanton and capricious experiments on public taste and indulgence, conceived it to be our duty to discourage their repetition by all the means in our power. We now see clearly, however, how the case stands; and, making up our minds, though with the most sincere pain and reluctance, to consider him as finally lost to the good cause of poetry, shall endeavour to be thankful for the occasional gleams of tenderness and beauty which the natural force of his imagination and affections must still shed over all his productions—and to which we shall ever turn with delight, in spite of the affectation and mysticism and prolixity, with which they are so abundantly contrasted.

Long habits of seclusion, and an excessive ambition of originality, can alone account for the disproportion which seems to exist between this author's taste and his genius; or for the devotion with which he has sacrificed so many precious gifts at the shrine of those paltry idols which he has set up for himself among his lakes and his mountains. Solitary musings, amidst such scenes, might no doubt be expected to nurse up the mind to the majesty of poetical conceptions (though it is remarkable, that all the greater poets lived, or had lived, in the full current of society); but the collision of equal minds—the admonition of prevailing impressions—seems necessary to reduce its redundancies, and repress that tendency to extravagance or puerility, into which the self-indulgence and self-admiration of genius is so apt to be betrayed, when it is allowed to wanton, without awe or restraint, in the triumph and delight of its own intoxication. That its flights should be graceful and glorious in the eyes of men, it seems almost to be necessary that they should be made in the consciousness that men's eyes are to behold them—and that the inward transport and vigour by which they are inspired, should be tempered by an occasional reference to what will be thought of them by those ultimate dispensers of glory. An habitual and general knowledge of the few settled and permanent maxims, which form the canon of general taste in all large and polished societies—a certain tact, which informs us at once that many things, which we still love and are moved by in secret, must necessarily be despised as childish, or derided as absurd, in all such societies, —though it will not stand in the place of genius, seems necessary to the success of its exertions; and though it will never enable any one to produce the higher beauties of art, can alone secure the talent which does produce them from errors that must render it useless. Those who have most of the talent, however, commonly acquire this knowledge with the greatest facility; and if Mr Wordsworth, instead of confining himself almost entirely to the society of the dalesmen and cottagers, and little children, who form the subjects of his book, had condescended to mingle a little more with the people that were to read and judge of it, we cannot help thinking that its texture might have been considerably improved; at least it appears to us to be absolutely impossible, that any one who had lived or mixed familiarly with men of literature and ordinary judgment in poetry (of course we exclude the coadjutors and disciples of his own school), could ever have fallen into such gross faults, or so long mistaken them for beauties. His first essays we looked upon in a good degree as poetical paradoxes, maintained experimentally, in order to display talent, and court notoriety—and so maintained, with no more serious belief in their truth, than is usually generated by an ingenious and animated defence of other paradoxes. But when we find that he has been for twenty years exclusively employed upon articles of this very fabric, and that he has still enough of raw material on hand to keep him so employed for twenty years to come, we cannot refuse him the justice of believing that he is a

sincere convert to his own system, and must ascribe the pecu-
liarities of his composition, not to any transient affectation, or
accidental caprice of imagination, but to a settled perversity
of taste or understanding, which has been fostered, if not alto-
gether created, by the circumstances to which we have alluded.

The volume before us, if we were to describe it very shortly,
we should characterize as a tissue of moral and devotional rav-
ings, in which innumerable changes are rung upon a few very
simple and familiar ideas: but with such an accompaniment of
long words, long sentences, and unwieldy phrases—and such a
hubbub of strained raptures and fantastical sublimities, that it
is often difficult for the most skilful and attentive student to
obtain a glimpse of the author's meaning—and altogether im-
possible for an ordinary reader to conjecture what he is about.
Moral and religious enthusiasm, though undoubtedly poetical
emotions, are at the same time but dangerous inspirers of
poetry; nothing being so apt to run into interminable dulness
or mellifluous extravagance, without giving the unfortunate
author the slightest intimation of his danger. His laudable
zeal for the efficacy of his preachments, he very naturally mis-
takes for the ardour of poetical inspiration—and, while deal-
ing out the high words and glowing phrases which are so
readily supplied by themes of this description, can scarcely
avoid believing that he is eminently original and impressive:
all sorts of commonplace notions and expressions are sanctified
in his eyes, by the sublime ends for which they are employed;
and the mystical verbiage of the Methodist pulpit is repeated,
till the speaker entertains no doubt that he is the chosen organ
of divine truth and persuasion. But if such be the common
hazards of seeking inspiration from those potent fountains,
it may easily be conceived what chance Mr Wordsworth had of
escaping their enchantment, with his natural propensities to
wordiness, and his unlucky habit of debasing pathos with
vulgarity. The fact accordingly is, that in this production he is
more obscure than a Pindaric poet of the seventeenth century;
and more verbose "than even himself of yore"; while the
wilfulness with which he persists in choosing his examples of
intellectual dignity and tenderness exclusively from the lowest

ranks of society, will be sufficiently apparent, from the circumstances of his having thought fit to make his chief prolocutor in this poetical dialogue, and chief advocate of Providence and virtue, *an old Scotch Pedlar*—retired indeed from business—but still rambling about in his former haunts, and gossiping among his old customers, without his pack on his shoulders. The other persons of the drama are, a retired military chaplain, who has grown half an atheist and half a misanthrope—the wife of an unprosperous weaver—a servant girl with her natural child—a parish pauper, and one or two other personages of equal rank and dignity.

The character of the work is decidedly didactic; and more than nine tenths of it are occupied with a species of dialogue, or rather a series of long sermons or harangues, which pass between the pedlar, the author, the old chaplain, and a worthy vicar, who entertains the whole party at dinner on the last day of their excursion. The incidents which occur in the course of it are few and trifling as can well be imagined; and those which the different speakers narrate in the course of their discourses, are introduced rather to illustrate their arguments or opinions, than for any interest they are supposed to possess of their own. The doctrine which the work is intended to enforce, we are by no means certain that we have discovered. In so far as we can collect, however, it seems to be neither more nor less than the old familiar one, that a firm belief in the providence of a wise and beneficent Being must be our great stay and support under all afflictions and perplexities upon earth—and that there are indications of His power and goodness in all the aspects of the visible universe, whether living or inanimate—every part of which should therefore be regarded with love and reverence, as exponents of those great attributes. We can testify, at least, that these salutary and important truths are inculcated at far greater length, and with more repetitions, than in any ten volumes of sermons that we have ever perused.   It is also maintained, with equal conciseness and originality, that there is frequently much good sense, as well as much enjoyment, in the humbler conditions of life; and that, in spite of great vices and abuses, there is a reasonable allowance both of happiness and

goodness in society at large. If there be any deeper or more
recondite doctrines in Mr Wordsworth's book, we must con-
fess that they have escaped us; and, convinced as we are of the
truth and soundness of those to which we have alluded, we
cannot help thinking that they might have been better enforced
with less parade and prolixity. His effusions on what may be
called the physiognomy of external nature, or its moral and
theological expression, are eminently fantastic, obscure, and
affected. It is quite time, however, that we should give the
reader a more particular account of this singular performance.

It opens with a picture of the author toiling across a bare
common in a hot summer day, and reaching at last a ruined
hut surrounded with tall trees, where he meets by appointment
with a hale old man, with an iron-pointed staff lying beside him.
Then follows, a retrospective account of their first acquaint-
ance—formed, it seems, when the author was at a village school
and his aged friend occupied "one room—the fifth part of a
house" in the neighbourhood. After this, we have the history
of this reverend person at no small length. He was born, we
are happy to find, in Scotland—among the hills of Athol; and
his mother, after his father's death, married the parish school-
master—so that he was taught his letters betimes: but then,
as it is here set forth with much solemnity,

> From his sixth year, the boy of whom I speak,
> In summer, tended cattle on the hills;

And again, a few pages after, that there may be no risk of mis-
take as to a point of such essential importance:

> From early childhood, even, as hath been said,
> From his *sixth year*, he had been sent abroad,
> *In summer*—to tend herds! Such was his task!

In the course of this occupation it is next recorded, that he
acquired such a taste for rural scenery and open air, that when
he was sent to teach a school in a neighbouring village, he
found it "a misery to him," and determined to embrace the
more romantic occupation of a Pedlar—or, as Mr Wordsworth
more musically expresses it,

> A vagrant merchant, bent beneath his load;

—and in the course of his peregrinations had acquired a very large acquaintance, which, after he had given up dealing, he frequently took a summer ramble to visit.

The author, on coming up to this interesting personage, finds him sitting with his eyes half shut; and, not being quite sure whether he is asleep or awake, stands "some minutes' space" in silence beside him. "At length," says he, with his own delightful simplicity:

> At length I hail'd him—*seeing that his hat*
> *Was moist* with water-drops, as if the brim
> Had newly scoop'd a running stream!—
> ————' "Tis," said I, "a burning day!
> My lips are parch'd with thirst; but you, I guess,
> Have somewhere found relief."

Upon this, the benevolent old man points him out, not a running stream but a well in a corner, to which the author repairs; and after minutely describing its situation, beyond a broken wall, and between two alders that "grew in a cold damp nook," he thus faithfully chronicles the process of his return:

> My thirst I slak'd; and from the cheerless spot
> Withdrawing, straightway to the shade return'd,
> Where sate the old man on the cottage bench.

The Pedlar then gives an account of the last inhabitants of the deserted cottage beside them. These were, a good industrious weaver and his wife and children. They were very happy for a while, till sickness and want of work came upon them; and then the father enlisted as a soldier, and the wife pined in that lonely cottage—growing every year more careless and desponding, as anxiety and fears for her absent husband, of whom no tidings ever reached her, accumulated. Her children died, and left her cheerless and alone; and at last she died also; and the cottage fell to decay. We must say, that there is very considerable pathos in the telling of this simple story; and that they who can get over the repugnance excited by the triteness of its incidents, and the lowness of its objects, will not fail to be struck with the author's knowledge of the human heart, and the power he possesses of stirring up its deepest and

gentlest sympathies. His prolixity, indeed, it is not so easy to
get over. This little story fills about twenty-five quarto pages;
and abounds, of course, with mawkish sentiment, and details
of preposterous minuteness. When the tale is told, the travel-
lers take their staffs, and end their first day's journey, without
further adventure, at a little inn.

The Second Book sets them forward betimes in the morning;
they pass by a Village Wake; and as they approach a more soli-
tary part of the mountains, the old man tells the author that he
is taking him to see an old friend of his, who had formerly
been chaplain to a Highland regiment—had lost a beloved wife
—been roused from his dejection by the first enthusiasm of the
French Revolution—had emigrated on its miscarriage, to
America—and returned disgusted to hide himself in the retreat
to which they were now ascending. That retreat is then most
tediously described—a smooth green valley in the heart of the
mountain, without trees, and with only one dwelling. Just as
they get sight of it from the ridge above, they see a funeral
train proceeding from the solitary abode, and hurry on with
some apprehension for the fate of the amiable misanthrope—
whom they find, however, in very tolerable condition at the
door, and learn that the funeral was that of an aged pauper who
had been boarded out by the parish in that cheap farm house,
and had died in consequence of long exposure to heavy rain.
The old chaplain, or, as Mr Wordsworth is pleased to call him,
the Solitary, tells this dull story at prodigious length; and after
giving an inflated description of an effect of mountain mists in
the evening sun, treats his visitors with a rustic dinner—and
they walk out to the fields at the close of the second book.

The Third makes no progress in the excursion. It is entirely
filled with moral and religious conversation and debate, and
with a more ample detail of the Solitary's past life than had
been given in the sketch of his friend. The conversation is,
in our judgment, exceedingly dull and mystical; and the Soli-
tary's confessions insufferably diffuse. Yet there is occasionally
very considerable force of writing and tenderness of sentiment
in this part of the work.

The Fourth Book is also filled with dialogues, ethical and

theological, and, with the exception of some brilliant and forcible expressions here and there, consists of an exposition of truism, more cloudy, wordy, and inconceivably prolix, than any thing we ever met with.

In the beginning of the Fifth Book, they leave the solitary valley, taking its pensive inhabitant along with them, and stray on to where the landscape sinks down into milder features, till they arrive at a church, which stands on a moderate elevation in the centre of a wide and fertile vale. Here they meditate for a while among the monuments, till the Vicar comes out and joins them—and, recognizing the Pedlar for an old acquaintance, mixes graciously in the conversation, which proceeds in a very edifying manner till the close of the book.

The Sixth contains a choice obituary, or characteristic account, of several of the persons who lie buried before this group of moralizers—an unsuccessful lover, who had found consolation in natural history—a miner, who worked on for twenty years, in despite of universal ridicule, and at last found the vein he had expected—two political enemies reconciled in old age to each other—an old female miser—a seduced damsel —and two widowers, one who had devoted himself to the education of his daughters, and one who had preferred marrying a prudent middle-aged woman to take care of them.

In the beginning of the Eighth Book, the worthy Vicar expresses, in the words of Mr Wordsworth's own epitome,

> his apprehensions that he had detained his auditors too long—invites them to his house—Solitary, disinclined to comply, rallies the Wanderer and somewhat playfully draws a comparison between his itinerant profession and that of a knight-errant—which leads to the Wanderer, giving an account of changes in the country, from the Manufacturing spirit—Its favourable effects—The other side of the picture, etc., etc.

After these very poetical themes are exhausted, they all go into the house, where they are introduced to the Vicar's wife and daughter; and while they sit chatting in the parlour over a family dinner, his son and one of his companions come in with a fine dish of trouts piled on a blue slate; and after being caressed by the company, are sent to dinner in the nursery. This ends the eighth book.

The Ninth and last Book is chiefly occupied with a mystical discourse of the Pedlar; who maintains, that the whole universe is animated by an active principle, the noblest seat of which is in the human soul; and moreover, that the final end of old age is to train and enable us

> To hear the mighty stream of *Tendency*
> Uttering, for elevation of our thoughts,
> A clear sonorous voice, inaudible
> To the vast multitude whose doom it is
> To run the giddy round of vain delight.

with other matters as luminous and emphatic. The hostess at length breaks off the harangue, by proposing that they should all make a little excursion on the lake, and they embark accordingly, and, after navigating for some time along its shores, and drinking tea on a little island, land at last on a remote promontory, from which they see the sun go down, and listen to a solemn and pious, but rather long prayer from the Vicar. They then walk back to the parsonage door, where the Author and his friend propose to spend the evening; but the Solitary prefers walking back in the moonshine to his own valley, after promising to take another ramble with them:

> If time, with free consent, be yours to give,
> And season favours.

And here the publication somewhat abruptly closes.

Nobody can be more disposed to do justice to the great powers of Mr Wordsworth than we are; and, from the first time that he came before us, down to the present moment, we have uniformly testified in their favour, and assigned indeed our high sense of their value as the chief ground of the bitterness with which we resented their perversion. That perversion, however, is now far more visible than their original dignity; and while we collect the fragments, it is impossible not to mourn over the ruins from which we are condemned to pick them. If any one should doubt of the existence of such a perversion, or be disposed to dispute about the instances we have hastily brought forward, we would just beg leave to refer him

F

to the general plan and character of the poem now before us. Why should Mr Wordsworth have made his hero a super-annuated Pedlar? What but the most wretched affectation, or provoking perversity of taste, could induce any one to place his chosen advocate of wisdom and virtue in so absurd and fantastic a condition? Did Mr Wordsworth really imagine, that his favourite doctrines were likely to gain any thing in point of effect or authority, by being put into the mouth of a person accustomed to higgle about tape, or brass sleeve-buttons? Or is it not plain, that, independent of the ridicule and disgust which such a personification must excite in many of his readers, its adoption exposes his work throughout to the charge of revolting incongruity, and utter disregard of probability or nature? For, after he has thus wilfully debased his moral teacher by a low occupation, is there one word that he puts into his mouth, or one sentiment of which he makes him the organ, that has the most remote reference to that occupation? Is there any thing in his learned, abstract, and logical harangues, that savours of the calling that is ascribed to him? Are any of their materials such as a pedlar could possibly have dealt in? Are the manners, the diction, the sentiments, in any the very smallest degree, accommodated to a person in that condition? or are they not eminently and conspicuously such as could not by possibility belong to it? A man who went about selling flannel and pocket-handkerchiefs in this lofty dictum, would soon frighten away all his customers; and would infallibly pass either for a madman, or for some learned and affected gentleman, who, in a frolic, had taken up a character which he was peculiarly ill qualified for supporting.

The absurdity in this case, we think, is palpable and glaring: but it is exactly of the same nature with that which infects the substance of the work—a puerile ambition of singularity engrafted on an unlucky predilection for truisms; and an affected passion for simplicity and humble life, most awkwardly combined with a taste for mystical refinements, and all the gorgeousness of obscure phraseology. His taste for simplicity is evinced by sprinkling up and down his interminable de-clamations a few descriptions of baby-houses, and of old hats with wet brims; and his amiable partiality for humble life, by assuring us that a wordy rhetorician, who talks about Thebes, and allegorizes all the heathen mythology, was once a pedlar—and making him break in upon his magnificent orations with two or three awkward notices of something that he had seen when selling winter raiment about the country—or of the changes in the state of society, which had almost annihilated his former calling.

From Wilson's "Vindication of Mr Wordworth's Letter to Mr Gray, on a new edition of Burns": *Blackwood's*, October 1817

There is here no call upon me to deviate into any discussion on the merits or demerits of Mr Jeffrey as a Critic. He probably would care as little for my opinion as I do for his; yet it is right that all liberal-minded men should, to a certain degree, respect each other's opinions. I therefore declare it to be my conviction, in direct opposition to that of Mr Wordsworth, that Mr Jeffrey is the best Professional Critic we now have, and that, so far from shewing gross incapacity when writing of works of original genius, that he has never, in one instance, withheld the praise of originality when it was due. Of Mr Wordsworth himself he has uniformly written in terms of far loftier commendation than any other contemporary Critic, and has placed him at all times in the first rank of Genius. It is true that he has committed innumerable mistakes, and occasionally exhibited a very perplexing ignorance, both when discussing the general question of Poetry, in reference to Mr Wordsworth's system, and when analysing individual poems and passages; but of many of the most striking and most admirable qualities of Mr Wordsworth's poetical character, he has shewn an acute and fine discernment, and poured himself out in praise of them with the most unrestrained and glowing enthusiasm. Those unmeaning sarcasms fitting the lively and ingenious turn of his mind, accustomed in his profession to a mode of thinking and feeling not very congenial with the simple and stately emotions of Poetry, can have no influence upon spirits capable and worthy of enjoying such Poems as the Lyrical Ballads, and such a Poem as the *Excursion*—while they may afford a suitable amusement to those pert and presuming persons, or those dull and obtuse ones, with whom genius holds no alliance, and to whom she can speak no intelligible language; but it is surely pleasanter to see such small folk contentedly swallowing the dole dealt out to them, in a moment of sprightliness, by a facetious Critic, than to see them laying their unprivileged hands on the viands of that Table which Wordsworth has spread for the rich and wealthy men in the Land of Intellect.

It should, however, be held in mind by Mr. Wordsworth's admirers, among whom are to be found every living Poet of any eminence, that, with all the fearlessness of original genius, he has burst and cast away the bonds which were worn very contentedly by many great writers. Mr Wordsworth is a man of too much original power not to have very often written ill; and it is incredible that, 'mid all his gigantic efforts to establish a system (even allowing that system to be a right one), he has never violated the principles of taste or reason. He has brought about a *revolution* in Poetry; and a revolution can no more be brought about in Poetry than in the Constitution, without the destruction or injury of many excellent and time-hallowed establishments. I have no doubt that, when all the rubbish is removed, and free and open space given to behold the structures which Mr Wordsworth has reared in all the grandeur of their proportions, that Posterity will hail him as a regenerator and a creator. But meanwhile some allowance must be made for them who, however ignorantly, adhere to their ancient idols; and for my own part, I can bear all manner of silly nonsense to be spoken about Wordsworth with the most unmoved tranquillity. I know that if he has often written ill, Milton and Shakespeare have done so before him. Johnson has said, that we cannot read many pages of Shakespeare "without contempt and indignation"; and Hume says, that the same divine Poet cannot, for two pages together, "preserve a reasonable propriety." The same critic says, that at least a third of *Paradise Lost* is "almost wholly devoid of harmony

and elegance—nay, of all vigour of imagination." Now,
neither Samuel Johnson nor David Hume were dunces. Let us
therefore believe that neither is Mr Francis Jeffrey a dunce—
and let Mr Wordsworth be contented with sharing the fate of
Milton and Shakespeare.

But in a subject of this nature, why should we dwell on any
disagreeable or painful altercations between men of Power.
Here there is a noble prospect, without any drawback or alloy,
to delight our souls and our imagination. A Poet distinguished
for the originality of his genius—for his profound knowledge
of the human heart, for his spiritual insight into all the grandeur
and magnificence of the external world, for a strain of the most
serene, undisturbed, and lofty morality, within whose control
no mind can come without being elevated, purified, and en-
lightened, for a religion partaking at once of all the solemnity
of faith, and all the enthusiasm of poetry—and, to crown all
with a perfect consummation, a Poet who has realized, in a life
of sublime solitude, the visions that have blessed the dreams of
his inspiration. He comes forward with a countenance and a
voice worthy of himself and the Being of whom he speaks, and
vindicates, from the confused admiration, or the vulgar re-
proaches of ordinary minds, a Bard who is the pride of his
native land, and a glory to human nature—while he speaks of
his failings with such reverential pity, of his virtues with such
noble praise, that we see Burns standing before us in all his
weakness and all his strength—the same warmhearted, affec-
tionate, headstrong, fervid, impassioned, imprudent, erring,
independent, noble, high-minded, and inspired Man, that won
or commanded every soul, and whose voice, omnipotent in life,
speaks with a yet more overpowering sound from the silence
of the grave.

COLERIDGE

'S.T.C.' was remarkably lacking in the literary man's appetite for publicity—"the scuffle," as a contemporary poet has called it, "for scraps of notice"—and, apart from the attack on Jeffrey in Chapter III of the *Biographia Literaria*, he gave no sign of any strong reaction to the criticism of his work that appeared in the periodicals. Nor was this, for the most part, of much interest or value. It is confessed on every hand that the twentieth century is only just beginning to piece together and comprehend the complex, yet unified, achievement of Coleridge's lifetime; evaluation of so much that was new, and so much that depended for elucidation on other works not yet published, perhaps not yet written, could hardly be expected from the contemporary reviewer. His poetry, indeed, stood some chance of being comprehended, or at least admired; and once the initial recoil from its extreme romanticism, as typified in Southey's dismissal of the *Ancient Mariner* as "a Dutch attempt at German sublimity" —once this had spent itself, the age did in fact produce some discerning tributes. In this the *Quarterly*, for once, led the way. Its article on Coleridge (August 1834) ought, strictly, to be excluded from this volume, for it is not criticism of a living writer; Coleridge had, tragically, died a few days before the issue appeared. But to exclude it would be a foolish pedantry. Its author, Henry Nelson Coleridge, brought to his work a deep devotion to S.T.C. combined with a knowledge of his mental processes, which, as his nephew and son-in-law, he had had the opportunity to study in conversation.

The *Edinburgh* has nothing very interesting to show, though Hazlitt's attack of 1816 is interesting enough to be reprinted. But it shows none of the qualities that make Hazlitt a good critic; and unfortunately Hazlitt reappears as co-author of the review of *Biographia Literaria* (August 1817) though this was predominantly Jeffrey's. In a footnote to the article Jeffrey answered, but without much conviction, Coleridge's strictures on his critical methods. It is an uninspiring chapter of the *Edinburgh's* story.

"Maga," with characteristic inconsistency, began by attacking Coleridge with the utmost fury (besides what is given below, the burlesque of *Christabel* in the issue for June 1819 is worth consulting), and later flattered him with equal vigour.

On the whole, the Reviewers did not show their powers to advantage in dealing with "the heaven-eyed creature." They did best by the small part of his work that was capable of being measured by the accepted standards of literary taste; both the attacks and the defences have some meaning; but, whereas in the case of Byron or Keats one feels that the contemporary critics revealed with tolerable accuracy the merits and faults of their work, leaving posterity to make some redistributions of emphasis, with Coleridge it is clear that they did not even begin to perform such a task. Their apparatus was not designed for it; though it may humble us to note that, even so, they came closer to providing a significant criticism of Coleridge than their counterparts before or since would have had the chance to do.

Hazlitt on *Kubla Khan*: *Edinburgh Review*, September 1816

Christabel: *Kubla Khan, a Vision. The Pains of Sleep.* By S. T. COLERIDGE Esq. London. Murray, 1816.

The advertisement by which this work was announced to the publick, carried in its front a recommendation from Lord Byron—who, it seems, has somewhere praised Christabel, as "a wild and singularly original and beautiful poem." Great as the noble bard's merits undoubtedly are in poetry, some of his latest *publications* dispose us to distrust his authority, where the question is what ought to meet the public eye; and the works before us afford an additional proof, that his judgment on such matters is not absolutely to be relied on. Moreover, we are a little inclined to doubt the value of the praise which one poet lends another. It seems now-a-days to be the practice of that once irritable race to laud each other without bounds; and one can hardly avoid suspecting, that what is thus lavishly advanced may be laid out with a view to being repaid with interest. Mr Coleridge, however, must be judged by his own merits.

[*The hostile analysis of "Christabel," which opens the article, has been omitted for reasons of space, but the reader will find it rewarding*].

Kubla Khan is given to the public, it seems, "at the request of a poet of great and deserved celebrity"; but whether Lord Byron the praiser of *the Christabel*, or the Laureate, the praiser of Princes, we are not informed. As far as Mr Coleridge's "own opinions are concerned," it is published, "not upon the ground of any *poetic* merits," but "as a *Psychological Curiosity*!" In these opinions of the candid author, we entirely concur; but for this reason we hardly think it was necessary to give the minute detail which the Preface contains, of the circumstances attending its composition. Had the question regarded *Paradise Lost*, or Dryden's *Ode*, we could not have had a more particular account of the circumstances in which it was composed. It was in the year 1797, and in the summer season. Mr Coleridge was in bad health; the particular disease is not given; but the careful reader will form his own conjectures. He had retired very prudently to a lonely farm-house; and whoever would see the place which gave birth to the "psychological curiosity," may find his way thither without a guide; for it is situated on the confines of Somerset and Devonshire, and on the Exmoor part of the boundary; and it is, moreover, between Porlock and Linton. In that farm-house, he had a slight indisposition, and had taken an anodyne, which threw him into a deep sleep in his chair (whether after dinner or not he omits to state), "at the moment that he was reading a sentence in Purchas's *Pilgrims*," relative to a palace of Kubla Khan. The effects of the anodyne, and the sentence together, were prodigious: They produced the "curiosity" now before us; for, during his three-hour sleep, Mr Coleridge "has the most vivid confidence that he could not have composed less than from two to three hundred lines." On awaking, he "instantly and eagerly" wrote down the verses here published; when he was (he says, "*unfortunately*") called out by a "person on business from Porlock, and detained by him above an hour"; and when he returned, the vision was gone. The lines here given smell strongly, it must be owned, of the anodyne; and, but that an under dose of a sedative produces contrary effects, we should inevitably have been lulled by them into forgetfulness of all things. Perhaps a dozen more such lines as the following would reduce the most irritable of critics to a state of inaction.

> A damsel with a dulcimer
> In a vision once I saw:
> It was an Abyssinian maid
> And on her dulcimer she play'd,
> Singing of Mount Abora.
> Could I revive within me
> Her symphony and song,
> To such a deep delight, 'twould win me
> That with music loud and long
> I would build that dome in air,
> That sunny dome! those caves of ice!
> And all who heard, should see them there,
> And all should cry, Beware! Beware!
> His flashing eyes, his floating hair!
> Weave a circle round him thrice,
> And close your eyes with holy dread:
> For he on honey-dew hath fed, *etc.*, *etc.*

There is a good deal more altogether as exquisite—and in particular a fine description of a wood, "ancient as the hills"; and "folding sunny spots of *greenery*!" But we suppose this specimen will be sufficient.

Persons in this poet's unhappy condition, generally feel the want of sleep as the worst of their evils; but there are instances too, in the history of the disease, of sleep being attended with new agony, as if the waking thoughts, how wild and turbulent soever, had still been under some slight restraint, which sleep instantly removed. Mr Coleridge appears to have experienced this symptom, if we may judge from the title of his third poem, *The Pains of Sleep*; and, in truth, from its composition—which is mere raving, without anything more affecting than a number of incoherent words, expressive of extravagance and incongruity. We need give no specimen of it.

Upon the whole, we look upon this publication as one of the most notable pieces of impertinence of which the press has lately been guilty; and one of the boldest experiments that has yet been made on the patience or understanding of the public. It is impossible, however, to dismiss it, without a remark or two. The other productions of the Lake School have generally exhibited talents thrown away upon subjects so mean, that no power of genius could ennoble them; or perverted and rendered useless by a false theory of poetical compositions. But even in the worst of them, if we except the *White Doe* of Mr Wordsworth and some of the laureate odes, there were always some gleams of feeling, or of fancy. But the thing now before us, is utterly destitute of value. It exhibits from beginning to end not a ray of genius; and we defy any man to point out a passage of poetical merit in any of the three pieces which it contains, except, perhaps, the following lines on p. 32, and even these are not very brilliant; nor is the leading thought original:

> Alas! they had been friends in youth;
> But whispering tongues can poison truth;
> And constancy lives in realms above;
> And life is thorny; and youth is vain;
> And to be wroth with one we love,
> Doth work like madness in the brain.

With this one exception, there is literally not one couplet in the publication before us which would be reckoned poetry, or even sense, were it found in the corner of a newspaper or upon the window of an inn. Must we then be doomed to hear such a mixture of raving and driv'ling, extolled as the work of a "wild and original" genius, simply because Mr Coleridge has now and then written fine verses, and a brother poet chooses, in his milder mood, to laud him from courtesy or from interest? And are such panegyrics to be echoed by the mean tools of a political faction, because they relate to one whose daily prose is understood to be dedicated to the support of all that courtiers think should be supported? If it be true that the author has thus earned the patronage of those liberal dispensers of bounty, we can have no objection that they should give him proper proofs of their gratitude; but we cannot help wishing, for his sake, as well as our own, that they would pay in solid pudding instead of empty praise; and adhere, at least in this instance, to the good old system of rewarding their champions with places and pensions, instead of puffing their bad poetry, and endeavouring to cram their nonsense down the throats of all the loyal and well affected.

John Wilson on *Biographia Literaria*: *Blackwood's*, October 1817

. . . Considered merely in a literary point of view, the work is most execrable. He rambles from one subject to another in the most wayward and capricious manner; either from indolence, or ignorance, or weakness, he has never in one single instance finished a discussion; and while he darkens what was dark before into tenfold obscurity, he so treats the most ordinary common-places as to give them the air of mysteries, till we no longer know the faces of our old acquaintances beneath their cowl and hood, but witness plain flesh and blood matters of fact miraculously converted into a troop of phantoms. That he is a man of genius is certain; but he is not a man of strong intellect nor of powerful talents. He has a great deal of fancy and imagination, but little or no real feeling, and certainly no judgment. He cannot form to himself any harmonious land-scape such as it exists in nature, but beautified by the serene light of the imagination. He cannot conceive simple and majestic groups of human figures and characters acting on the theatre of real existence. But his pictures of nature are fine only as imaging the dreaminess, and obscurity, and confusion of dis-tempered sleep; while all his agents pass before our eyes like shadows, and only impress and affect us with a phantasmagorial splendour.

It is impossible to read many pages of this work without thinking that Mr Coleridge conceives himself to be a far greater man than the Public is likely to admit; and we wish to waken him from what seems to us a most ludicrous delusion. He seems to believe that every tongue is wagging in his praise, that

every ear is open to imbibe the oracular breathings of his in-
spiration. Even when he would fain convince us that his soul
is wholly occupied with some other illustrious character, he
breaks out into laudatory exclamations concerning himself;
no sound is so sweet to him as that of his own voice: the ground
is hallowed on which his footsteps tread; and there seems to
him something more than human in his very shadow. He will
read no books that other people read; his scorn is as misplaced
and extravagant as his admiration; opinions that seem to tally
with his own wild ravings are holy and inspired; and, unless
agreeable to his creed, the wisdom of ages is folly; and wits,
whom the world worships, dwarfed when they approach his
venerable side. His admiration of nature or of man—we had
almost said his religious feelings towards his God—are all
narrowed, weakened, and corrupted and poisoned by inveter-
ate and diseased egotism; and instead of his mind reflecting the
beauty and glory of nature, he seems to consider the mighty
universe itself as nothing better than a mirror, in which, with a
grinning and idiot self-complacency, he may contemplate the
Physiognomy of Samuel Taylor Coleridge. Though he has yet
done nothing in any one department of human knowledge,
yet he speaks of his theories, and plans, and views, and dis-
coveries, as if he had produced some memorable revolution
in Science. He at all times connects his own name in Poetry
with Shakespeare, and Spenser, and Milton; in politics with
Burke, and Fox, and Pitt; in metaphysics with Locke, and
Hartley, and Berkeley, and Kant—feeling himself not only to
be the worthy compeer of those illustrious Spirits, but to unite,
in his own mighty intellect, all the glorious powers and facul-
ties by which they were separately distinguished, as if his soul
were endowed with all human power, and was the depository
of the aggregate, or rather the essence, of all human know-
ledge. So deplorable a delusion as this has only been equalled
by that of Joanna Southcote, who mistook a complaint in the
bowels for the divine *afflatus*; and believed herself about to give
birth to the regenerator of the world, when sick unto death of
an incurable and loathsome disease.

The truth is, that Mr Coleridge is but an obscure name in

English literature. In London he is well known in literary society, and justly admired for his extraordinary loquacity: he has his own little circle of devoted worshippers, and he mistakes their foolish babbling for the voice of the world. His name too has been often foisted into Reviews, and accordingly is known to many who never saw any of his works. In Scotland few know or care anything about him; and perhaps no man who has spoken and written so much, and occasionally with so much genius and ability, ever made so little impression on the public mind. Few people know how to spell or pronounce his name; and were he to drop from the clouds among any given number of well informed and intelligent men north of the Tweed, he would find it impossible to make any intelligible communication respecting himself; for of him and his writings there would prevail only a perplexing dream, or the most untroubled ignorance. We cannot see in what the state of literature would have been different, had he been cut off in childhood, or had he never been born; for, except a few wild and fanciful ballads, he has produced nothing worthy of remembrance. Yet, insignificant as he assuredly is, he cannot put pen to paper without a feeling that millions of eyes are fixed upon him; and he scatters his Sibylline Leaves around him, with as majestical an air as if a crowd of enthusiastic admirers were rushing forward to grasp the divine promulgations, instead of their being, as in fact they are, coldly received by the accidental passenger, like a lying lottery puff or a quack advertisement.

This most miserable arrogance seems, in the present age, confined almost exclusively to the original members of the Lake School, and is, we think, worthy of especial notice, as one of the leading features of their character. It would be difficult to defend it either in Southey or Wordsworth; but in Coleridge it is altogether ridiculous. Southey has undoubtedly written four noble Poems—*Thalaba*, *Madoc*, *Kehama*, and *Roderick*; and if the Poets of this age are admitted, by the voice of posterity, to take their places by the side of the Mighty of former times in the Temple of Immortality, he will be one of that sacred company. Wordsworth, too, with all his manifold errors and defects, has, we think, won to himself a great name, and, in point of originality, will be considered as second to no man of this age. They are entitled to think highly of themselves, in comparison with their most highly gifted contemporaries; and therefore, though their arrogance may be offensive, as it often is, it is seldom or never utterly ridiculous. But Mr Coleridge stands on much lower ground, and will be known to future times only as a man who overrated and abused his talents—who saw glimpses of that glory which he could not grasp—who presumptuously came forward to officiate as High Priest at mysteries beyond his ken—and who carried himself as if he had been familiarly admitted into the Penetralia of Nature, when in truth he kept perpetually stumbling at the very Threshold.

. . . It would seem, that in truly great souls all feeling of self-importance, in its narrowest sense, must be incompatible with the consciousness of a mighty achievement. The idea of the mere faculty or power is absorbed as it were in the idea of the work performed. That work stands out in its glory from the mind of its Creator; and in the contemplation of it, he forgets that he himself was the cause of its existence, or feels only a dim but sublime association between himself and the object of his admiration; and when he does think of himself in conjunction with others, he feels towards the scoffer only a pitying sorrow for his blindness—being assured, that though at all times there will be weakness, and ignorance, and worthlessness, which can hold no communion with him or with his thoughts, so will there be at all times the pure, the noble, and the pious, whose delight will be to love, to admire, and to imitate; and that never, at any point of time, past, present, or to come, can a true Poet be defrauded of his just fame.

But we need not speak of Poets alone (though we have done so at present to expose the miserable pretensions of Mr Coleridge), but look through all the bright ranks of men distinguished by mental power, in whatever department of human science. It is our faith, that without moral there can be no intellectual grandeur; and surely the self-conceit and arrogance which we have been exposing, are altogether incompatible with lofty feelings and majestic principles. It is the Dwarf alone who endeavours to strut himself into the height of the surrounding company; but the man of princely stature seems unconscious of the strength in which nevertheless he rejoices, and only sees his superiority in the gaze of admiration which he commands. Look at the most inventive spirits of this country—those whose intellect have achieved the most memorable triumphs. Take, for example, Leslie in physical science, and what airs of majesty does he ever assume? What is Samuel Coleridge compared to such a man? What is an ingenious and fanciful versifier to him who has, like a magician, gained command over the very elements of nature, who has realized the fictions of Poetry, and to whom Frost and Fire are ministering and obedient spirits? But of this enough. It is a position that doubtless might require some modification, but in the main, it is and must be true, that real Greatness, whether in Intellect, Genius, or Virtue, is dignified and unostentatious; and that no potent spirit ever whimpered over the blindness of the age to his merits, and, like Mr Coleridge, or a child blubbering for the moon, with clamorous outcries implored and imprecated reputation.

. . . .

We have done. We have felt it our duty to speak with severity of this book and its author, and we have given our readers ample opportunities to judge of the justice of our strictures. We have not been speaking in the cause of Literature only, but, we conceive, in the cause of Morality and Religion. For it is not fitting that he should be held up as an example to the rising generation (but, on the contrary, it is most fitting that he should be exposed as a most dangerous model), who has alternately embraced, defended, and thrown aside all systems of Philosophy, and all creeds of Religion; who seems to have no power of retaining an opinion—no trust in the principles which he defends—but who fluctuates from theory to theory, according as he is impelled by vanity, envy, or diseased desire of change and who, while he would subvert and scatter into dust those structures of knowledge, reared by

the wise men of this and other generations, has nothing to erect
in their room but the baseless and air-built fabrics of a dreaming
imagination.

Blackwood's, February 1819

The Rime of the Auncient Waggonere

In Four Parts

Part First

It is an auncient waggonere,
  And hee stoppeth one of nine:
"Now wherefore dost thou grip me soe
  With that horny fist of thine?"

An auncient waggonere stoppeth ane tailore going to a wedding, whereat he hath been appointed to be the best manne, and to take a hand in the casting of the slippere.

"The bridegroom's doors are opened
  wide,
  And thither I must walke;
Soe, by youre leave, I muste be gone,
  I have noe time for talke!"

The waggonere in mood for chate, and admits of no excuse.

Hee holds him with his horny fist—
  "There was a wain," quothe hee,
"Hold offe thou raggamouffine tykke,"—
  Eftsoones his fist dropped hee.

The tailore seized with the ague.

Hee satte him downe upon a stone,
  With ruefulle looks of feare;
And thus began this tippsye manne,
  The red nosed waggonere.

He listeneth like a three yeares and a half child.

"The wain is fulle, the horses pulle,
  Merrilye did we trotte
Alonge the bridge, alonge the road,
  A jolly crewe I wotte:"—
And here the tailore smotte his breaste,
  He smelte the cabbage potte!

The appetite of the tailore whetted by the smell of cabbage.

"The nighte was darke, like Noe's arke,
  Oure waggone moved alonge;
The hail pour'd faste, loude roared the
    blaste,
  Yet stille we moved alonge;
And sung in chorus, 'Cease loud Borus,'
  A very charminge songe.

The waggonere, in talkinge anent Boreas, maketh bad orthographye.

"'Bravoe, bravissimoe,' I cried,
  The sounde was quite elatinge;
But, in a trice, upon the ice,
  We heard the horses skaitinge.

Their mirth interrupted;

"The ice was here, the ice was there,
  It was a dismal mattere,
To see the cargoe, one by one,
  Flounderinge in the wattere!

And the passengers exercise themselves in the pleasant art of swimminge, as doeth also their prog, to witte, great store of colde roasted beef; item, ane beefstake pye; item, viii choppines of usquebaugh.

"With rout and roare, we reached the
    shore,
  And never a soul did sinke;
But in the rivere, gone for evere,
  Swum our meate and drinke.

"At lengthe we spied a goode grey
    goose,
  Thorough the snow it came;
And with the butte ende of my whippe,
  I hailed it in Goddhis name.

The waggonere hailethe ane goose, with ane novelle salutatione.

"It staggered as it had been drunke,
  So dexterous was it hitte;
Of brokene boughs we made a fire,
  Thenne Loncheone roasted itte."—

G

"Be done, thou tipsye waggonere,
  To the feaste I must awaye."—
The waggonere seized him bye the
  coatte,
  And forced him there to staye,
Begginge, in gentlemanlie style,
  Butte halfe ane hours delaye.

The tailore impatient to be gone, but is forcibly persuaded to remain.

Part Second

"The crimsone sunne was risinge o'er
  The verge of the horizon;
Upon my worde, as faire a sunne
  As ever I clapped eyes onne.

The waggonere's bowels yearn towards the sunne.

"'Twill bee ane comfortable thinge,"
  The mutinous crewe 'gan crye;
"'Twill be ane comfortable thinge,
  Within the jaile to lye;
"Ah! execrable wretche," saide they,
  "Thatte caused the goose to die!

The passengers throwe the blame of the goose massacre on the innocente waggonere.

"The day was drawing near itte's
  close,
  The sunne was well nighe settinge;
When lo! it seemed, as iffe his face
  Was veiled with fringe-warke-nettinge.

The sunne suffers ane artificial eclipse, and horror follows, the same not being mentioned in the Belfaste Almanacke.

"Somme saide itte was ane apple tree,
  Laden with goodlye fruite,
Somme swore itte was ane foreigne birde,
  Some said it was ane brute;
Alas! it was ane bumbailiffe,
  Ridinge in pursuite!

Various hypotheses on the subject, frome which the passengers draw wronge conclusions.

"A hue and crye sterte uppe behind,
  Whilke smote oure ears like thunder,
Within the waggone there was drede,
  Astonishmente and wonder.

Ane lovelye sound ariseth; ittes effects described.

"One after one, the rascalls rane,
   And from the carre did jump;
One after one, one after one,
   They felle with heavye thump.

The passengers throw
somersets.

"Six miles ane houre theye offe did
     scoure,
   Like shippes on ane stormye ocean,
Theire garments flappinge in the winde,
   With ane shorte uneasy motion.

"Their bodies with their legs did flye,
   Theye fled withe feare and glyffe;
Whye star'st thoue soe?—with one
    goode blow,
   I felled the bumbailiffe."

The waggonere compli-
menteth the bumbail-
liffe with ane Mendoza.

Part Third

"I feare thee, auncient waggonere,
   I feare thy hornye fiste,
For itte is stained with gooses gore,
   And bailiffe's blood, I wist.

"I fear to gette ane fisticuffe
   From thy leathern knuckles brown,
With that the tailore strove to ryse—
   The waggonere thrusts him down.

The tailore meeteth Cor-
poral Feare.

'Thou craven, if thou mov'st a limbe,
   I'll give thee cause for feare;'—
And thus went on, that tipsye man,
   The red-billed waggonere.

"The bumbailliffe so beautifull!
   Declared itte was no joke,
For, to his knowledge, both his legs,
   And fifteen ribbes were broke.

The bailiffe complaineth
of considerable derange-
ment of his animal econ-
omye.

"The lighte was gone, the nighte came
    on,
  Ane hundrede lantherns sheen,
Glimmered upon the kinge's highwaye.
  Ane lovelye sighte I ween.

Policemen, with their lanthernes, pursue the waggonere.

"'Is it he,' quoth one, 'Is this the
    manne,
  I'll laye the rascalle stiffe;
With cruel stroke the beak he broke
  Of the harmless bumbailiffe.'

"The threatening of the saucye rogue
  No more I coulde abide.
Advancing forthe my good right legge,
  Three paces and a stride,
I sent my lefte foot dexterously
  Seven inches thro' his side.

steppeth 20 feete in imitatione of the Admirable Crichtoun.

"Up came the seconde from the vanne;
  We had scarcely fought a round,
When some one smote me from behinde,
  And I fell down in a swound:

Complaineth of foul play and falleth down in ane trance.

"And when my head began to clear,
  I heard the yemering crew—
Quoth one, 'This man hath penance done
  And penance more shall do.'"

One acteth the parte of Job's comfortere.

Part Fourth

"Oh! Freedom is a glorious thing!—
  And, tailore, by the bye,
I'd rather in a halter swing,
  Than in a dungeon lie.

The waggonere maketh ane shrewd observation.

"The jailore came to bring me foode,
  Forget it will I never,
How he turned uppe the white o' his eye,
  When I stuck him in the liver.

The waggonere tickleth the spleen of the jailor, who daunces ane Fandango.

"His threade of life was snapt; once
    more
  I reached the open streete;
The people sung out 'Gardyloo'
  As I ran down the streete.
Methought the blessed air of heaven
  Never smelte so sweete.

Rejoicethe in the fragrance of the aire.

"Once more upon the broad high-
    waye,
  I walked with feare and drede;
And every fifteen steppes I tooke
  I turned about my heade.
For feare the corporal of the guarde
  Might close behind me trede!

Dreadeth Shoan Dhu, the corporal of the guarde.

"Behold, upon the western wave,
  Setteth the broad bright sunne;
So I must onward, as I have
  Full fifteen miles to runne;—

"And should the bailiffes hither come
  To aske whilke waye I've gone,
Tell them I took the othere road,
  Said hee, and trotted onne."

The waggonere taketh leave of the tailore,

The tailore rushed into the roome,
  O'erturning three or foure;
Fractured his skulle against the walle,
  And worde spake never more!!

to whome ane small accidente happeneth. Whereupon followeth the morale very proper to be had in minde by all members of the Dilettanti Society when they come over the bridge at these houres. Wherefore let them take heed and not lay blame where it lyeth nott.

Morale

Such is the fate of foolish men,
  The danger all may see,
Of those, who list to waggoneres,
  And keepe bade companye.

Blackwood's, October 1819

The longest poem in the collection of the Sibylline Leaves, is the *Rime of the Ancient Mariner*—and to our feeling, it is by far the most wonderful also—the most original—and the most touching of all the productions of its author. From it alone, we are inclined to think an idea of the whole poetical genius of Mr Coleridge might be gathered, such as could scarcely receive any very important addition either of extent or of distinctness, from a perusal of the whole of his other works. To speak of it at all is extremely difficult; above all the poems with which we are acquainted in any language—it is a poem to be felt—cherished—mused upon—not to be talked about—not capable of being described—analyzed—or criticized. It is the wildest of all the creations of genius—it is not like a thing of the living, listening, moving world—the very music of its words is like the melancholy mysterious breath of something sung to the sleeping ear—its images have the beauty—the grandeur—the incoherence of some mighty vision. The loveliness and the terror glide before us in turns—with, at one moment, the awful shadowy dimness—at another, the yet more awful distinctness of a majestic dream.

Dim and shadowy, and incoherent, however, though it be—how blind, how wilfully, or how foolishly blind must they have been who refused to see any meaning or purpose in the Tale of the Mariner!

Quarterly Review, August 1834: from the article on Coleridge's *Poetical Works* by Henry Nelson Coleridge

We lately reviewed the life, and mean hereafter to review the works, of our departed Crabbe. Let us be indulged, in the mean time, in this opportunity of making a few remarks on the genius of the extraordinary man whose poems, now for the first time completely collected, are named at the head of this article. The larger part of this publication is, of course, of old date, and the author still lives; yet, besides the considerable amount of new matter in this edition, which might of itself, in the present dearth of anything eminently original in verse, justify our notice, we think the great, and yet somewhat hazy, celebrity of Coleridge, and the ill-understood character of his poetry, will be, in the opinion of a majority of our readers, more than an excuse for a few elucidatory remarks upon the subject. Idolized by many, and used without scruple by more, the poet of *Christabel* and the *Ancient Mariner* is but little truly known in that common literary world, which, without the prerogative of conferring fame hereafter, can most surely give or prevent popularity for the present. In that circle he commonly passes for a man of genius, who has written some very beautiful verses, but whose original powers, whatever they were, have been long since lost or confounded in the pursuit of metaphysic dreams. We ourselves venture to think very differently of Mr Coleridge, both as a poet and a philosopher, although we are well enough aware that nothing which we can say will, as matters now stand, much advance his chance of becoming a fashionable author.

Indeed, as we rather believe, we should earn small thanks from him for our happiest exertions in such a cause; for certainly, of all the men of letters whom it has been our fortune to know, we never met any who was so utterly regardless of the reputation of the mere author as Mr Coleridge—one so lavish and indiscriminate in the exhibition of his own intellectual wealth before any and every person, no matter who—one so reckless who might reap where he had most prodigally sown and watered. "God knows," as we once heard him exclaim upon the subject of his unpublished system of philosophy, "God knows, I have no author's vanity about it. I should be absolutely glad if I could hear that the *thing* had been done before me." It is somewhere told of Virgil, that he took more pleasure in the good verses of Varius and Horace than in his own. We would not answer for that; but the story has always occurred to us, when we have seen Mr Coleridge criticizing and amending the work of a contemporary author with much more zeal and hilarity than we ever perceived him to display about anything of his own.

Perhaps our readers may have heard repeated a saying of Wordsworth's, that many men of this age had done wonderful *things*, as Davy, Scott, Cuvier, etc.; but that Coleridge was the only wonderful *man* he ever knew. Something, of course, must be allowed in this as in all other cases for the antithesis; but we believe the fact really to be, that the greater part of those who have occasionally visited Mr Coleridge have left him with a feeling akin to the judgment indicated in the above remark. They admire the man more than his works, or they forget the works in the absorbing impression made by the living author. And no wonder. Those who remember him in his more vigorous days can bear witness to the peculiarity and transcendant power of his conversational eloquence. It was unlike anything that could be heard elsewhere; the kind was different, the degree was different, the manner was different. The boundless range of scientific knowledge, the brilliancy and exquisite nicety of illustration, the deep and ready reasoning, the strangeness and immensity of bookish lore—were not all; the dramatic story, the joke, the pun, the festivity must be added—and with these the clerical-looking dress, the thick waving silver hair, the youthful-coloured cheek, the indefinable mouth and lips, the quick yet steady and penetrating greenish grey eye, the slow and continuous enunciation, and the everlasting music of his tones—all went to make up the image and to constitute the living presence of the man. He is now no longer young, and bodily infirmities, we regret to know, have pressed heavily upon him. His natural force is indeed abated; but his eye is not dim, neither is his mind yet enfeebled. "O youth!" he says in one of the most exquisitely finished of his later poems:

> O youth! for years so many and sweet,
> 'Tis known that thou and I were one,
> I'll think it but a fond conceit—
> It cannot be that thou art gone!
> Thy vesper bell hath not yet tolled:
> And thou wert aye a masker bold!
> What strange disguise hast now put on,
> To make believe that thou art gone?

I see these locks in silvery slips,
This drooping gait, this altered size;
But springtide blossoms on thy lips,
And tears take sunshine from thine eyes!
Life is but thought: so think I will
That Youth and I are house-mates still.

Mr Coleridge's conversation, it is true, has not now all the brilliant versatility of his former years; yet we know not whether the contrast between his bodily weakness and his mental power does not leave a deeper and a more solemnly affecting impression, than his most triumphant displays in youth could ever have done. To see the pain-stricken countenance relax, and the contracted frame dilate under the kindling of intellectual fire alone—to watch the infirmities of the flesh shrinking out of sight, or glorified and transfigured in the brightness of the awakening spirit—is an awful object of contemplation; and in no other person did we ever witness such a distinction—nay, alienation of mind from body—such a mastery of the purely intellectual over the purely corporeal, as in the instance of this remarkable man. Even now his conversation is characterized by all the essentials of its former excellence; there is the same individuality, the same *unexpectedness*, the same universal grasp; nothing is too high, nothing too low for it: it glances from earth to heaven, from heaven to earth, with a speed and a splendour, an ease and a power, which almost seem inspired; yet its universality is not of the same kind with the superficial ranging of the clever talkers whose criticism and whose information are called forth by, and spent upon, the particular topics in hand. No; in this more, perhaps, than in anything else is Mr Coleridge's discourse distinguished: that it springs from an inner centre, and illustrates by light from the soul. His thoughts are, if we may say so, as the radii of a circle, the centre of which may be in the petals of a rose, and the circumference as wide as the boundary of things visible and invisible. In this it was that we always thought another eminent light of our time, recently lost to us, an exact contrast to Mr Coleridge as to quality and style of conversation. You could not in all London or England hear a more fluent, a

more brilliant, a more exquisitely elegant converser than Sir
James Mackintosh; nor could you ever find him unprovided.
But, somehow or other, it always seemed as if all the sharp and
brilliant things he said were poured out of so many vials filled
and labelled for the particular occasion; it struck us, to use a
figure, as if his mind were an ample and well-arranged *hortus
siccus*, from which you might have specimens of every kind of
plant, but all of them cut and dried for store. You rarely saw
nature working at the very moment in him. With Coleridge it
was and still is otherwise. He may be slower, more rambling,
less pertinent; he may not strike at the instant as so eloquent;
but then, what he brings forth is fresh coined; his flowers are
newly gathered, they are wet with dew, and, if you please, you
may almost see them growing in the rich garden of his mind. The
projection is visible; the enchantment is done before your eyes.
To listen to Mackintosh was to inhale perfume; it pleased, but
did not satisfy. The effect of an hour with Coleridge is to set you
thinking; his words haunt you for a week afterwards; they are
spells, brightenings, revelations. In short, it is, if we may ven-
ture to draw so bold a line, the whole difference between talent
and genius.

A very experienced short-hand writer was employed to take
down Mr Coleridge's lectures on Shakespeare, but the manu-
script was almost entirely unintelligible. Yet the lecturer was,
as he always is, slow and measured. The writer—we have some
notion it was no worse an artist than Mr Gurney himself—gave
this account of the difficulty: that with regard to every other
speaker whom he had ever heard, however rapid or involved, he
could almost always, by long experience in his art, guess the
form of the latter part, or apodosis, of the sentence by the form
of the beginning; but that the conclusion of every one of
Coleridge's sentences was a *surprise* upon him. He was obliged
to listen to the last word. Yet this unexpectedness, as we termed
it before, is not the effect of quaintness or confusion of con-
struction: so far from it, that we believe foreigners of different
nations, especially Germans and Italians, have often borne
very remarkable testimony to the grammatical purity and sim-
plicity of his language, and have declared that they generally

understood what he said much better than the sustained conversation of any other Englishman whom they had met. It is the uncommonness of the thoughts or the image which prevents your anticipating the end.

We owe, perhaps, an apology to our readers for the length of the preceding remarks; but the fact is, so very much of the intellectual life and influence of Mr Coleridge has consisted in the oral communications of his opinions, that no sketch could be reasonably complete without a distinct notice of the peculiar character of his powers in this particular. We believe it has not been the lot of any other literary man in England, since Dr Johnson, to command the devoted admiration and steady zeal of so many and such widely-differing disciples—some of them having become, and others being likely to become, fresh and independent sources of light and moral action in themselves upon the principles of their common master. One half of these affectionate disciples have learned their lessons of philosophy from the teacher's mouth. He has been to them as an old oracle of the Academy or Lyceum. The fulness, the inwardness, the ultimate scope of his doctrines has never yet been published in print, and if disclosed, it has been from time to time in the higher moments of conversation, when occasion and mood, and person begot an exalted crisis. More than once has Mr Coleridge said, that with pen in hand he felt a thousand checks and difficulties in the expression of his meaning; but that—authorship aside—he never found the smallest hitch or impediment in the fullest utterance of his most subtle fancies by word of mouth. His abstrusest thoughts became rhythmical and clear when chaunted to their own music. But let us proceed now to the publication before us.

.   .   .   .   .

He does not belong to that grand division of poetry and poets which corresponds with painting and painters; of which Pindar and Dante are the chief—those masters of the picturesque, who, by a felicity inborn, view and present everything in the completeness of actual objectivity—and who have a class derived from and congenial with them, presenting few pictures indeed, but always full of picturesque matter; of which secondary class Spenser and Southey may be mentioned as eminent instances. To neither of these does Mr Coleridge belong; in his *Christabel*, there certainly are several *distinct pictures* of great beauty; but he, as a poet, clearly comes within the other division which answers to music and the musician, in which you have a magnificent mirage of words with the subjective associations of the poet curling, and twisting, and creeping round, and through, and above every part of it. This is the class to which Milton belongs, in whose poems we have heard Mr Coleridge say that he remembered but two proper pictures—Adam bending over the sleeping Eve at the beginning of the fifth book of the *Paradise Lost*, and Dalilah approaching Samson towards the end of the *Agonistes*. But when we point out the intense personal feeling, the self-projection, as it were, which characterizes Mr Coleridge's poems, we mean that such feeling is the soul and spirit, not the whole body and form, of his poetry. For surely no one has ever more earnestly and constantly borne in mind the maxim of Milton, that poetry ought to be *simple, sensuous, and impassioned*. The poems in these volumes are no authority for that dreamy, half-swooning style of verse which was criticized by Lord Byron (in language too strong for print) as the fatal sin of Mr John Keats, and which, unless abjured betimes, must prove fatal to several younger aspirants—male and female—who for the moment enjoy some popularity. The poetry before us is distinct and clear, and accurate in its imagery; but the imagery is rarely or never exhibited for description's sake alone; it is rarely or never exclusively objective; that is to say, put forward as a spectacle, a picture on which the mind's eye is to rest and terminate. You may if your sight is short, or your imagination cold, regard the imagery in itself and go no farther; but the poet's intention is that you should feel and imagine a great deal more than you see. His aim is to awaken in the reader the same mood of mind, the same cast of imagination and fancy whence issued the associations which animate and enlighten his pictures. You must think with him, must suffer yourself to be lifted out of your own school of opinion or faith, and fall back upon your own consciousness, an unsophisticated man. If you decline this, *non tibi spirat*. From his earliest youth to this day, Mr Coleridge's poetry has been a faithful mirror reflecting the images of his mind. Hence he is so original, so individual. With a little trouble, the zealous reader of the *Biographia Literaria* may trace in these volumes the whole course of mental struggle and self-evolvement narrated in that odd but interesting work; but he will see the track marked in light; the notions become images, the images glorified, and not unfrequently the abstruse position stamped clearer by the poet than by the psychologist. No student of Coleridge's philosophy can fully understand it without a perusal of the illuminating, and if we may so say, *popularizing* commentary of his poetry. It is the Greek put into the vulgar tongue. And we must say, it is somewhat strange to hear any one condemn those philisophical principles as altogether unintelligible, which are inextricably interwoven in every page of a volume of poetry which he professes to admire.

No writer has ever expressed the great truth that man makes his world, or that it is the imagination which shapes and colours all things—more vividly than Coleridge. Indeed, he is the first who, in the age in which we live, brought forward that position into light and action. It is nearly forty years ago that he wrote the following passage in his *Ode on Dejection*, one of the most characteristic and beautiful of his lyric poems:

A grief without a pang, void, dark, and drear,
  A stifled, drowsy, unimpassioned grief,
  Which finds no natural outlet, no relief,
    In word, or sigh, or tear:
O Lady! in this wan and heartless mood,
To other thoughts by yonder throstle wooed,
  All this long eve, so balmy and serene,
Have I been gazing on the western sky
  And its peculiar tint of yellow green;
And still I gaze—and with how blank an eye!
And those thin clouds above, in flakes and bars,
That give away their motion to the stars;
Those stars that glide behind them or between,
Now sparkling, now bedimmed, but always seen;

Yon crescent moon, as fixed as if it grew
In its own cloudless, starless lake of blue;
I see them all so excellently fair,
I see, not feel, how beautiful they are!
    My genial spirits fail;
    And what can these avail
To lift the smothering weight from off my breast?
    It were a vain endeavour,
    Though I should gaze for ever
On that green light that lingers in the west:
I may not hope from outward forms to win
The passion and the life, whose fountains are within.

    O Lady! we receive but what we give,
And in our life alone does nature live;
Ours is her wedding garment, ours her shroud!
    And would we aught behold of higher worth
Than that inanimate cold world allowed
To the poor loveless ever-anxious crowd,
    Ah! from the soul itself must issue forth
A light, a glory, a fair luminous cloud,
    Enveloping the Earth—
And from the soul itself must there be sent
    A sweet and potent voice of its own birth,
Of all sweet sounds the life and element!

    O pure of heart! thou need'st not ask of me
What this strong music in the soul may be!
What and wherein it doth exist,
This light, this glory, this fair luminous mist,
This beautiful and beauty-making power.
    Joy, virtuous Lady! Joy that ne'er was given
Save to the pure, and in their purest hour,
Life, and Life's effluence, cloud at once and shower,
Joy, Lady, is the spirit and the power
Which wedding nature to us gives in dower,
    A new Earth and new Heaven,
Undreamt of by the sensual and the proud;
Joy is the sweet voice—Joy the luminous cloud—
    We in ourselves rejoice!
And thence flows all that charms or ear or sight,
    All melodies the echoes of that voice,
All colours a suffusion from that light.

vol. i, p. 238

To this habit of intellectual introversion we are very much inclined to attribute Mr Coleridge's never having seriously undertaken a great heroic poem. The *Paradise Lost* may be thought to stand in the way of our laying down any general rule on the subject; yet that poem is as peculiar as Milton himself, and does not materially affect our opinion, that the pure epic can hardly be achieved by the poet in whose mind the reflecting turn *greatly* predominates. The extent of the action in such a poem requires a free and fluent stream of narrative verse; description, purely objective, must fill a large space in it, and its permanent success depends on a rapidity, or at least a liveliness, of movements which is scarcely compatible with much of what Bacon calls *inwardness* of meaning. The reader's attention could not be preserved; his journey being long, he expects his road to be smooth and unembarrassed. The condensed passion of the ode is out of place in heroic song. Few persons will dispute that the two great Homeric poems are the most delightful of epics; they may not have the sublimity of the *Paradise Lost*, nor the picturesqueness of the *Divine Comedy*, not the etherial brilliancy of the *Orlando*; but, dead, as they are in language, metre, accent—obsolete in religion, manners, costume, and country—they nevertheless even now *please* all those who can read them beyond all other narrative poems. There is a salt in them which keeps them sweet and incorruptible throughout every change. They are the most popular of all the remains of ancient genius, and translations of them for the twentieth time are amongst the very latest productions of our contemporary literature. From beginning to end, these marvellous poems are exclusively objective; everything is in them, except the poet himself. It is not to Vico or Wolfe that we refer, when we say that *Homer* is *vox et praeterea nihil*; as musical as the nightingale, and as invisible.

If any epic subject would have suited Mr Coleridge's varied powers and peculiar bent of mind, it might, perhaps, have been that which he once contemplated, and for which he made some preparations—*The Fall of Jerusalem*. The splendid drama which has subsequently appeared under that name by a younger poet, has not necessarily precluded an attempt on the epic scale by a master genius. Yet the difficulties of the undertaking are appalling from their number and peculiarity; and not the least overwhelming of them are involved in the treatment of those very circumstances and relations which constitute its singular attraction. We have twice heard Mr Coleridge express his opinion on this point. "The destruction of Jerusalem," he said upon one occasion:

> is the only subject now remaining for an epic poem; a subject which, like Milton's Fall of Man, should interest all Christendom, as the Homeric War of Troy interested all Greece. There would be difficulties, as there are in all subjects; and they must be mitigated and thrown into the shade, as Milton has done with the numerous difficulties in the *Paradise Lost*. But there would be a greater assemblage of grandeur and splendour than can now be found in any other theme. As for the mythology, *incredulus odi*; and yet there must be a mythology, or a quasi-mythology, for an epic poem. Here there would be the completion of the prophecies; the termination of the first revealed national religion under the violent assault of Paganism, itself the immediate forerunner and condition of the spread of a revealed mundane religion; and then you would have the character of the Roman and the Jew, and the awfulness, the completeness, the justice. I schemed it at twenty-five, but, alas! *venturum expectat.*

Upon another occasion, Mr Coleridge spoke more discouragingly.

> This subject, with all its great capabilities, has this one grand defect— that, whereas a poem, to be epic, must have a personal interest—in the *Destruction of Jerusalem* no genius or skill could possibly preserve the interest for the hero from being merged in the interest for the event. The fact is, the event itself is too sublime and overwhelming.

We think this is fine and just criticism; yet we ardently wish the critic had tried the utmost strength of his arm in executing the magnificent idea of his early manhood. Even now—vain as we fear any such appeal is—we cannot keep ourselves back from making a respectful call upon this great poet to consider whether his undiminished powers of verse do not seem to demand from him something beyond the little pieces, sweet as they are, which he has alone produced since his middle manhood. We know and duly value the importance of the essays in which his philosophical views have as yet been imperfectly developed, and we look with anxiety to the publication of the whole, or a part, of that great work in which, we are told, the labour of his life has been expended in founding and completing a truly catholic "System of philosophy for a Christian man." We would not, for the chance of an epic fragment, interfere with the consummation of this grand and long-cherished design. But is there any necessary incompatibility between the full action of the poet and the philosopher in Mr Coleridge's particular case? He, of all men, would deny that the character of his studies alone tended to enfeeble the imagination, or to circumscribe the power of expression; and if that be so, what is there to prevent—what is there not rather to induce—a serious devotion of some portion, at least, of his leisure to the planning and execution of some considerable poem? *Poterit si posse videtur*; and could Mr Coleridge but seem to himself as capable as he seems to others, we believe he would not leave the world without a legacy of verse even richer than aught that has yet come from him.

H

BYRON

IT was natural that the most celebrated and notorious poet of his age should be discussed frequently and at length in the Reviews and Magazines; particularly as the first poem with which Byron reached a more than microscopic public was a furious onslaught on the Reviewers and their ways. His early volume, *Hours of Idleness*, had been the object of a scornful notice in the *Edinburgh* for January 1808; Byron, already intensely avid for fame, was deeply stung, but set to work immediately to relieve his feelings. He had already (October 1807) completed a poem entitled *British Bards*, but now he withheld publication while he extended the scope of his satire to include the Reviewers, publishing the poem in its enlarged form in March 1809 as *English Bards and Scotch Reviewers*. Its success evidently pleased him, for he at once prepared a second edition, still more enlarged, before setting out on his travels in July; it appeared in October, and was followed in his absence by two more editions; on his return, in July 1811, he revised it again and issued it a fifth time. Then, with a characteristically sudden change of mind, he devoted his energies to suppressing the poem, ordering his publisher, Cawthorn, to burn all the remaining copies. (The poem survives because, of course, a large number of copies had reached general circulation, and even of this ill-fated fifth impression, a few escaped to become the basis of subsequent reprints.)

After this bad beginning, however, Byron's relations with the Reviewers were far from unhappy. For the rest of his life he regretted *English Bards and Scotch Reviewers*—"this miserable record of misplaced anger and indiscriminate acrimony," he called it in 1816—and made especial amends to Jeffrey, to whom he had been inclined to attribute the authorship of the offending article. (Actually it was by Lord Brougham). Years

later, in the tenth canto of *Don Juan*, he addressed Jeffrey in
terms of positive affection:

> And all our little feuds, at least all *mine*,
> Dear Jeffrey, once my most redoubted foe
> (As far as rhyme and criticism combine
> To make such puppets of us things below),
> Are over: Here's a health to 'Auld Lang Syne.'
> I do not know you, and may never know
> Your face—but you have acted on the whole
> Most nobly, and I own it from my soul.
>
> . . . And though, as you remember, in a fit
> Of wrath and rhyme, when juvenile and curly,
> I rail'd at Scots to show my wrath and wit,
> Which must be own'd was sensitive and surly,
> Yet 'tis in vain such sallies to permit,
> They cannot quench young feelings fresh and early;
> I *scotch'd not kill'd* the Scotchman in my blood,
> And love the land of 'mountain and of flood.'

Poor lines, but valuable as a generous expression of feeling
from one who, though quick to take offence, was not, despite
the 'Scotchman in his blood,' a good hater.

To retrace our steps a little: the *Edinburgh* never replied to
English Bards and Scotch Reviewers, even though Byron insist-
ently challenged Jeffrey to come forward and defend himself.
"My Northern friends," he wrote in his postscript to the
second edition of the poem,

> have accused me, with justice, of personality towards their great
> literary Anthropophagus, *Jeffrey*: but what else was to be done with him
> and his dirty pack, who feed by 'lying and slandering,' and slake their
> thirst by 'evil speaking'?

But the *Edinburgh* continued on its majestic way, and the great
series of articles in which Jeffrey later examined Byron's poetry,
articles which might well stand as the model for all subsequent
criticism of the poet, contained no hint of personal rancour.

With the *Quarterly* Byron's relations were good from the
first. He was neither a Radical in politics nor a 'Laker' in
poetry; and furthermore, poet and reviewer had, in this case,
the same publisher—a fact which helps to explain why the
Quarterly chose to ignore *Don Juan* instead of joining in the

chorus of shocked vituperation that greeted it. Another reason for the favourable tone of the *Quarterly's* early reviews of Byron was that his books were, naturally, handed over to Scott, whose articles on *Childe Harold's Pilgrimage* are fine examples of serious reviewing. Again, Byron, who was always glad to emphasize the great differences of taste and temperament that separated him from the other 'Romantics,' professed, and no doubt even felt, a profound respect for Gifford, frequently sending good wishes to him in his letters to Murray. So matters stood until Byron's continual defiance of the proprieties, a defiance so persistent as to reveal the ingrained conventionality of the man (a true mark of the 'Scotchman in his blood'), set the whole of respectable opinion against him. His dramas were handed over to a churchman, Reginald Heber, who produced a long, cross-grained and worthless article (vol. xxvii, p. 476 ff.), and valuable criticism of his work ceased to appear in the Review.

Blackwood's, in the person of Wilson, produced readable criticism of *Manfred* (see below) and led the attack on the poet's 'immorality' in *Don Juan*. Wilson also reviewed *Childe Harold*, Part IV, in the *Edinburgh* for June 1818; but he was, on the whole, not at his best in dealing with Byron, and Jeffrey's articles remain far above all other contemporary criticism of 'the Childe.' It is, however, only fair to add that the contemporary mind which most keenly penetrated to the inner nature of Byron's work was that of Shelley, as his scattered remarks show; if he had ever written a formal *critique* of his friend's poetry, it would have left very little for succeeding generations to add.

Scott: in the *Quarterly Review*, October 1816

Childe Harold's Pilgrimage, Canto III. 8vo. *The Prisoner of Chillon, a Dream; and other Poems.* By LORD BYRON. 8vo. John Murray: London.

Distinguished by title and descent from an illustrious line of ancestry, Lord Byron shewed, even in his earliest years, that nature had added to those advantages the richest gifts of genius and fancy. His own tale is partly told in two lines of *Lara*:

> Left by his Sire, too young such loss to know,
> Lord of himself, that heritage of woe.

His first literary adventure and its fate are well remembered. The poems which he published in his minority had, indeed, those faults of conception and diction which are inseparable from juvenile attempts, and in particular might rather be considered as imitations of what had caught the ear and fancy of the youthful author, than as exhibiting originality of conception and expression. It was like the first essay of the singing bird catching at and imitating the notes of its parent, ere habit and time have given the fullness of tone, confidence, and self-possession which renders assistance unnecessary. Yet though there were many, and those not the worst judges, who discerned in these juvenile productions, a depth of thought and felicity of expression which promised much at a more mature age, the errors did not escape the critical lash; and certain brethren of ours yielded to the opportunity of pouncing upon a titled author, and to that which most readily besets our fraternity, and to which we dare not pronounce ourselves wholly inaccessible, the temptation, namely, of shewing our own wit, and entertaining our readers with a lively article without much respect to the feelings of the author, or even to the indications of merit which the work may exhibit. The review was read and raised mirth; the poems were neglected, the author was irritated, and took his revenge in keen iambics, not only on the offending critic, but on many others, in whose conduct or writings the juvenile bard had found, or imagined he had found, some cause of offence. The satire, which has been since suppressed, as containing opinions hastily expressed, contained a spirit at least sufficiently poignant for all the purposes of reprisal; and although the verses might, in many respects, be deemed the offspring of hasty and indiscriminating resentment, they bore a strong testimony to the ripening talents of the author. Having thus vented his indignation against the critics and their readers, and put many, if not all the laughers upon his side, Lord Byron went abroad, and the controversy was forgotten for some years.

It was in 1812, when Lord Byron returned to England, that *Childe Harold's Pilgrimage* made its first appearance, producing an effect upon the public, at least equal to any work which has appeared within this or the last century. Reading is indeed so general among all ranks and classes, that the impulse received by the public mind on such occasions is instantaneous through all but the very lowest classes of society, instead of being slowly communicated from one set of readers to another, as was the case in the days of our fathers. *The Pilgrimage*, acting on such an extensive medium, was calculated to rouse and arrest the attention in a peculiar degree. The fictitious personage, whose sentiments, however, no one could help identifying with those of the author himself, presented himself with an avowed disdain of all the attributes which most men would be gladly supposed to possess. Childe Harold is represented as one satiated by indulgence in pleasure, and seeking in change of place and clime a relief from the tedium of a life which glided on without an object. The assuming of such a character as the medium of communicating his poetry and his sentiments indicated a feeling towards the public, which, if it fell short of contemning their favour, disdained, at least, all attempts to propitiate them. Yet the very audacity of this repulsive personification, joined to the energy with which it was supported, and to the indications of a bold, powerful, and original mind which glanced through every line of the poem, electrified the mass of readers, and placed at once upon Lord Byron's head the garland for which other men of genius have toiled long, and which they have gained late. He was placed pre-eminent among the literary men of his country by general acclamation. Those who had so rigorously censured his juvenile essays, and perhaps "dreaded such another field," were the first to pay warm and, we believe, sincere homage to his matured efforts; while others, who saw in the sentiments of Childe Harold much to regret and to censure, did not withhold their tribute of applause to the depth of thought, the power and force of expression, the beauty of description, and the energy of sentiment which animated the

Pilgrimage. If the volume was laid aside for a moment, under
the melancholy and unpleasing impression that it seemed cal-
culated to chase hope from the side of man, and to dim his
prospects both of this life and of futurity, it was immediately
and almost involuntarily assumed again, as our feeling of the
author's genius predominated over our dislike to contemplate
the gloomy views of human nature which it was his pleasure
to place before us. Something was set down to the angry recol-
lection of his first failure, which might fairly authorize so high
a mind to hold the world's opinion in contempt; something
was allowed for the recent family losses to which the poem
alluded, and under the feeling of which it had been partly
written: and it seemed to most readers as if gentler and more
kindly features were, at times, seen to glance from under the
cloud of misanthropy, which the author had flung around his
hero. Thus, as all admired the Pilgrimage of Childe Harold, all
were prepared to greet the author with that fame which is the
poet's best reward, and which is chieflv and most justly due to
one who, in these exhausted days, strikes out a new and original
line of composition.

It was amidst such feelings of admiration that Lord Byron
entered, we may almost say for the first time, the public stage
on which he has, for four years, made so distinguished a figure.
Every thing in his manner, person, and conversation, tended
to maintain the charm which his genius had flung around him;
and those admitted to his conversation, far from finding that
the inspired poet sunk into ordinary mortality, felt themselves
attached to him, not only by many noble qualities, but by the
interest of a mysterious, undefined, and almost painful curiosity.

. . . It is another remarkable property of the poetry of Lord
Byron, that although his manner is frequently varied—
although he appears to have assumed for an occasion the char-
acteristic stanza and style of several contemporaries, yet not
only is his poetry marked in every instance by the strongest cast
of originality, but in some leading particulars, and especially
in the character of his heroes, each story so closely resembles
the other, that managed by a writer of less power, the effect
would have been an unpleasing monotony. All, or almost all,

his heroes, have somewhat the attributes of Childe Harold: all or almost all, have minds which seem at variance with their fortunes, and exhibit high and poignant feelings of pain and pleasure; a keen sense of what is noble and honourable, and an equally keen susceptibility of injustice or injury, under the garb of stoicism or contempt of mankind. The strength of early passion, and the glow of youthful feeling, are uniformly painted as chilled or subdued by a train of early imprudences or of darker guilt, and the sense of enjoyment tarnished, by too intimate and experienced an acquaintance with the vanity of human wishes. These general attributes mark the stern features of all Lord Byron's heroes, from those which are shaded by the scalloped hat of the illustrious Pilgrim, to those which lurk under the turban of Alp, the Renegade. The public, ever anxious in curiosity or malignity to attach to fictitious characters real prototypes, were obstinate in declaring that in these leading traits of character Lord Byron copied from the individual features reflected in his own mirror. On this subject the noble author entered, on one occasion, a formal protest, though, it will be observed, without entirely disavowing the ground on which the conjecture was formed.

With regard to my story, and stories in general, I should have been glad to have rendered my personages more perfect and amiable, if possible, inasmuch as I have been sometimes criticised, and considered no less responsible for their deeds and qualities than if all had been personal. Be it so—if I have deviated into the gloomy vanity of "drawing from self," the pictures are probably like, since they are unfavourable; and if not, those who know me are undeceived. I have no particular desire that any but my acquaintance should think the author better than the beings of his imaginings; but I cannot help a little surprize, and perhaps amusement, at some odd critical exceptions in the present instance, when I see several bards (far more deserving, I allow) in very reputable plight, and quite exempt from all participation in the faults of those heroes, who, nevertheless, might be found with little more morality than *The Giaour*, and perhaps—but no—I must admit Childe Harold to be a very repulsive personage; and as to his identity, those who like it must give him whatever 'alias' they please.

It is difficult to say whether we are to receive this passage as an admission or a denial of the opinion to which it refers: but Lord Byron certainly did the public injustice, if he supposed it imputed to him the criminal actions with which many of his heroes were stained. Men no more expected to meet in Lord Byron the Corsair, who "knew himself a villian," than they looked for the hypocrisy of Kehama on the shores of the Der-went Water, or the profligacy of Marmion on the banks of the Tweed: yet even in the features of Conrad, those who have looked on Lord Byron will recognise some likeness.

>   . . . to the sight
> No giant frame sets forth his common height;
> Yet, in the whole, who paused to look again,
> Saw more than marks the crowd of vulgar men;
> They gaze and marvel how—and still confess
> That thus it is, but why they cannot guess.
> Sun-burnt his check, his forehead high and pale
> The sable curls in wild profusion veil;
> And oft perforce his rising lip reveals
> The haughtier thought it curbs, but scarce conceals.
> Though smooth his voice, and calm his general mien,
> Still seems there something he would not have seen:
> His features' deepening lines and varying hue
> At times attracted, yet perplexed the view.
>   *The Corsair*, p. 11.

And the ascetic regimen which the noble author himself observed, was no less marked in the description of Conrad's fare.

> Ne'er for his lip the purpling cup they fill,
> That goblet passes him untasted still—
> And for his fare—the rudest of his crew
> Would that, in turn, have passed untasted too;
> Earth's coarsest bread, the garden's homeliest roots,
> And scarce the summer luxury of fruits,
> His short repast in humbleness supply
> With all a hermit's board would scarce deny.—*Ibid* p. 4.

The following description of Lara suddenly and unexpect-edly returned from distant travels, and reassuming his station in the society of his own country, has in like manner strong points of resemblance to the part which the author himself seemed occasionally to bear amid the scenes where the great mingle with the fair.

> ... 'tis quickly seen
> Whate'er he be, 'twas not what he had been;
> That brow in furrow'd lines had fix'd at last,
> And spake of passions, but of passions past;
> The pride, but not the fire, of early days,
> Coldness of mien, and carelessness of praise;
> A high demeanour, and a glance that took
> Their thoughts from others by a single look;
> And that sarcastic levity of tongue,
> The stinging of a heart the world hath stung,
> That darts in seeming playfulness around,
> And makes those feel that will not own the wound;
> All these seem'd his, and something more beneath
> Than glance could well reveal, or accent breathe:
> Ambition, glory, love, the common aim
> That some can conquer, and that all would claim,
> Within his breast appear'd no more to strive,
> Yet seem'd as lately they had been alive;
> And some deep feeling it were vain to trace
> At moments lighten'd o'er his livid face. *Lara*, 6-7.

We are not writing Lord Byron's private history, though from the connection already stated between his poetry and his character, we feel ourselves forced upon considering his literary life, his deportment, and even his personal appearance. But we know enough of his private story to give our warrant that, though his youth may have shared somewhat too largely in the indiscretions of those left too early masters of their own actions and fortunes, falsehood and malice alone can impute to him any real cause for hopeless remorse or gloomy misanthropy. To what, then, are we to ascribe the singular peculiarity which induced an author of such talent, and so well skilled in tracing the darker impressions which guilt and remorse leave on the human character, so frequently to affix features peculiar to himself to the robbers and corsairs which he sketched with a pencil as forcible as that of Salvator? More than one answer may be returned to this question; nor do we pretend to say which is best warranted by the facts. The practice may arise from a temperament which radical and constitutional melancholy has, as in the case of Hamlet, predisposed to identify its *owner* with scenes of that deep and arousing interest which arises from the stings of conscience contending with the stubborn energy of pride, and delighting to be placed in supposed situations of guilt and danger, as some men love instinctively to tread the giddy edge of a precipice, or, holding by some frail twig, to stoop forward over the abyss into which the dark torrent discharges itself. Or it may be that these disguises were assumed capriciously as a man might chuse the cloak, poniard, and dark-lantern of a bravo, for his disguise at a masquerade. Or feeling his own powers in painting the sombre and the horrible, Lord Byron assumed in his fervour the very semblance of the characters he describes, like an actor who presents on the stage at once his own person and the tragic character with which for the time he is invested. Nor is it altogether incompatible with his character to believe that, in contempt of the criticisms which on this account had attended *Childe Harold*, he was determined to shew to the public how little he was affected by them, and how effectually it was in his power to compel attention and respect, even when imparting a portion of his own likeness and his own peculiarities to pirates—and outlaws.

But although we do not pretend to ascertain the motive on which Lord Byron acted in bringing the peculiarities of his own sentiments and feeling so frequently before his readers, it is with no little admiration that we regard these extraordinary powers, which, amidst this seeming uniformity, could continue to rivet the public attention, and secure general and continued applause. The versatility of authors who have been able to draw and support characters as different from each other as from their own, has given to their productions the inexpressible charm of variety, and has often secured them against that neglect which in general attends what is technically called mannerism. But it was reserved to Lord Byron to present the same character on the public stage again and again, varied only by the exertions of that powerful genius, which searching the springs of passion and of feeling in their innermost recesses, knew how to combine their operations, so that the interest was eternally varying, and never abated, although the most important personage of the drama retained the same lineaments. It will one day be considered as not the least remarkable literary phenomenon of this age, that during a period of four years, notwithstanding the quantity of distinguished poetical talent of which we may be permitted to boast, a single author, and he managing his pen with the careless and negligent ease of a man of quality, and chusing for his theme subjects so very similar, and personages bearing so close a resemblance to each other, did, in despite of these circumstances, of the unamiable attributes with which he usually invested his heroes, and of the proverbial fickleness of the public, maintain the ascendency in their favour, which he had acquired by his first matured production. So however it indisputably has been; and these comparatively small circles of admirers excepted, which assemble naturally around individual poets of eminence, Lord Byron has been for that time, and may for some time continue to be, the Champion of the English Parnassus. If his empire over the public mind be in any measure diminished, it arises from no literary failure of his own, and from no triumph of his competitors, but from other circumstances so frequently alluded to in the publications before us, that they cannot pass without some notice, which we will study to render as brief as it is impartial.

The poet thus gifted, thus honoured, thus admired, no longer entitled to regard himself as one defrauded of his just fame, and expelled with derision from the lists in which he had stood forward a candidate for honour, but crowned with all which the public could bestow, was now in a situation apparently as enviable as could be attained through mere literary celebrity. The sequel may be given in the words in which the author, adopting here more distinctly the character of Childe Harold than in the original poem, has chosen to present it to us, and to assign the cause why Childe Harold has resumed his pilgrim's staff when it was hoped he had sat down for life a denizen of his native country. The length of the quotation will be pardoned by those who can feel at once the moral interest and poetical beauty with which it abounds.

[*Quotes stanzas* 8–16.]

The commentary through which the meaning of this melancholy tale is rendered obvious, has been long before the public, and is still in vivid remembrance; for the errors of those who excel their fellows in gifts and accomplishments are not soon forgotten. Those scenes, ever most painful to the bosom, were rendered yet more so by public discussion; and it is at least possible that amongst those who exclaimed most loudly on this unhappy occasion, were some in whose eyes literary superiority exaggerated Lord Byron's offence. The scene may be described in a few words: the wise condemned—the good regretted—the multitude, idly or maliciously inquisitive, rushed from place to place, gathering gossip, which they mangled and exaggerated while they repeated it; and impudence, ever ready to hitch itself into notoriety, *hooked on*, as Falstaff enjoins Bardolph, blustered, bullied, and talked of "pleading a cause" and "taking a side."

The family misfortunes which have for a time lost Lord Byron to his native land have neither chilled his poetical fire, nor deprived England of its benefit. The Third Canto of *Childe Harold* exhibits, in all its strength and in all its peculiarity, the wild, powerful and original vein of poetry which, in the preceding cantos, first fixed the public attention upon the author. If there is any difference, the former seem to us to have been rather more sedulously corrected and revised for publication, and the present work to have been dashed from the author's pen with less regard to the subordinate points of expression and versification. Yet such is the deep and powerful strain of passion, such the original tone and colouring of description, that the want of polish in some of its minute parts rather adds to than deprives the poem of its energy. It seems, occasionally, as if the consideration of mere grace was beneath the care of the poet, in his ardour to hurry upon the reader the "thoughts that glow and words that burn"; and that the occasional roughness of the verse corresponded with the stern tone of thought, and of mental suffering which it expresses. We have remarked the same effect produced by the action of Mrs Siddons, when, to give emphasis to some passage of overwhelming passion, she has seemed wilfully to assume a position constrained, stiffened, violent, diametrically contrary to the rules of grace, in order, as it were, to concentrate herself for the utterance of grief, or passion which disdained embellishment.

In the same manner, versification, in the hands of a master-bard, is as frequently correspondent to the thoughts it expresses as to the action it describes, and the "line labours and the words move slow" under the heavy and painful thought; wrung as it were, from the bosom, as when Ajax is heaving his massy rock. It is proper, however, to give some account of the plan of the poem before we pursue these observations.

The subject is the same as in the preceding Cantos of the *Pilgrimage*. Harold wanders over other fields and amid other scenery, and gives vent to the various thoughts and medita-tions, which they excite in his breast. The poem opens with a beautiful and pathetic, though abrupt, invocation to the infant daughter of the author, and bespeaks at once our interest and our sympathy for the self-exiled Pilgrim.

I

Is thy face like thy mother's, my fair child?
Ada! sole daughter of my house and heart?
When last I saw thy young blue eyes they smiled,
And then we parted, not as now we part,
But with a hope.
      Awaking with a start,
The waters heave around me; and on high
The winds lift up their voices: I depart,
Whither I know not; but the hour's gone by,
When Albion's lessening shores could grieve or glad mine eye.

II

Once more upon the waters! yet once more!
And the waves bound beneath me as a steed
That knows his rider. Welcome, to their roar!
Swift be their guidance, wheresoe'er it lead!
Though the strain'd mast should quiver as a reed,
And the rent canvass fluttering strew the gale,
Still must I on; for I am as a weed,
Flung from the rock, on Ocean's foam, to sail
Where'er the surge may sweep, the tempest's breath prevail.
      Canto III, pp. 3-4.

The theme of *Childe Harold* is then resumed, and the stanzas follow which we have already quoted, and which, it must be

allowed, identify the noble author with the creature of his
imagination more intimately than in the former Cantos. We do
not mean to say that all Childe Harold's feelings and adven-
tures must be considered as those of Lord Byron, but merely
that there is much of Lord Byron in the supposed Pilgrim.

.   .   .   .   .

Childe Harold, though he shuns to celebrate the victory of
Waterloo, gives us a most beautiful description of the evening
which preceded the battle of Quatre Bras, the alarm which
called out the troops, and the hurry and confusion which pre-
ceded their march. We are not sure that any verses in our lan-
guage surpass the following in vigour and in feeling. The
quotation is again a long one, but we must not and dare not
curtail it.

XXI

There was a sound of revelry by night
And Belgium's capital had gathered then
Her Beauty and her Chivalry, and bright
The lamps shone o'er fair women and brave men;
A thousand hearts beat happily; and when
Music arose with its voluptuous swell,
Soft eyes look'd love to eyes which spake again,
And all went merry as a marriage-bell;
But hush! hark! a deep sound strikes like a rising knell!

XXII

Did ye not hear it?—No; 'twas but the wind
Or the car rattling o'er the stony street;
On with the dance! Let joy be unconfined;
No sleep till morn, when Youth and Pleasure meet
To chase the glowing Hours with flying feet—
But hark!—that heavy sound breaks in once more,
As if the clouds its echo would repeat;
And nearer, clearer, deadlier than before!
Arm! arm! it is—it is—the cannon's opening roar!

XXIII

Within a window'd niche of that high hall
Sate Brunswick's fated chieftain; he did hear
That sound the first amidst the festival,
And caught its tone with Death's prophetic ear;
And when they smiled because he deem'd it near,
His heart more truly knew that peal too well
Which stretch'd his father on a bloody bier,
And roused the vengeance blood alone could quell:
He rush'd into the field, and, foremost fighting, fell.

XXIV

Ah! then and there was hurrying to and fro,
And gathering tears, and tremblings of distress,
And cheeks all pale, which but an hour ago
Blush'd at the praise of their own loveliness;
And there were sudden partings, such as press
The life from out young hearts, and choking sighs
Which ne'er might be repeated; who could guess
If ever more meet those mutual eyes,
Since upon night so sweet such awful morn could rise?

XXV

And there was mounting in hot haste: the steed,
The mustering squadron, and the clattering car,
Went pouring forward with impetuous speed,
And swiftly forming in the ranks of war;
And the deep thunderpeal on peal afar;
And near, the beat of the alarming drum
Roused up the soldier ere the morning star;
While throng'd the citizens with terror dumb,
Or whispering, with white lips—"The foe! They come! they
come!"

XXVI

And wild and high the "Cameron's gathering" rose!
The war-note of Lochiel, which Albyn's hills
Have heard, and heard, too, have her Saxon foes:
How in the noon of night that pibroch thrills,
Savage and shrill! But with the breath which fills
Their mountain-pipe, so fill the mountaineers
With the fierce native daring which instils
The stirring memory of a thousand years,
And Evan's, Donald's fame rings in each clansman's ears!

XXVII

And Ardennes waves above them her green leaves,
Dewy with nature's tear-drops, as they pass,
Grieving, if aught inanimate e'er grieves,
Over the unreturning brave—alas!
Ere evening to be trodden like the grass
Which now beneath them, but above shall grow
In its next verdure, when this fiery mass
Of living valour, rolling on the foe
And burning with high hope, shall moulder cold and low.

XXVIII

Last noon beheld them full of lusty life,
Last eve in Beauty's circle proudly gay,
The midnight brought the signal-sound of strife,
The morn the marshalling in arms—the day
Battle's magnificently-stern array!
The thunder clouds close o'er it, which when rent
The earth is covered thick with other clay,
Which her own clay shall cover, heaped and pent,
Rider and horse—friend, foe—in one red burial blent!

A beautiful elegiac stanza on the Honourable Major Howard, a relation of Lord Byron; and several verses in which the author contemplates the character and fall of Napoleon, close the meditations suggested by the field of Waterloo. The present situation of Buonaparte ought to exempt him (unless when, as in the following pages, he is brought officially before us) from such petty warfare as we can wage. But if Lord Byron supposes that Napoleon's fall was occasioned, or even precipitated by a "just habitual scorn of men and their thoughts," too publicly and rashly expressed, or as he has termed it in a note, "the continued obtrusion on mankind of his want of all community of feeling with or for them," we conceive him to be under a material error. Far from being deficient in that necessary branch of the politician's art, which soothes the passions and conciliates the prejudices of those whom they wish to employ as instruments, Buonaparte possessed it in exquisite perfection. He seldom missed finding the very man that was fittest for his immediate purpose; and he had

I

in a peculiar degree, the art of moulding him to it. It was not, then, because he despised the means necessary to gain his end that he finally fell short of attaining it, but because confiding in his stars, his fortune, and his strength, the ends which he proposed were unattainable even by the gigantic means which he possessed. But if we are to understand that the projects of Napoleon intimated, too plainly for the subsistence of his power, how little he regarded human life or human happiness in the accomplishment of his personal views, and that this conviction heated his enemies and cooled his friends, his indeed may be called a *scorn*, but surely not a *just scorn* of his fellow-mortals.

. . . . . .

The poem proceeds to describe, in a tone of great beauty and feeling, a night-scene witnessed on the Lake of Geneva; and each natural object, from the evening grasshopper to the stars, "the poetry of heaven," suggests the contemplation of the connection between the Creator and his works. The scene is varied by the "fierce and fair delight" of a thunder-storm, described in verse almost as vivid as its lightnings. We had marked it for transcript, as one of the most beautiful passages of the poem; but quotation must have bounds, and we have been already liberal. But the "live thunder leaping among the rattling crags"—the voice of mountains, as if shouting to each other—the plashing of the big rain—the gleaming of the wide lake, lighted like a phosphoric sea—present a picture of sublime terror, yet of enjoyment, often attempted, but never so well, certainly never better, brought out in poetry. The Pilgrim reviews the characters of Gibbon and Voltaire, suggested by their residences on the lake of Geneva, and concludes by reverting to the same melancholy tone of feeling with which the poem commenced. Childe Harold, though not formally dismissed, glides from our observations; and the poet, in his own person, renews the affecting address to his infant daughter:

CXV

My daughter! with thy name this song begun—
My daughter! with thy name thus much shall end.
I see thee not—I hear thee not—but none
Can be so wrapt in thee; thou art the friend
To whom the shadows of far years extend:
Albeit my brow thou never should'st behold,
My voice shall with thy future visions blend,
And reach into thy heart—when mine is cold,
A token and a tone, even from thy father's mould.

He proceeds in the same tone for several stanzas, and then concludes with this paternal benediction:

Sweet be thy cradled slumbers o'er the sea,
And from the mountains where I now respire,
Fain would I waft such blessings upon thee,
As with a sigh I deem thou might'st have been to me.

Having thus finished the analysis of this beautiful poem, we have the difficult and delicate task before us, of offering some remarks on the tone and feeling in which it is composed. But before discharging this part of our duty, we must give some account of the other *fasciculus* with which the fertile genius of Lord Byron has supplied us.

The collection to which the *Prisoner of Chillon* gives name, inferior in interest to the continuation of Childe Harold, is marked nevertheless, by the peculiar force of Lord Byron's genius. It consists of a series of detached pieces, some of them fragments, and rather poetical prolusions, than finished and perfect poems . . .

It will readily be allowed that this singular poem [*The Prisoner of Chillon*] is more powerful than pleasing. The dungeon of Bonnivard, is, like that of Ugolino, a subject too dismal for even the power of the painter or poet to counteract its horrors. It is the more disagreeable as affording human hope no anchor to rest upon, and describing the sufferer, though a man of talents and virtues, as altogether inert and powerless under his accumulated sufferings. Yet as a picture, however gloomy the colouring, it may rival any which Lord Byron has drawn, nor is it possible to read it without a sinking of the heart, corresponding with that which he describes the victim to have suffered.

Scott on *Childe Harold IV*: *Quarterly Review*, April 1818

... From the copious specimens which we have given, the reader will be enabled to judge how well the last part of this great poem has sustained Lord Byron's high reputation. Yet we think it possible to trace a marked difference, though none in the tone of thought and expression, betwixt this canto and the first three. There is less of passion, more of deep thought and sentiment, at once collected and general. The stream which in its earlier course bounds over cataracts and rages through narrow and rocky defiles, deepens, expands, and becomes less turbid as it rolls on, losing the aspect of terror and gaining that of sublimity. Eight years have passed between the appearance of the first volume and the present which concludes the work, a lapse of time which, joined with other circumstances, may have contributed somewhat to moderate the tone of Childe Harold's quarrel with the world, and, if not to reconcile him to his lot, to give him, at least, the firmness which endures it without loud complaint. To return however, to the proposition with which we opened our criticism, certain it is, that whether as Harold or as Lord Byron no author has ever fixed upon himself personally so intense a share of the public attention. His descriptions of present and existing scenes however striking and beautiful, his recurrence to past actions however important and however powerfully described, become interesting chiefly from the tincture which they receive from the mind of the author. The grot of Egeria, the ruins of the Palatine, are but a theme for his musings, always deep and powerful though sometimes gloomy even to sullenness. This cast of solemnity may not perhaps be justly attributed to the native disposition of the author, which is reported to be as lively as, judging from this single poem at least, we might pronounce it to be grave. But our ideas of happiness are chiefly caught by reflection from the minds of others, and hence it may be observed that those enjoy the most uniform train of good spirits who are thinking

much of others and little of themselves. The contemplation of
our minds, however salutary for the purposes of self-examina-
tion and humiliation, must always be a solemn task, since the
best will find enough for remorse, the wisest for regret, the
most fortunate for sorrow. And to this influence more than
to any natural disposition to melancholy, to the pain which
necessarily follows this anatomizing of his own thoughts and
feelings which is so decidedly and peculiarly the characteristic
of the Pilgrimage, we are disposed in a great measure to ascribe
that sombre tint which pervades the poem. The poetry which
treats of the actions and sentiments of others may be grave
or gay according to the light in which the author chuses to
view his subject, but he who shall mine long and deeply for
materials in his own bosom will encounter abysses at the depth
of which he must necessarily tremble. This moral truth ap-
pears to us to afford, in a great measure, a key to the peculiar
tone of Lord Byron. How then, will the reader ask, is our pro-
position to be reconciled to that which preceded it? If the
necessary result of an inquiry into our own thoughts be the
conviction that all is vanity and vexation of spirit, why should
we object to a style of writing, whatever its consequences may
be, which involves in it truths as certain as they are melan-
choly? If the study of our own enjoyments leads us to doubt
the reality of all except the indisputable pleasures of sense, and
inclines us therefore towards the Epicurean system—it is
nature, it may be said, and not the poet which urges us upon
the fatal conclusion. But this is not so. Nature, when she
created man a social being, gave him the capacity of drawing
that happiness from his relations with the rest of his race,
which he is doomed to seek in vain in his own bosom. These
relations cannot be the source of happiness to us if we despise
or hate the kind with whom it is their office to unite us more
closely. If the earth be a den of fools and knaves, from whom
the man of genius differs by the more mercurial and exalted
character of his intellect, it is natural that he should look down
with pitiless scorn on creatures so inferior. But if, as we believe,
each man, in his own degree, possesses a portion of the ethereal
flame, however smothered by unfavourable circumstances, it is

or should be enough to secure the most mean from the scorn
of genius as well as from the oppression of power, and such
being the case, the relations which we hold with society
through all their gradations are channels through which the
better affections of the loftiest may, without degradation,
extend themselves to the lowest. Farther, it is not only our
social connections which are assigned us in order to qualify
that contempt of mankind, which too deeply indulged tends
only to intense selfishness; we have other and higher motives
for enduring the lot of humanity—sorrow, and pain, and
trouble—with patience of our own griefs and commiseration
for those of others. The wisest and the best of all ages have
agreed that our present life is a state of trial not of enjoyment,
and that we now suffer sorrow that we may hereafter be par-
takers of happiness. If this be true, and it has seldom been long,
or at least ultimately, doubted by those who have turned their
attention to so serious an investigation, other and worthier
motives of action and endurance must necessarily occur to the
mind than philosophy can teach or human pride supply. It is
not our intention to do more than merely indicate so ample a
topic for consideration. But we cannot forbear to add, that the
vanishing of Lord Byron's Pilgrim strongly reminded us of the
close of another work, the delight of our childhood. Childe
Harold, a prominent character in the first volume of the Pil-
grimage, fades gradually from the scene like the spectre asso-
ciate who performed the first stages of his journey with a
knight-errant, bearing all the appearance of a living man, but
who lessened to the sight by degrees, and became at length
totally invisible when they approached the cavern where his
mortal remains were deposited.

CLXIV

But where is he, the Pilgrim of my song,
The being who upheld it through the past?
Methinks he cometh late and tarries long.
He is no more—these breathings are his last;
His wanderings done, his visions ebbing fast
And he himself as nothing: if he was
Aught but a phantasy, and could be class'd
With forms which live and suffer—let that pass—
His shadow fades away into Destruction's mass. (p. 85)

In the corresponding passage of the Tales of the Genii, Ridley, the amiable author or compiler of the collection, expresses himself to the following purport, for we have not the book at hand to do justice to his precise words:

> Reader, the Genii are no more, and Horam, but the phantom of my mind, fiction himself and fiction all that he seemed to write, speaks not again. But lament not their loss, since if desirous to see virtue guarded by miracles, Religion can display before you scenes tremendous, wonderful and great, more worthy of your sight than aught that human fancy can conceive—the moral veil rent in twain and the Sun of Righteousness arising from the thick clouds of heathen darkness.

In the sincere spirit of admiration for Lord Byron's talents, and regard for his character which has dictated the rest of our criticism, we here close our analysis of *Childe Harold*.

Our task respecting Lord Byron's poetry is finished, when we have mentioned the subject, quoted passages of superior merit, or which their position renders most capable of being detached from the body of the poem. For the character of his style and versification once distinctly traced (and we have had repeated occasion to consider it) cannot again be dwelt on without repetition. The harmony of verse, and the power of numbers, nay, the selection and arrangement of expressions, are all so subordinate to the thought and sentiment, as to become comparatively light in the scale. His poetry is like the oratory which hurries the hearers along without permitting them to pause on its solecisms or singularities. Its general structure is bold, severe, and as it were Doric, admitting few ornaments but those immediately suggested by the glowing imagination of the author, rising and sinking with the tones of his enthusiasm, roughening into argument, or softening into the melody of feeling and sentiment, as if the language fit for either were alike at the command of the poet, and the numbers not only came uncalled, but arranged themselves with little care on his part into the varied modulation which the subject requires. Many of the stanzas, considered separately from the rest, might be objected to as involved, harsh, and overflowing into each other beyond the usual license of the Spenserian stanza. But considering the various matter of which the poet had to treat—considering the monotony of a long-continued smoothness of sound, and accurate division of the sense according to the stanzas—considering also that the effect of the general harmony is, as in music, improved by the judicious introduction of discords wherewith it is contrasted, we cannot join with those who state this occasional harshness as an objection to Lord Byron's poetry. If the line sometimes "labours and the words move slow," it is in passages where the sense is correspondent to these laborious movements. A highly finished strain of versification resembles a dressed pleasure ground, elegant—even beautiful—but tame and insipid compared to the majesty and interest of a woouland chase, where scenes of natural loveliness are rendered sweeter and more interesting by the contrast of irregularity and wildness.

Wilson on *Manfred*: *Blackwood's*, June 1817

LORD BYRON has been elected by acclamation to the throne of poetical supremacy; nor are we disposed to question his title to the crown. There breathes over all his genius an air of kingly dignity; strength, vigour, energy, are his attributes; and he wields his faculties with a proud consciousness of their power, and a confident anticipation of their effects. Living poets perhaps there are, who have taken a wider range, but none who have achieved such complete, such perfect triumphs. In no great attempt has he ever failed; and, soon as he begins his flight, we feel that he is to soar upon unflagging wings—that when he has reached the black and tempestuous elevation of his favourite atmosphere, he will, eagle-like, sail on undisturbed through the heart of clouds, storms, and darkness.

To no poet was there ever given so awful a revelation of the passions of the human soul. He surveys, with a stern delight, that tumult and conflict of terrible thoughts from which other highly gifted and powerful minds have involuntarily recoiled; he calmly and fearlessly stands upon the brink of that abyss from which the soul would seem to shrink with horror; and he looks down upon, and listens to, the everlasting agitation of the howling waters. There are in his poetry feelings, thoughts, sentiments, and passions, that we at once recognise to be human though we know not whence they come: they break upon us like the sudden flash of a returning dream—like some wild cry from another world. And even those whose lives have had little experience of the wilder passions, for a moment feel that an unknown region of their own souls has been revealed to them, and that there are indeed fearful mysteries in our human nature.

When this dark and powerful spirit for a while withdraws from the contemplation of his own wild world, and conde-scends to look upon the ordinary shews and spectacles of life, he often seems unexpectedly to participate in the feelings and emotions of beings with whom it might be thought he could claim no kindred; and thus many passages are to be found in his poetry, of the most irresistible and overpowering pathos, in which the depth of his sympathy with common sorrows and common sufferers, seems as profound as if his nature knew nothing more mournful than sighs and tears.

We have no intention of drawing Lord Byron's poetical character, and have been led, we know not how, into these very general and imperfect observations. But perhaps the little we have said may in some degree shew, why hitherto this great poet has dealt so seldom with the forms of the external world. He has so deeply looked into the soul of man, and so intensely sympathized with all the struggles there—that he has had no feelings or passions to fling away on the mere earth he inhabits. But it is evident that the same powers, which he has so glori-ously exerted upon man as their subject, would kindle up and enlighten, or darken and disturb, the features of external nature; and that, if he so willed it, his poetry, instead of being rife with wrath, despair, remorse, and all other agitating pas-sions, might present an equally sublime assemblage of woods, glens, and mountains—of lakes and rivers, cataracts and oceans. In the third canto of *Childe Harold*, accordingly, he has delivered up his soul to the impulses of Nature, and we have seen how that high communion has elevated and sublimed it. He instantly penetrated into her heart, as he had before into the heart of Man; and, in a few months of solitary wandering among the Alps, his soul became as deeply embued with her glory and magnificence, as if, from youth, he had dedicated himself to no other power, and had for ever devoutly worshipped at her altar. He leapt at once into the first rank of descriptive poets. He came into competition with Wordsworth upon his own ground, and with his own weapons; and in the first encounter he vanquished and over threw him. His description of the stormy night among the Alps—of the blending—the mingling—the fusion of his own soul, with the raging elements around him—is alone worth all the dull metaphysics of the *Excursion*, and shews that he might enlarge the limits of human consciousness regarding the operations of matter upon mind, as widely as he has enlarged them regarding the operations of mind upon itself.

In the very singular, and, we suspect, very imperfect poem, of which we are about to give a short account, Lord Byron has pursued the same course as in the third canto of *Childe Harold*, and put out his strength upon the same objects. The action is laid among the mountains of the Alps—the characters are all, more or less, formed and swayed by the operations of the magnificent scenery around them, and every page of the poem teems with imagery and passion, though, at the same time, the mind of the poet is often overborne, as it were, by the strength and novelty of his own conceptions; and thus the composition, as a whole, is liable to many and fatal objections.

But there is a still more novel exhibition of Lord Byron's powers in this extraordinary drama. He has here burst into the world of spirits; and, in the wild delight with which the elements of nature seem to have inspired him, he has endeavoured to embody and call up before him their ministering agents, and to employ these wild Personifications, as he formerly employed the feelings and passions of man. We are not prepared to say, that, in this daring attempt, he has completely succeeded. We are inclined to think, that the plan he has conceived, and the principal Character which he has wished to delineate, would require a fuller development than is here given to them; and accordingly, a sense of imperfection, incompleteness, and confusion, accompanies the mind through-

out the perusal of the poem, owing either to some failure on
the part of the poet, or to the inherent mystery of the subject.
But though on that account it is difficult to comprehend dis-
tinctly the drift of the composition, and almost impossible to
give any thing like a distinct account of it, it unquestionably
exhibits many noble delineations of mountain scenery—many
impressive and terrible pictures of passion—and many wild
and awful visions of imagery and horror.

From Jeffrey's review of three of Byron's plays: *Edin-
burgh Review*, February 1822

The charge we bring against Lord Byron, in short, is, that
his writings have a tendency to destroy all belief in the reality
of virtue—and to make all enthusiasm and constancy of affec-
tion ridiculous; and this not so much by direct maxims and
examples, of an imposing or seducing kind, as by the constant
exhibition of the most profligate heartlessness in the persons
who had been transiently represented as actuated by the purest
and most exalted emotions—and in the lessons of that very
teacher who had been, but a moment before, so beautifully
pathetic in the expression of the loftiest conceptions. When a
gay voluptuary descants, somewhat too freely, on the intoxica-
tions of love and wine, we ascribe his excesses to the efferve-
scence of youthful spirits, and do not consider him as seriously
impeaching either the value or the reality of the severer vir-
tues; and in the same way, when the satirist deals out his sar-
casms against the sincerity of human professions, and unmasks
the secret infirmities of our bosoms, we consider this as aimed
at hypocrisy, and not at mankind: or, at all events, and in
either case, we consider the Sensualist and the Misanthrope as
wandering, each in his own delusion—and are contented to pity
those who have never known the charms of a tender or gener-
ous affection. The true antidote to such seductive or revolting
views of human nature, is to turn to the scenes of its nobleness
and attraction; and to reconcile ourselves again to our kind,
by listening to the accents of pure affection and incorruptible

honour. But if those accents have flowed in all their sweetness, from the very lips that instantly open again to mock and blaspheme them, the antidote is mingled with the poison, and the draught is the more deadly for the mixture!

The reveller may pursue his orgies, and the wanton display her enchantments, with comparative safety to those around them, as long as they know or believe that there are purer and higher enjoyments, and teachers and followers of a happier way. But if the Priest pass from the altar, with persuasive exhortations to peace and purity still trembling on his tongue, to join familiarly in the grossest and most profane debauchery—if the Matron, who has charmed all hearts by the lovely sanctimonies of her conjugal and maternal endearments, glides out from the circle of her children, and gives bold and shameless way to the most abandoned and degrading vices—our notions of right and wrong are at once confounded—our confidence in virtue shaken to the foundation—and our reliance on truth and fidelity at an end for ever.

This is the charge which we bring against Lord Byron. We say that, under some strange misapprehension as to the truth, and the duty of proclaiming it, he has exerted all the powers of his powerful mind to convince his readers, both directly and indirectly, that all ennobling pursuits, and disinterested virtues, are mere deceits or illusions—hollow mockeries for the most part, and, at best, but laborious follies. Religion, love, patriotism, valour, devotion, constancy, ambition—all are to be laughed at, disbelieved in, and despised!—and nothing is really good, so far as we can gather, but a succession of dangers to stir the blood, and of banquets and intrigues to soothe it again! If this doctrine stood alone, with its examples, it would revolt, we believe, more than it would seduce: but the author of it has the unlucky gift of personating all those sweet and lofty illusions, and that with such grace and force, and truth to nature, that it is impossible not to suppose, for the time, that he is among the most devoted of their votaries—till he casts off the character with a jerk—and, the moment after he has moved and exalted us to the very height of our conception, resumes his mockery of all things serious or sublime—and lets

us down at once on some coarse joke, hard-hearted sarcasm, or
fierce and relentless personality—as if on purpose to show

Whoe'er was edified, himself was not—

or to demonstrate practically as it were, and by example, how
possible it is to have all fine and noble feelings, or their appear-
ance, for a moment, and yet retain no particle of respect for
them—or of belief in their intrinsic worth or permanent reality.
Thus, we have an indelicate but very clever scene of young
Juan's concealment in the bed of an amorous matron, and of the
torrent of "rattling and audacious eloquence" with which she
repels the too just suspicions of her jealous lord. All this is
merely comic and a little coarse: but then the poet chooses to
make this shameless and abandoned woman address to her
young gallant an epistle breathing the very spirit of warm,
devoted, pure, and unalterable love—thus profaning the holiest
language of the heart, and indirectly associating it with the
most hateful and degrading sensuality. In like manner, the
sublime and terrific description of the Shipwreck is strangely
and disgustingly broken by traits of low humour and buffoon-
ery; and we pass immediately from the moans of an agonizing
father fainting over his famished son, to facetious stories of
Juan's begging a paw of his father's dog—and refusing a slice
of his tutor!—as if it were a fine thing to be hard-hearted—and
pity and compassion were fit only to be laughed at. In the same
spirit, the glorious Ode on the aspirations of Greece after
liberty, is instantly followed up by a strain of dull and cold-
blooded ribaldry; —and we are hurried on from the distrac-
tion and death of Haidee to merry scenes of intrigue and mas-
querading in the seraglio. Thus all good feelings are excited
only to accustom us to their speedy and complete extinction;
and we are brought back, from their transient and theatrical
exhibition, to the staple and substantial doctrine of the work—
the non-existence of constancy in women or honour in men,
and the folly of expecting to meet with any such virtues, or of
cultivating them, for an undeserving world; and all this mixed
up with so much wit and cleverness, and knowledge of human
nature, as to make it irresistibly pleasant and plausible—while

there is not only no antidote supplied, but every thing that might have operated in that way has been anticipated, and presented already in as strong and engaging a form as possible—but under such associations as to rob it of all efficacy, or even turn it into an auxiliary of the poison.

This is our sincere opinion of much of Lord Byron's most splendid poetry—a little exaggerated perhaps in the expression, from a desire to make our exposition clear and impressive—but, in substance, we think merited and correct. We have already said, and we deliberately repeat, that we have no notion that Lord Byron had any mischievous intention in these publications —and readily acquit him of any wish to corrupt the morale, or impair the happiness of his readers. Such a wish, indeed, is in itself altogether inconceivable; but it is our duty, nevertheless, to say, that much of what he has published appears to us to have this tendency—and that we are acquainted with no writings so well calculated to extinguish in young minds all generous enthusiasm and gentle affection—all respect for themselves, and all love for their kind—to make them practise and profess hardily what it teaches them to suspect in others—and actually to persuade them that it is wise and manly and knowing to laugh, not only at self-denial and restraint, but at all aspiring ambition, and all warm and constant affection.

Jeffrey on *Childe Harold III* and *The Prisoner of Chillon*: *Edinburgh Review*, December 1816

If the finest poetry be that which leaves the deepest impression on the minds of its readers—and this is not the worst test of its excellence—Lord Byron, we think, must be allowed to take precedence of all his distinguished contemporaries. He has not the variety of Scott—nor the delicacy of Campbell—nor the absolute truth of Crabbe—nor the polished sparkling of Moore; but in force of diction, and inextinguishable energy of sentiment, he clearly surpasses them all. "Words that breathe, and thoughts that burn," are not merely the ornaments, but the common staple of his poetry; and he is not inspired or impressive only in some happy passages, but through the whole body and tissue of his composition. It was an unavoidable condition, perhaps, of this higher excellence, that his scenes should be narrow, and his persons few. To compass such ends as he had in view, it was necessary to reject all ordinary agents, and all trivial combinations. He could not possibly be amusing, or ingenious, or playful; or hope to maintain the requisite pitch of interest by the recitation of sprightly adventures, or the opposition of common characters. To produce great effects, in short, he felt that it was necessary to deal only with the greater passions—with the exaltations of a daring fancy; and the errors of a lofty intellect—with the pride, the terrors, and the agonies of strong emotion—the fire and air alone of our human elements.

In this respect, and in his general notion of the end and the means of poetry, we have sometimes thought that his views fell more in with those of the Lake poets, than of any other existing party in the poetical commonwealth: and, in some of his later productions, especially, it is impossible not to be struck with his occasional approaches to the style and manner of this class of writers. Lord Byron, however, it should be observed, like all other persons of a quick sense of beauty, and sure enough of their own originality to be in no fear of paltry imputations, is a great mimic of styles and manners, and a great borrower of external character. He and Scott, accordingly, are full of imitations of all writers from whom they have ever derived gratification; and the two most original writers of the age might appear, to superficial observers, to be the most deeply indebted to their predecessors. In this particular instance, we have no fault to find with Lord Byron: for undoubtedly the finer passages of Wordsworth and Southey have in them wherewithal to lend an impulse to the utmost ambition of rival genius; and their diction and manner of writing is frequently both striking and original. But we must say, that it would afford us still greater pleasure to find these tuneful gentlemen returning the compliment which Lord Byron has here paid to their talents; and forming themselves on the model rather of his imitations, than of their own originals. In those imitations they will find that, though he is sometimes abundantly mystical, he never, or at least very rarely, indulges in absolute nonsense—never takes his lofty flights upon mean or ridiculous occasions—and, above all, never dilutes his strong conceptions, and magnificent imaginations, with a flood of oppressive verbosity. On the contrary, he is, of all living writers, the most concise and condensed; and, we would fain hope, may go far, by his example, to redeem the great reproach of our modern literature —its intolerable prolixity and redundance. In his nervous and manly lines, we find no elaborate amplification of common sentiments—no ostentatious polishing of pretty expressions; and we really think that the brilliant success which has rewarded his disdain of those paltry artifices, should put to shame for ever that puling and self-admiring race, who can live through half a volume on the stock of a single thought, and expatiate over diverse fair quarto pages with the details of one tedious description. In Lord Byron, on the contrary, we have a perpetual stream of thick-coming fancies—an eternal spring of fresh-blowing images, which seem called into existence by the sudden flash of those glowing thoughts and overwhelming emotions, that struggle for expression through the whole flow of his poetry—and impart to a diction that is often abrupt and irregular, a force and a charm which frequently realize all that is said of inspiration.

With all these undoubted claims to our admiration, however, it is impossible to deny that the noble author before us has still something to learn, and a good deal to correct. He is frequently abrupt and careless, and sometimes obscure. There are marks, occasionally, of effort and straining after an emphasis, which is generally spontaneous; and, above all, there is far too great a monotony in the moral colouring of his pictures, and too much repetition of the same sentiments and maxims. He delights too exclusively in the delineation of a certain morbid exaltation of character and of feeling—a sort of demoniacal sublimity, not without some traits of the ruined Archangel. He is haunted almost perpetually with the image of a being feeding and fed upon by violent passions, and the recollections of the catastrophes they have occasioned; and, though worn out by

their past indulgence, unable to sustain the burden of an exist-
ence which they do not continue to animate:—full of pride,
and revenge, and obduracy—disdaining life and death, and
mankind and himself—and trampling, in his scorn, not only
upon the falsehood and formality of polished life, but upon its
tame virtues and slavish devotion: yet envying, by fits, the very
beings he despises, and melting into mere softness and com-
passion, when the helplessness of childhood or the frailty of
woman make an appeal to his generosity. Such is the person
with whom we are called upon almost exclusively to sympa-
thize in all the greater productions of this distinguished writer:
in *Childe Harold*—in *The Corsair*—in *Lara*—in the *Siege of
Corith*—in *Parisina*, and in most of the smaller pieces.

It is impossible to represent such a character better than
Lord Byron has done in all these productions—or indeed to
represent any thing more terrible in its anger, or more attrac-
tive in its relenting. In point of effect, we readily admit, that
no one character can be more poetical or impressive: but it is
really too much to find the scene perpetually filled by one char-
acter—not only in all the acts of each several drama, but in all
the different dramas of the series; and, grand and impressive
as it is, we feel at last that these very qualities make some relief
more indispensable, and oppress the spirits of ordinary mortals
with too deep an impression of awe and repulsion. There is too
much guilt, in short, and too much gloom, in the leading char-
acter; and though it be a fine thing to gaze, now and then, on
stormy seas, and thunder-shaken mountains, we should prefer
passing our days in sheltered valleys, and by the murmur of
calmer water.

We are aware that these metaphors may be turned against
us—and that, without metaphor, it may be said that men do not
pass their days in reading poetry—and that, as they may look
into Lord Byron only about as often as they look abroad upon
tempests, they have no more reason to complain of him for
being grand and gloomy, than to complain of the same quali-
ties in the glaciers and volcanoes which they go so far to visit.
Painters, too, it may be said, have often gained great reputation
by their representations of tigers and other ferocious animals,

K

or of caverns and banditti—and poets should be allowed, without reproach, to indulge in analogous exercises. We are far from thinking that there is no weight in these considerations; and feel how plausibly it may be said, that we have no better reason for a great part of our complaint, than that an author, to whom we are already very greatly indebted, has chosen rather to please himself, than us, in the use he makes of his talents.

This, no doubt, seems both unreasonable and ungrateful: but it is nevertheless true, that a public benefactor becomes a debtor to the public; and is, in some degree, responsible for the employment of those gifts which seem to be conferred upon him, not merely for his own delight, but for the delight and improvement of his fellows through all generations. Independent of this, however, we think there is a reply to the apology. A great living poet is not like a distant volcano, or an occasional tempest. He is a volcano in the heart of our land, and a cloud that hangs over our dwellings; and we have some reason to complain, if, instead of genial warmth and grateful shade, he voluntarily darkens and inflames our atmosphere with perpetual fiery explosions and pitchy vapours. Lord Byron's poetry, in short, is too attractive and too famous to lie dormant or inoperative; and, therefore, if it produce any painful or pernicious effects, there will be murmurs, and ought to be suggestions of alteration. Now, though an artist may draw fighting tigers and hungry lions in as lively and natural a way as he can, without giving any encouragement to human ferocity, or even much alarm to human fear, the case is somewhat different, when a poet represents men with tiger-like dispositions—and yet more so, when he exhausts the resources of his genius to make this terrible being interesting and attractive, and to represent all the lofty virtues as the natural allies of his ferocity. It is still worse when he proceeds to show, that all these precious gifts of dauntless courage, strong affection, and high imagination, are not only akin to guilt, but the parents of misery—and that those only have any chance of tranquillity or happiness in this world, whom it is the object of his poetry to make us shun and despise.

These, it appears to us, are not merely errors in taste, but

perversions of morality; and, as a great poet is necessarily a
moral teacher, and gives forth his ethical lessons, in general,
with far more effect and authority than any of his graver
brethren, he is peculiarly liable to the censures reserved for
those who turn the means of improvement to purposes of
corruption.

It may no doubt be said that poetry in general tends less to
the useful than the splendid qualities of our nature—that a
character poetically good has long been distinguished from one
that is morally so—and that, ever since the time of Achilles,
our sympathies, on such occasions, have been chiefly engrossed
by persons whose deportment is by no means examplary; and
who in many points approach to the temperament of Lord
Byron's ideal hero. There is some truth in this suggestion also.
But other poets, in the *first* place, do not allow their favourites
so outrageous a monopoly of the glory and interest of the
piece—and sin less therefore against the laws either of poetical
or distributive justice. In the *second* place, their heroes are not,
generally, either so bad or so good as Lord Byron's—and do
not indeed very much exceed the standard of truth and nature,
in either of the extremes. His, however, are as monstrous and
unnatural as centaurs, and hippogriffs—and must ever figure
in the eye of sober reason as so many bright and hateful impos-
sibilities. But the most important distinction is, that the other
poets who deal in peccant heroes, neither feel nor express that
ardent affection for them, which is visible in the whole of this
author's delineations; but merely make use of them as necessary
agents in the extraordinary adventures they have to detail, and
persons whose mingled vices and virtues are requisite to bring
about the catastrophe of their story. In Lord Byron, however,
the interest of the story, where there happens to be one, which
is not always the case, is uniformly postponed to that of the
character itself—into which he enters so deeply, and with so
extraordinary a fondness, that he generally continues to speak
in its language, after it has been dismissed from the stage; and
to inculcate, on his own authority, the same sentiments which
had been previously recommended by its example. We do not
consider it unfair, therefore, to say that Lord Byron appears to

us to be the zealous apostle of a certain fierce and magnificent misanthropy; which has already saddened his poetry with too deep a shade, and not only led to a great misapplication of great talents, but contributed to render popular some very false estimates of the constituents of human happiness and merit.

"Remarks on Don Juan": *Blackwood's*, August 1819

It has not been without much reflection and overcoming many reluctancies, that we have at last resolved to say a few words more to our readers concerning this very extraordinary poem. The nature and causes of our difficulties will be easily understood by those of them who have read any part of *Don Juan*— but despair of standing justified as to the conclusion at which we have arrived, in the opinion of any but those who have read and understood the whole of a work, in the composition of which there is unquestionably a more thorough and intense infusion of genius and vice—power and profligacy—than in any poem which had ever before been written in the English, or indeed in any other modern language. Had the wickedness been less inextricably mingled with the beauty and the grace, and the strength of a most inimitable and incomprehensible muse, our task would have been easy: But *Silence* would be a very poor and a very useless chastisement to be inflicted by us, or by any one, on a production, whose corruptions have been so effectually embalmed—which, in spite of all that critics can do or refrain from doing, nothing can possibly prevent from taking a high place in the literature of our country, and remaining to all ages a perpetual monument of the exalted intellect, and the depraved heart, of one of the most remarkable men to whom that country has had the honour and the disgrace of giving birth.

That Lord Byron has never written any thing more decisively and triumphantly expressive of the greatness of his genius, will be allowed by all who have read this poem. That (laying all its manifold and grievous offences for a moment out of our view) it is by far the most admirable specimen of the mixture of ease, strength, gayety, and seriousness extant in the whole body of English poetry, is a proposition to which, we are almost as well persuaded, very few of them will refuse their assent. With sorrow and humiliation do we speak it—the poet has devoted his powers to the worst of purposes and passions; and it increases his guilt and our sorrow, that he has devoted them entire. What the immediate effect of the poem may be on contemporary literature, we cannot pretend to guess—too happy could we hope that its lessons of boldness and vigour in language, and versification, and conception, might be attended to, as they deserve to be—without any stain being suffered to fall on the purity of those who minister to the general shape and culture of the public mind, from the mischievous insults against all good principle and all good feeling, which have been unworthily embodied in so many elements of fascination.

The moral strain of the whole poem is pitched in the lowest key—and if the genius of the author lifts him now and then out of his pollution, it seems as if he regretted the elevation, and made all haste to descend again. To particularize the offences committed in its pages would be worse than vain—because the great genius of the man seems to have been throughout exerted to its utmost strength, in devising every possible method of pouring scorn upon every element of good or noble nature in the hearts of his readers. Love—honour—patriotism—religion, are mentioned only to be scoffed at and derided, as if their sole resting-place were, or ought to be, in the bosoms of fools. It appears, in short, as if this miserable man, having exhausted every species of sensual gratification—having drained the cup of sin even to its bitterest dregs, were resolved to shew us that he is no longer a human being, even in his frailities; but a cool unconcerned fiend, laughing with a detestable glee over the whole of the better and worse elements of which human life is composed—treating well nigh with equal derision the most pure of virtues, and the most odious of vices—dead alike to the beauty of the one, and the deformity of the other—a mere heartless despiser of that frail but noble humanity, whose type was never exhibited in a shape of more deplorable degradation than in his own contemptuously distinct delineation of himself. To confess in secret to his Maker, and weep over in secret agonies the wildest and most phantastic transgressions of heart and mind, is the part of a conscious sinner, in whom sin has not become the sole principle of life and action—of a soul for which there is yet hope. But to lay bare to the eye of man and of *woman* all the hidden convulsions of a wicked spirit—thoughts too abominable, we would hope, to have been imagined by any but him that has expressed them —and to do all this without one symptom of pain, contrition, remorse, or hesitation, with a calm careless ferociousness of contented and satisfied depravity—this was an insult which no wicked man of genius had ever before dared to put upon his Creator or his Species. This highest of all possible exhibitions of self-abandonment has been set forth in mirth and gladness, by one whose name was once pronounced with pride and veneration by every English voice. This atrocious consummation was reserved for Byron.

It has long been sufficiently manifest, that this man is devoid of religion. At times, indeed, the power and presence of the Deity, as speaking in the sterner workings of the elements, seems to force some momentary consciousness of their existence into his labouring breast—a spirit in which there breathes so much of the divine, cannot always resist the majesty of its Maker. But of true religion terror is a small part—and of all religion, that founded on mere terror, is the least worthy of such a man as Byron. We may look in vain through all his works for the slightest evidence that his soul had ever listened to the *gentle voice* of the oracles. His understanding has been subdued into conviction by some passing cloud; but his heart has never been touched. He has never written one line that savours of the spirit of meekness. His faith is but for a moment—"he believes and trembles," and relapses again into his gloom of unbelief—a gloom in which he is at least as devoid of *Hope* and *Charity* as he is of *Faith*. The same proud hardness of heart which makes the author of *Don Juan* a despiser of the Faith for which his fathers bled, has rendered him a scorner of the better part of woman; and therefore it is that his love poetry

is a continual insult to the beauty that inspires it. The earthy
part of the passion is all that has found a resting place within
his breast—His idol is all of clay—and he dashes her to pieces
almost in the moment of his worship. Impiously railing
against his God—madly and meanly disloyal to his Sovereign
and his country—and abruptly outraging all the best feelings
of female honour, affection, and confidence—how small a part
of chivalry is that which remains to the descendant of the
Byrons—a gloomy vizor, and a deadly weapon!

Of these offences, however, or of such as these, Lord Byron
had been guilty abundantly before, and for such he has before
been rebuked in our own, and in other more authoritative
pages. There are other and newer sins with which the author of
Don Juan has stained himself—sins of a class, if possible, even
more despicable than any he had before committed; and in
regard to which it is matter of regret to us, that as yet our
periodical critics have not appeared to express themselves with
any seemly measure of manly and candid indignation.

Those who are acquainted (as who is not?) with the main
incidents in the private life of Lord Byron—and who have not
seen this production (and we are aware, that very few of our
Northern readers have seen it)—will scarcely believe, that the
odious malignity of this man's bosom should have carried him
so far, as to make him commence a filthy and impious poem,
with an elaborate satire on the character and manners of his
wife—from whom, even by his own confession, he has been
separated only in consequence of his own cruel and heartless
misconduct. It is in vain for Lord Byron to attempt in any way
to justify his own behaviour in that affair; and, now that he has
so openly and audaciously invited inquiry and reproach, we do
not see any good reason why he should not be plainly told so by
the general voice of his countrymen. It would not be an easy
matter to persuade any Man who has any knowledge of the
nature of Woman, that a female such as Lord Byron has him-
self described his wife to be, would rashly, or hastily, or lightly
separate herself, from the love by which she had once been in-
spired for such a man as he is, or was. Had he not heaped insult
upon insult, and scorn upon scorn—had he not forced the iron of

his contempt into her very soul—there is no woman of delicacy and virtue, as he *admitted* Lady Byron to be, who would not have hoped all things and suffered all things from one, her love of whom must have been inwoven with so many exalting elements of delicious pride, and more delicious humility. To offend the love of such a woman was wrong—but it might be forgiven; to desert her was unmanly—but he might have returned and wiped for ever from her eyes the tears of her desertion; but to injure, and to desert, and then to turn back and wound her widowed privacy with unhallowed strains of cold-blooded mockery—was brutally, fiendishly, inexpiably mean. For impurities there might be some possibility of pardon, were they supposed to spring only from the reckless buoyancy of young blood and fiery passions, for impiety there might at least be pity, were it visible that the misery of the impious soul were as great as its darkness; but for offences such as this, which cannot proceed either from the madness of sudden impulse, or the bewildered agonies of self-perplexing and self-despairing doubt—but which speak the wilful and determined spite of an unrepenting, unsoftened, smiling, sarcastic, joyous sinner—for such diabolical, such slavish vice, there can be neither pity nor pardon. Our knowledge that it is committed by one of the most powerful intellects our island ever has produced, lends intensity a thousand fold to the bitterness of our indignation. Every high thought that was ever kindled in our breasts by the muse of Byron—every pure and lofty feeling that ever responded from within us to the sweep of his majestic inspiration—every remembered moment of admiration and enthusiasm is up in arms against him. We look back with a mixture of wrath and scorn to the delight with which we suffered ourselves to be filled by one who, all the while he was furnishing us with delight, must, we cannot doubt it, have been mocking us with a cruel mockery—less cruel only, because less peculiar, than that with which he has now turned him from the lurking-place of his selfish and polluted exile, to pour the pitiful chalice of his contumely on the surrendered devotion of a virgin-bosom, and the holy hopes of the mother of his child. The consciousness of the insulting deceit which has been

practised upon us, mingles with the nobler pain arising from
the contemplation of perverted and degraded genius—to make
us wish that no such being as Byron ever had existed. It is
indeed a sad and an humiliating thing to know, that in the
same year there proceeded from the same pen two productions,
in all things so different, as the Fourth Canto of *Childe Harold*
and this loathsome *Don Juan*.

Lady Byron, however, has one consolation still remaining,
and yet we fear she will think it but a poor one. She shares
the scornful satire of her husband, not only with all that is
good, and pure, and high, in human nature—its principles and
its feeling; but with every individual also, in whose character
the predominance of these blessed elements has been sufficient
to excite the envy, or exacerbate the despair of this guilty man.
We shall not needlessly widen the wound by detailing its
cruelty; we have mentioned one, and, all will admit, the worst
instance of the private malignity which has been embodied in
so many passages of *Don Juan*; and we are quite sure, lofty-
minded and virtuous men whom Lord Byron has debased him-
self by insulting, will close the volume which contains their
own injuries, with no feelings save those of pity for Him that
has inflicted them, and for Her who partakes so largely in the
same injuries; and whose hard destiny has deprived her for
ever of that proud and pure privilege, which enables themselves
to despise them. As to the rest of the world, we know not that
Lord Byron could have invented any more certain means of
bringing down contempt inexpiable on his own head, than by
turning the weapons of his spleen against men whose virtues
few indeed can equal, but still fewer are so lost and unworthy
as not to love and admire.

SHELLEY

OF the three periodicals with which we are chiefly concerned in his volume, one was whole-heartedly against Shelley, one (with reservations) for him, and the third neutral. The *Quarterly* attacked him furiously, *Blackwood's* found something to say in his defence, and the *Edinburgh* never mentioned him at all.

The idea that Shelley's work was neglected in his own lifetime was thoroughly exploded in 1938 by the publication of Professor White's vast collection of contemporary reviews and references, *The Unextinguished Hearth*, which lists hundreds of mentions and a large number of long reviews. *Blackwood's* in particular gave sustained attention to his work, reviewing every publication to which he set his name. Nevertheless, there is little evidence that any of this mass of criticism was any use to Shelley; he appears never to have revised his work, or altered his methods, as a result of it; indeed, owing to his residence in Italy from 1818 until his death, it is uncertain how much of it he even saw.

One article, however, certainly reached him. "The droll remarks of the *Quarterly*," he wrote to his publishers, the brothers Ollier, on October 15, 1819,

> and Hunt's kind defence, arrived as safe as such poison, and safer than such an antidote usually do. . . . Southey wrote the article in question, I am well aware. Observe the impudence of the man in speaking of himself. The only remark worth notice in this piece is the assumption that I imitate Wordsworth.

The 'piece' referred to is the notorious *Quarterly* article (April, 1819), in which, in the course of a review of *The Revolt of Islam*, Shelley's personal character and conduct are attacked. Hunt's "kind defence" was contained in three articles in his *Examiner* (September 26, October 3, and October 10). And if Shelley's opponents could retort that, Hunt being a Radical and a Cockney, such a defence was a mere confirmation of their suspicions, the same charge could certainly not be brought against the new and formidable ally who appeared immediately afterwards. In November, John Wilson opened fire from the columns of *Blackwood's*. "I am glad," wrote Shelley to Charles Ollier (December 15), "to see the *Quarterly* cut up, and that by one of their own people."

There is no doubt that the *Quarterly's* brutality offended Shelley deeply. For the rest of his life he was on the look-out to see if he could discover the reviewer's identity. His first guess, Southey, was a bad one, and by 1821 he was on another scent. "I have discovered," he wrote to Charles Ollier (June 11), "that my calumniator in the *Quarterly Review* was the Rev. Mr Milman. Priests and eunuchs have their privilege." (Milman, a scholar and author of third-rate plays, was a clergyman who later became Dean of St Paul's). But Shelley was still wrong. The author was Sir John Taylor Coleridge, a former school-fellow at Eton. It shows, indeed, the peculiar blend of spite and patronage that artists commonly receive from those who knew them in childhood. *The Revolt of Islam* is in fact a revised version of a poem originally entitled *Laon and Cythna*, which Shelley was prevailed upon to alter, cutting out its most dangerous revolutionary passages. A few copies of the poem in its original form, however, had been issued in 1818, under the title *Laon and Cythna*; or, *The Revolution of the Golden City*: *A Vision of the Nineteenth Century*. It was this that the *Quarterly* selected for review, though well aware that it had been withdrawn; for "our duty requires us to use his own evidence against himself, to interpret him when he is obscure now, by himself where he was plain before"; clear evidence, as the late Professor White indicated, of "a special desire to overwhelm the author."

Blackwood's, on the other hand, has a good record as regards its criticism of Shelley. Little as they could stomach his political ideas, Lockhart, Wilson, and Maginn were quick to appreciate the power and originality of his poetry. The article on *Prometheus Unbound*, represented below, is a fair specimen of their horrified recoil from the one, and eager praise of the other.

Quarterly Review, April 1819

Art. vii. 1. *Laon and Cythna, or the Revolution of the Golden City.*
A vision of the Nineteenth Century, in the Stanza of Spenser. By
Percy B. Shelley. London. 1818.

2. *The Revolt of Islam.* A Poem in Twelve Cantos. By Percy Bysshe
Shelley. London. 1818.

This is one of that industrious knot of authors, the tendency
of whose works we have in our late Numbers exposed to the
caution of our readers—novel, poem, romance, letters, tours,
critique, lecture and essay follow one another, framed to the
same measure, and in subjection to the same key-note, while
the sweet undersong of the weekly journal, filling up all
pauses, strengthening all weaknesses, smoothing all abrupt-
nesses, harmonizes the whole strain. Of all his brethren Mr
Shelley carries to the greatest length the doctrines of the sect.
He is, for this and other reasons, by far the least pernicious of
them; indeed there is a *naïveté* and openness in his manner of
laying down the most extravagant positions, which in some
measure deprives them of their venom; and when he enlarges
on what certainly are but necessary results of opinions more
guardedly delivered by others, he might almost be mistaken for
some artful advocate of civil order and religious institutions.
This benefit indeed may be drawn from his book, for there is
scarcely any more persuasive argument for truth than to carry
out to all their legitimate consequences the doctrines of error.
But this is not Mr Shelley's intention; he is, we are sorry to say,
in sober earnest:—with perfect deliberation, and the steadiest
perseverance he perverts all the gifts of his nature, and does all
the injury, both public and private, which his faculties enable
him to perpetrate.

Laon and Cythna is the same poem with the *Revolt of Islam*—
under the first name it exhibited some features which made
"the experiment on the temper of the public mind," as the
author calls it, somewhat too bold and hazardous. This knight-
errant in the cause of "a liberal and comprehensive morality"
had already sustained some "perilous handling" in his en-

counters with Prejudice and Error, and acquired in consequence
of it a small portion of the better part of valour. Accordingly
Laon and Cythna withdrew from circulation; and happy had it
been for Mr Shelley if he had been contented with his failure,
and closed his experiments. But with minds of a certain class,
notoriety, infamy, any thing is better than obscurity; baffled in
a thousand attempts after fame, they will still make one more at
whatever risk—and they end commonly like an awkward
chemist who perseveres in tampering with his ingredients, till,
in an unlucky moment, they take fire, and he is blown up by
the explosion.

Laon and Cythna has accordingly re-appeared with a new
name, and a few slight alterations. If we could trace in these
any signs of an altered spirit, we should have hailed with the
sincerest pleasure the return of one whom nature intended for
better things, to the ranks of virtue and religion. But Mr
Shelley is no penitent; he has reproduced the same poison, a
little, and but a little, more cautiously disguised, and as it is
thus intended only to do the more mischief at less personal
risk to the author, our duty requires us to use his own evidence
against himself, to interpret him where he is obscure now, by
himself where he was plain before, and to exhibit the "fearful
consequences" to which he would bring us, as he drew them
in the boldness of his first conception.

Before, however, we do this, we will discharge our duty to
Mr Shelley as poetical critics—in a case like the present, indeed,
where the freight is so pernicious, it is but a secondary duty to
consider the 'build' of the vessel which bears it; but it is a duty
too peculiarly our own to be wholly neglected. Though we
should be sorry to see the *Revolt of Islam* in our readers' hands,
we are bound to say that it is not without beautiful passages,
that the language is in general free from errors of taste, and the
versification smooth and harmonious. In these respects it
resembles the latter productions of Mr Southey, though the
tone is less subdued, and the copy altogether more luxuriant
and ornate than the original. Mr Shelley indeed is an unspar-
ing imitator; and he draws largely on the rich stores of another
mountain poet, to whose religious mind it must be matter, we

think, of perpetual sorrow to see the philosophy which comes pure and holy from his pen, degraded and perverted, as it continually is, by this miserable crew of atheists or pantheists, who have just sense enough to abuse its terms, but neither heart nor principle to comprehend its import, or follow its application. We shall cite one of the passages to which we alluded above, in support of our opinion: perhaps it is that which has pleased us more than any other in the whole poem.

> An orphan with my parents lived, whose eyes
> Were loadstars of delight, which drew me home
> When I might wander forth, nor did I prize
> Aught (any) human thing beneath Heaven's mighty dome
> Beyond this child; so when sad hours were come,
> And baffled hope like ice still clung to me;
> Since kin were cold, and friends had now become
> Heartless and false, I turned from all, to be,
> Cythna, the only source of tears and smiles to thee.

> What wert thou then? a child most infantine,
> Yet wandering far beyond that innocent age
> In all but its sweet looks, and mien divine;
> Even then, methought with the world's tyrant rage
> A patient warfare thy young heart did wage,
> When those soft eyes of scarcely conscious thought
> Some tale or thine own fancies would engage
> To overflow with tears, or converse fraught
> With passion o'er their depths its fleeting light had wrought.

> She moves upon this earth, a shape of brightness,
> A power, that from its object scarcely drew
> One impulse of her being—in her lightness
> Most like some radiant cloud of morning dew
> Which wanders through the waste air's pathless blue
> To nourish some far desert; she did seem
> Beside me, gathering beauty as she grew
> Like the bright shade of some immortal dream
> Which walks, when tempest sleeps, the waves of life's dark stream.

> As mine own shadow was this child to me,
> A second self—far dearer and more fair,
> Which clothed in undissolving radiancy
> All those steep paths, which languor and despair
> Of human things had made so dark and bare,

But which I trod alone—nor, till bereft
Of friends and overcome by lonely care,
Knew I what solace for that loss was left,
Though by a bitter wound my trusting heart was cleft. (p. 42).

These, with all their imperfections, are beautiful stanzas; they are, however, of rare occurrence: had the poem many more such, it could never, we are persuaded, become popular. Its merits and its faults equally conspire against it; it has not much ribaldry or voluptuousness for prurient imaginations, and no personal scandal for the malicious; and even those on whom it might be expected to act most dangerously by its semblance of enthusiasm, will have stout hearts to proceed beyond the first canto. As a whole, it is insupportably dull, and laboriously obscure; its absurdities are not of the kind which provoke laughter, the story is almost wholly devoid of interest, and very meagre; nor can we admire Mr Shelley's mode of making up for this defect—as he has but one incident where he should have ten, he tells that one so intricately, that it takes the time of ten to comprehend it.

Mr Shelley is a philosopher by the courtesy of the age, and has a theory of course respecting the government of the world; we will state in as few words as we can the general outlines of that theory, the manner in which he demonstrates it, and the practical consequences, which he proposes to deduce from it. It is to the second of these divisions that we would beg his attention; we despair of convincing him directly that he has taken up false and pernicious notions; but if he pays any deference to the common laws of reasoning, we hope to shew him that, let the goodness of his cause be what it may, his manner of advocating it is false and unsound. This may be mortifying to a teacher of mankind; but a philosopher seeks the truth, and has no vanity to be mortified.

The existence of evil, physical and moral, is the grand problem of all philosophy; the humble find it a trial, the proud make it a stumbling-block; Mr Shelley refers it to the faults of those civil institutions and religious creeds which are designed to regulate the conduct of man here, and his hopes in a hereafter. In these he seems to make no distinction, but considers them all as bottomed upon principles pernicious to man and unworthy of God, carried into details the most cruel, and upheld only by the stupidity of the many on the one hand, and the selfish conspiracy of the few on the other. According to him the earth is a boon garden needing little care or cultivation, but pouring forth spontaneously and inexhaustibly all innocent delights and luxuries to her innumerable children; the seasons have no inclemencies, the air no pestilences for man in his proper state of wisdom and liberty; his business here is to enjoy himself, to abstain from no gratification, to repent of no sin, hate no crime, but be wise, happy and free, with plenty of "lawless love." This is man's natural state, the state to which Mr Shelley will bring us, if we will but break up the "crust of our outworn opinions," as he calls them, and put them into his magic cauldron. But kings have introduced war, legislators crime, priests sin; the dreadful consequences have been that the earth has lost her fertility, the seasons their mildness, the air its salubrity, man his freedom and happiness. We have become a foul-feeding carnivorous race, are foolish enough to feel uncomfortable after the commission of sin; some of us even go so far as to consider vice odious; and we all groan under a multiplied burthen of crimes *merely conventional*; among which Mr Shelley specifies with great *sang froid* the commission of *incest*!

We said that our philosopher makes no distinction in his condemnation of creeds; we should rather have said, that he makes no exception; distinction he does make, and it is to the prejudice of that which we hold. In one place indeed he assembles a number of names of the founders of religions, to treat them all with equal disrespect.

> And through the host contention wild befell,
> As each of his own God the wondrous works did tell;
> [1] And Oromaze and Christ and Mahomet.
> Moses and Buddh, Zerdusht, and Brahm and Foh,
> A tumult of strange names, *etc.* (p. 227).

[1] "And Oromaze, Joshua and Mahomet," p. 227, *Revolt of Islam*. This is a very fair specimen of Mr Shelley's alterations, which we see are wholly prudential, and artfully so, as the blasphemy is still preserved entire.

But in many places he manifests a dislike to Christianity which is frantic, and would be, if in such a case any thing could be, ridiculous. When the votaries of all religions are assembled with one accord (this unanimity by the bye is in a vision of the nineteenth century) to stifle the first breathings of liberty, and execute the revenge of a ruthless tyrant, he selects a Christian priest to be the organ of sentiments outrageously and pre-eminently cruel. The two characteristic principles upon which Christianity may be said to be built are repentance and faith. Of repentance he speaks thus:

> Reproach not thine own soul, but know thyself;
> Nor hate another's crime, nor loathe thine own.
> It is the dark idolatry of self
> Which, when our thoughts and actions once are gone,
> Demands that we should weep and bleed and groan;
> O vacant expiation! be at rest—
> The past is death's—the future is thine own;
> And love and joy can make the foulest breast
> A paradise of flowers where peace might build her nest.
> (p. 188).

Repentance then is selfishness in an extreme which amounts to idolatry! but what is Faith? our readers can hardly be pre-pared for the odious accumulation of sin and sorrow which Mr Shelley conceives under this word. "Faith is the Python, the Ogress, the Evil Genius, the Wicked Fairy, the Giantess of our children's tales"; whenever any thing bad is to be ac-counted for, any hard name to be used, this convenient mono-syllable fills up the blank.

> Beneath his feet, 'mong ghastliest forms, represt
> Lay Faith, an obscene worm (p. 188).
> sleeping there
> With lidless eyes lie Faith, and Plague and Slaughter,
> A ghastly brood conceived of Lethe's sullen water (p. 220).

> And underneath thy feet writhe Faith and Folly,
> Custom and Hell, and mortal Melancholy. (p. 119).

> Smiled on the flowery grave, in which were lain
> Fear, Faith, and Slavery. (p. 172).

Enough of Mr Shelley's theory. We proceed to examine the

L

manner in which the argument is conducted, and this we cannot do better than by putting a case.

Let us suppose a man entertaining Mr Shelley's opinions as to the causes of existing evil, and convinced of the necessity of a change in all the institutions of society, of his own ability to produce and conduct it, and of the excellence of that system which he would substitute in their place. These indeed are bold convictions for a young and inexperienced man, imperfectly educated, irregular in his application, and shamefully dissolute in his conduct; but let us suppose them to be sincere; the change, if brought about at all, must be effected by a concurrent will, and that, Mr Shelley will of course tell us, must be produced by an enlightened conviction. How then would a skilful reasoner, assured of the strength of his own ground, have proceeded in composing a tale of fiction for this purpose? Undoubtedly he would have taken the best laws, the best constitution, and the best religion in the known world; such at least as they most loved and venerated whom he was addressing; when he had put all these together, and developed their principles candidly, he would have shewn that under all favourable circumstances, and with all the best propensities of our nature to boot, still the natural effects of his combination would be to corrupt and degrade the human race. He would then have drawn a probable inference, that if the most approved systems and creeds under circumstances more advantageous than could ever be expected to concur in reality, still produced only vice and misery, the fault lay in them, or at least mankind could lose nothing by adventuring on a change. We say with confidence that a skilful combatant would and must have acted thus; not merely to make victory final, but to gain it in any shape. For if he reasons from what we acknowledge to be bad against what we believe to be good; if he puts a government confessedly despotic, a religion monstrous and false, if he places on the throne a cruel tyrant, and at the altar a bigoted and corrupt priesthood, how can his argument have any weight with those who think they live under a paternal government and a pure faith, who look up with love and gratitude to a beneficent monarch, and reverence a zealous and upright priesthood? The

laws and government on which Mr Shelley's reasoning pro-
ceeds, are the Turkish, administered by a lawless despot; his
religion is the Mohammedan, maintained by servile hypocrites;
and his scene for their joint operation Greece, the land full
beyond all others of recollections of former glory and inde-
pendence, now covered with shame and sunk in slavery. We
are Englishmen, Christians, free, and independent; we ask Mr
Shelley how his case applies to us? or what we learn from it to
the prejudice of our own institutions?

His residence at Oxford was a short one, and, if we mistake
not, rather abruptly terminated; yet we should have thought
that even in a freshman's term he might have learned from
Aldrich not to reason from a particular to an universal; and
any one of our fair readers we imagine who never heard of
Aldrich, would see the absurdity of inferring that all of her own
sex were the victims of the lust and tyranny of the other, from
the fact, if it be a fact, that young women of Greece were car-
ried off by force to the seraglio of Constantinople. This, how-
ever, is the sum and substance of the argument, as far as it
attempts to prove the causes of existing evil. Mr Shelley is
neither a dull, nor, considering all his disadvantages, a very
ignorant man; we will frankly confess, that with every disposi-
tion to judge him charitably, we find it hard to convince our-
selves of his belief in his own conclusions.

We have seen how Mr Shelley argues for the necessity of a
change; we must bestow a word or two upon the manner in
which he brings that change about, before we come to the
consequences which he derives from it. *Laon and Cythna*, his
hero and heroine, are the principal, indeed, almost the sole
agents. The latter by her eloquence rouses all of her own sex to
assert their liberty and independence; this perhaps was no diffi-
cult task; a female tongue in such a cause may be supposed to
have spoken fluently at least, and to have found a willing
audience; by the same instrument, however, she disarms the
soldiers who are sent to seize and destroy her,

> even the torturer who had bound
> Her meek calm frame, ere yet it was impaled
> Loosened her weeping then, nor could be found
> One human hand to harm her. (p. 84).

The influence of her voice is not confined to the Golden City, it travels over the land, stirring and swaying all hearts to its purpose:

> in hamlets and in towns
> The multitudes collect tumultuously,—
> Blood soon, although unwillingly, to shed. (p. 85).

These peaceable and tender advocates for "Universal Suffrage and no representation" assemble in battle-array under the walls of the Golden City, keeping night and day strict blockade (which Mr Shelley calls "a watch of love") around the desperate bands who still adhere to the maintenance of the iron-hearted monarch on the throne. Why the eloquence of Cythna had no power over them, or how the monarch himself, who had been a slave to her beauty, and to whom this model of purity and virtue had borne a child, was able to resist the spell of her voice, Mr Shelley leaves his readers to find out for themselves. In this pause of affairs Laon makes his appearance to complete the revolution; Cythna's voice had done wonders, but Laon's was still more powerful; the "sanguine slaves" of page 96, who stabbed ten thousand in their sleep, are turned in page 99 to fraternal bands; the power of the throne crumbles into dust, and the united hosts enter the city in triumph. A good deal of mummery follows, of national fêtes, reasonable rites, altars of federation, etc. borrowed from that store-house of cast-off mummeries and abominations, the French revolution. In the mean time all the kings of the earth, pagan and christian, send more sanguine slaves, who slaughter the sons of freedom in the midst of their merry-making; Plague and Famine come to slaughter them in return; and Laon and Cythna, who had chosen this auspicious moment in a ruined tower for the commencement of their "reign of love," surrender themselves to the monarch and are burnt alive.

Such is Mr Shelley's victory, such its security, and such the means of obtaining it! These last, we confess, are calculated to throw a damp upon our spirits, for if the hopes of mankind must depend upon the exertion of super-eminent eloquence, we have the authority of one who had well considered the subject, for believing that they could scarcely depend upon any thing of more rare occurrence. *Plures in omnibus rebus, quam in dicendo admirabiles*, was the remark of Cicero a great many ages ago, and the experience of all those ages has served but to confirm the truth of it.

Mr Shelley, however, is not a man to propose a difficult remedy without suggesting the means of procuring it. If we mistake not, Laon and Cythna, and even the sage (for there is a sort of good stupid Archimago in the poem) are already provided, and intent to begin their mission if we will but give them hearing. In short, Mr Shelley is his own Laon: this is clear from many passages of the preface and dedication. The lady to whom the poem is addressed is certainly the original of Cythna: we have more consideration for her than she has had for herself, and will either mortify her vanity, or spare her feelings, by not producing her before the public; it is enough for the philanthropist to know that when the season arrives she will be forth-coming. Mr Shelley says of himself and her, in a simile picturesque in itself, but laughable in its application,

> thou and I,
> Sweet friend, can look from our tranquillity,
> Like lamps, into the world's tempestuous night—
> Two tranquil stars, while clouds are passing by
> Which wrap them from the foundering seaman's sight,
> That burn from year to year with unextinguished light.
> (p. xxxii).

Neither will the reader be much at a loss to discover what sapient personage is dimly shadowed out in Archimago; but a clue is afforded even to the uninitiate by a note in the preface, in which we are told that Mr Malthus by his last edition has reduced the *Essay on Population* to a commentary illustrative of the unanswerableness of Political Justice.

With such instruments doubtless the glorious task will be speedily accomplished—and what will be the issue? this indeed is a serious question; but, as in most schemes of reform, it is easier to say what is to be removed, and destroyed, than what is to be put in its place. Mr Shelley would abrogate our laws— this would put an end to felonies and misdemeanours at a blow; he would abolish the rights of property, of course there could thenceforward be no violations of them, no heart-burnings between the poor and the rich, no disputed wills, no litigated inheritances, no food in short for sophistical judges, or hireling lawyers; he would overthrow the constitution, and then we should have no expensive court, no pensions or sine-cures, no silken lords or corrupt commoners, no slavish and enslaving army or navy; he would pull down our churches, level our Establishment, and burn our bibles—then we should pay no tithes, be enslaved by no superstitions, abused by no priestly artifices: marriage he cannot endure, and there would at once be a stop put to the lamented increase of adulterous con-nections amongst us, whilst by repealing the canon of heaven against incest, he would add to the purity, and heighten the ardour of those feelings with which brother and sister now regard each other; finally, as the basis of the whole scheme, he would have us renounce our belief in our religion, extinguish, if we can, the light of conscience within us, which embitters our joys here, and drown in oblivion the hopes and fears that hang over our hereafter. This is at least intelligible; but it is not so easy to describe the structure, which Mr Shelley would build upon this vast heap of ruins. "Love," he says, "is to be the sole law which shall govern the moral world"; but Love is a wide word with many significations, and we are at a loss as to which of them he would have it now bear. We are loath to understand it in its lowest sense, though we believe that as to the issue this would be the correctest mode of interpreting it; but this at least is clear, that Mr Shelley does not mean it in its highest sense: he does not mean that love, which is the fulfilling of the law, and which walks after the commandments, for he would erase the Decalogue, and every other code of laws; not the love which is said to be of God, and which is beautifully coupled with "joy, peace, long suffering, gentleness, goodness, faith, meekness, temperance," for he pre-eminently abhors that religion, which is built on that love and inculcates it as the essence of all duties, and its own fulfilment.

It is time to draw to an end. We have examined Mr Shelley's system slightly, but, we hope, dispassionately; there will be

those, who will say that we have done so coldly. He has in-
deed, to the best of his ability, wounded us in the tenderest
part. As far as in him lay, he has loosened the hold of our
protecting laws, and sapped the principles of our venerable
policy; he has invaded the purity and chilled the unsuspecting
ardour of our fireside intimacies; he has slandered, ridiculed
and blasphemed our holy religion; yet these are all too sacred
objects to be defended bitterly or unfairly. We have learned
too, though not in Mr Shelley's school, to discriminate be-
tween a man and his opinions, and while we shew no mercy to
the sin, we can regard the sinner with allowance and pity . . .

Blackwood's, November 1819

Alastor; or, the Spirit of Solitude; and other Poems. by Percy Bysshe
Shelley. London, Baldwin, Craddock and Joy, and Carpenter and
Sons. 1816.

We believe this little volume to be Mr Shelley's first publica-
tion; and such of our readers as have been struck by the power
and splendour of genius displayed in the *Revolt of Islam*, and
by the frequent tenderness and pathos of *Rosalind and Helen*,
will be glad to observe some of the earliest efforts of a mind
destined, in our opinion, under due discipline and self-manage-
ment, to achieve great things in poetry. It must be encour-
aging to those who, like us, cherish high hopes of this gifted
but wayward young man, to see what advances his intellect
has made within those few years, and to compare its powerful
though still imperfect display, in his principal poem with its
first gleamings and irradiations throughout this production
almost of his boyhood. In a short preface, written with all the
enthusiasm and much of the presumption of youth, Mr Shelley
gives a short explanation of the subject of "Alastor; or, the
Spirit of Solitude," which we cannot say throws any very
great light upon it, but without which, the poem would be, we
suspect, altogether unintelligible to ordinary readers. Mr
Shelley is too fond of allegories; and a great genius like his

should scorn, now that it has reached the maturity of manhood, to adopt a species of poetry in which the difficulties of the art may be so conveniently blinked, and weakness find so easy a refuge in obscurity.

[*Here follow four and a half closely printed pages mainly occupied by quotations from the volume, interspersed with comments of the order of " Several of the smaller poems contain beauties of no ordinary kind— but they are almost all liable to the charge of vagueness and obscurity.*"]

We beg leave, in conclusion, to say a few words about the treatment which Mr Shelley has, in his poetical character, received from the public. By our periodical critics he has either been entirely overlooked, or slightingly noticed, or grossly abused. There is not so much to find fault with in the mere silence of critics; but we do not hesitate to say, with all due respect for the general character of that journal, that Mr Shelley has been infamously and stupidly treated in the *Quarterly Review*. His Reviewer there, whoever he is, does not shew himself a man of such lofty principles as to entitle him to ride the high horse in company with the author of the *Revolt of Islam*. And when one compares the vis inertiae of his motionless prose with the "eagle-winged raptures" of Mr Shelley's poetry, one does not think indeed of Satan reproving Sin, but one does think, we will say it in plain words and without a figure, of a dunce rating a man of genius. If that critic does not know that Mr Shelley is a poet, almost in the very highest sense of that mysterious word, then, we appeal to all those whom we have enabled to judge for themselves, if he be not unfit to speak of poetry before the people of England. If he does know that Mr Shelley is a great poet, what manner of man is he who, with such conviction, brings himself, with the utmost difficulty, to admit that there is any beauty at all in Mr Shelley's writings, and is happy to pass that admission off with an accidental and niggardly phrase of vague and valueless commendation. This is manifest and mean—glaring and gross injustice on the part of a man who comes forward as the champion of morality, truth, faith, and religion. This is being guilty of one of the very worst charges of which he accuses another; nor will any man who loves and honours genius, even though that genius may have occasionally suffered itself to be both stained and led astray, think but with contempt and indignation and scorn of a critic who, while he pretends to wield the weapons of honour, virtue, and truth, yet clothes himself in the armour of deceit, hypocrisy, and falsehood. He *exults* to calumniate Mr Shelley's moral character, but he *fears* to acknowledge his genius. And therefore do we, as the sincere though sometimes sorrowing friends of Mr Shelley, scruple not to say, even though it may expose us to the charge of personality from those from whom alone such a charge could at all affect our minds, that the critic shews himself by such conduct as far inferior to Mr Shelley as a man of worth, as the language in which he utters his falsehood and uncharitableness shews him to be inferior as a man of intellect.

In the present state of public feeling, with regard to poets and poetry, a critic cannot attempt to defraud a poet of his fame, without paying the penalty either of his ignorance or his injustice. So long as he confines the expression of his envy or stupidity to works of moderate or doubtful merit, he may escape punishment; but if he dare to insult the spirit of England by contumelious and scornful treatment of any one of her gifted sons, that contumely and that scorn will most certainly be flung back upon himself, till he be made to shrink and to shiver beneath the load. It is not in the power of all the critics alive to blind one true lover of poetry to the splendour of Mr Shelley's genius—and the reader who, from mere curiosity, should turn to the *Revolt of Islam*, to see what sort of trash it was so moved the wrath and the spleen and the scorn of the Reviewer, would soon feel, that to understand the greatness of the poet, and the littleness of his traducer, nothing more was necessary than to recite to his delightful sense any six successive stanzas of that poem, so full of music, imagination, intellect, and passion. We care comparatively little for injustice offered to one moving majestical in the broad day of fame—it is the injustice done to the great, while their greatness is unknown or misunderstood, that a generous nature most abhors, in as much as it seems more basely wicked to wish that genius might never raise its head, than to envy the glory with which it is encircled.

There is, we firmly believe, a strong love of genius in the people of this country, and they are willing to pardon to its possessor much extravagance and error——nay, even more serious transgressions. Let both Mr Shelley and his critics think of that—let it encourage the one to walk onwards to his bright destiny, without turning into dark or doubtful or wicked ways—let it teach the other to feel a proper sense of his own insignificance, and to be ashamed, in the midst of his own weaknesses and deficiencies and meannesses, to aggravate the faults of the highly-gifted, and to gloat with a sinful satisfaction on the real or imaginery debasement of genius and intellect.

And here we ought, perhaps, to stop. But the Reviewer has dealt out a number of dark and oracular denunciations against the Poet, which the public can know nothing about, except that they imply a charge of immorality and wickedness. Let him speak out plainly, or let him hold his tongue. There are many wicked and foolish things in Mr Shelley's creed, and we have not hitherto scrupled, nor shall we henceforth scruple, to expose that wickedness and that folly. But we do not think that he believes his own creed—at least, that he believes it fully and to utter conviction— and we doubt not but the scales will yet fall from his eyes. The Reviewer, however, with a face of most laughable horror, accuses Mr Shelley in the same breath of some nameless act of atrocity, and of having been rusticated, or expelled, or warned to go away from the University of Oxford! He seems to shudder with the same holy fear at the violation of the laws of morality and the breaking of college rules. He forgets that in the world men do not wear caps and gowns as at Oriel or Exeter. He preaches not like Paul—but like a Proctor.

Once more, then we bid Mr Shelley farewell. Let him come forth from the eternal city, where, we understand, he has been sojourning—in his strength, conquering and to conquer. Let his soul watch his soul, and listen to the voice of its own noble nature—and there is no doubt that the future will make amends for the past, whatever its errors may have been—and that the Poet may yet be good, great, and happy.

Blackwood's, September 1820

Prometheus Unbound

Whatever may be the difference of men's opinions concern-
ing the measure of Mr Shelley's poetical power, there is one
point in regard to which all must be agreed, and that is his
Audacity. In the old days of the exulting genius of Greece,
Æschylus dared two things which astonished all men, and
which still astonish them—to exalt contemporary men into
the personages of majestic tragedies—and to call down and
embody into tragedy, without degradation, the elemental
spirits of nature and the deeper essences of Divinity. We
scarcely know whether to consider the *Persians* or the *Prome-
theus Bound* as the most extraordinary display of what has always
been esteemed the most audacious spirit that ever expressed
its workings in poetry. But what shall we say of the young
English poet who has now attempted, not only a flight as high
as the highest of Æschylus, but the very flight of that father of
tragedy—who has dared once more to dramatise Prometheus—
and, most wonderful of all, to dramatise the deliverance of
Prometheus—which is known to have formed the subject of a
lost tragedy of Æschylus no ways inferior in mystic elevation
to that of the Δεσμώτης.

Although a fragment of that perished master-piece be still
extant in the Latin version of Attius—it is quite impossible to
conjecture what were the personages introduced in the tragedy
of Æschylus, or by what train of passions and events he was
able to sustain himself on the height of that awful scene with
which his surviving Prometheus terminates. It is impossible,
however, after reading what is left of that famous trilogy,[1] to
suspect that the Greek poet symbolized any thing whatever by
the person of Prometheus, except the native strength of human
intellect itself—its strength of endurance above all others—its

[1] There was another and an earlier play of Æschylus, *Prometheus the Fire-
Stealer*, which is commonly supposed to have made part of the series; but the
best critics, we think, are of opinion, that that was entirely a satirical piece.

sublime power of patience. *Strength* and *Force* are the two agents who appear on this darkened theatre to bind the too benevolent Titan—Wit and Treachery, under the forms of Mercury and Oceanus, endeavour to prevail upon him to make himself free by giving up his dreadful secret; but Strength and Force, and Wit and Treason, are all alike powerless to overcome the resolution of that suffering divinity, or to win from him any acknowledgment of the new tyrant of the skies. Such was this simple and sublime allegory in the hands of Æschylus. As to what had been the original purpose of the framers of the allegory, that is a very different question, and would carry us back into the most hidden places of the history of mythology. No one, however, who compares the mythological systems of different races and countries, can fail to observe the frequent occurrence of certain great leading Ideas and leading Symbolisations of ideas too—which Christians are taught to contemplate with a knowledge that is the knowledge of reverence. Such, among others, are unquestionably the ideas of an Incarnate Divinity suffering on account of mankind—conferring benefits on mankind at the expense of his own suffering—the general idea of vicarious atonement itself—and the idea of the dignity of suffering as an exertion of intellectual might—all of which may be found, more or less obscurely shadowed forth, in the original Μῦθος of Prometheus the Titan, the enemy of the successful rebel and usurper Jove. We might have also mentioned the idea of a deliverer, waited for patiently through ages of darkness, and at last arriving in the person of the child of Io—but, in truth, there is no pleasure, and would be little propriety, in seeking to explain all this at greater length, considering, what we cannot consider without deepest pain, the very different views which have been taken of the original allegory by Mr Percy Bysshe Shelley.

It would be highly absurd to deny, that this gentleman has manifested very extraordinary powers of language and imagination in his treatment of the allegory, however grossly and miserably he may have tried to pervert its purpose and meaning. But of this more anon. In the meantime, what can be more deserving of reprobation than the course which he is allowing his intellect to take, and that too at the very time when he ought to be laying the foundations of a lasting and honourable name. There is no occasion for going round about the bush to hint what the poet himself has so unblushingly and sinfully blazoned forth in every part of his production. With him, it is quite evident that the Jupiter whose downfall has been predicted by Prometheus, means nothing more than Religion in general, that is, every human system of religious belief; and that, with the fall of this, he considers it perfectly necessary (as indeed we also believe, though with far different feelings) that every system of human government also should give way and perish. The patience of the contemplative spirit in Prometheus is to be followed by the daring of the active Demagorgon, at whose touch all "old thrones" are at once and for ever to be cast down into the dust. It appears too that Mr Shelley looks forward to an unusual relaxation of all moral rules—or rather, indeed, to the extinction of all moral feelings, except that of a certain mysterious indefinable kindliness, as the natural and necessary result of the overthrow of all civil government, and religious belief. It appears, still more wonderfully, that he contemplates this state of things as the ideal *summum bonum*. In short, it is quite impossible that there should exist a more pestiferous mixture of blasphemy, sedition, and sensuality, than is visible in the whole structure and strain of this poem—which, nevertheless, and notwithstanding all the detestation its principles excite, must and will be considered by all that read it attentively, as abounding in poetical beauties of the highest order—as presenting many specimens not easily to be surpassed, of the moral sublime of eloquence—as overflowing with pathos, and most magnificent in description. Where can be found a spectacle more worthy of sorrow than such a man performing and glorying in the performance of such things? His evil ambition—from all he has yet written, but most of all, from what he has last and best written, his *Prometheus*—it appears to be no other, than that of attaining the highest place among those poets—enemies, not friends of their species—who, as a great and virtuous poet has well said (putting evil consequences close after evil cause).

> Profane the God-given strength, and mar
> the lofty line.

. . . .

We cannot conclude without saying a word or two in regard to an accusation which we have lately seen brought against ourselves in some one of the London Magazines; we forget which at this moment. We are pretty sure we know who the author of that most false accusation is—of which more hereafter. He has the audacious insolence to say, that we praise Mr Shelley, although we dislike his principles, just because we know that he is not in a situation of life to be in any danger of suffering pecuniary inconveniences from being run down by critics; and, vice versa, abuse Hunt, Keats, and Hazlitt, and so forth, because we know that they are poor men; a fouler imputation could not be thrown on any writer than this creature has dared to throw on us; nor a more utterly false one; we repeat the word again—than this is when thrown upon us.

We have no personal acquaintance with any of these men, and no personal feelings in regard to any one of them, good or bad. We never even saw any one of their faces. As for Mr Keats, we are informed that he is in a very bad state of health, and that his friends attribute a great deal of it to the pain he has suffered from the critical castigation his *Endymion* drew down on him in this magazine. If it be so, we are most heartily sorry for it, and have no hesitation in saying, that had we suspected that young author, of being so delicately nerved, we should have administered our reproof in a much more lenient shape and style. The truth is, we from the beginning saw marks of feeling and power in Mr Keats' verses, which made us think it very likely, he might become a real poet of England, provided he could be persuaded to give up all the tricks of Cockneyism, and forswear for ever the thin potations of Mr Leigh Hunt. We, therefore, rated him as roundly as we decently could do, for the flagrant affectations, of those early productions of his. In the last volume he has published, we find more beauties than in the former, both of language and of thought, but we are sorry to say, we find abundance of the same absurd affectations also, and superficial conceits which first displeased us in his writings; and which we are again very sorry to say, must in our opinion, if persisted in, utterly and entirely prevent Mr Keats from ever taking his place among the pure and classical poets of his mother tongue. It is quite ridiculous to see how the vanity of these Cockneys makes them over-rate their own importance, even in the eyes of us, that have always expressed such plain unvarnished contempt for them, and who do feel for them all, a contempt too calm and profound, to admit of any admixture of any thing like anger or personal spleen. We should just as soon think of being wroth with vermin, independently of their coming into our apartment, as we should of having any feelings at all about any of these people, other than what are excited by seeing them in the shape of authors. Many of them, considered in any other character than that of authors, are, we have no doubt, entitled to be considered as very worthy people in their own way. Mr Hunt is said to be a very amiable man in his own sphere, and we believe him to be so willingly. Mr Keats we have often heard spoken of in terms of great kindness, and we have no doubt his manners and feelings are calculated to make his friends love him. But what has all this to do with our opinion of their poetry? What, in the name of wonder, does it concern us, whether these men sit among themselves, with mild or with sulky faces, eating their mutton steaks, and drinking their porter at Highgate, Hampstead or Lisson Green? What is there that should prevent us, or any other person, that happens not to have been educated in the University of Little Britain, from expressing a simple, undisguised, and impartial opinion, concerning the merits or demerits of men that we never saw, nor thought of for one moment, otherwise than as in their capacity of authors? What should hinder us from saying, since we think so, that Mr Leigh Hunt is a clever wrongheaded man, whose vanities have got inwoven so deeply into him, that he has no chance of ever writing one line of classical English, or thinking one genuine English thought, either about poetry or politics? What is the spell that must seal our lips, from uttering an opinion equally plain and perspicuous concerning Mr John Keats, viz. that nature possibly meant him to be a much better poet than Mr Leigh Hunt ever could have been, but that, if he persists in imitating the faults of that writer, he must be contented to share his fate, and be like him forgotten? Last of all, what should forbid us to announce our opinion, that Mr Shelley, as a man of genius, is not merely superior, either to Mr Hunt, or to Mr Keats, but altogether out of their sphere, and totally incapable of ever being brought into the most distant comparison with either of them. It is very possible, that Mr Shelley himself might not be inclined to place himself so high above these men as we do, but that is his affair, not ours. We are afraid that he shares, (at least with one of them) in an abominable system of belief, concerning Man and the World, the sympathy arising out of which common belief, may probably sway more than it ought to do on both sides. But the truth of the matter is this, and it is impossible to conceal it were we willing to do so, that Mr Shelley is destined to leave a great name behind him, and that we, as lovers of true genius, are most anxious that this name should ultimately be pure as well as great.

KEATS

"Who killed John Keats?" asked Byron in July 1821, and answered himself:

> "I," says the Quarterly,
> So savage and tartarly,
> "'Twas one of my feats."

And the tradition that Keats was "snuffed out by an article," to quote Byron again, died sufficiently hard. The fate of Keats became caught up in the rapidly expanding Romantic myth, soon to be sentimentalized and vamped up by the Victorians, of the outcast poet. Thomas Chatterton, the poetic prodigy who committed suicide at the age of nineteen in the dawn of the Romantic era, was quickly taken up by the generation that followed, and his fate was idealized from a simple tragedy of disappointment and injured pride into a symbol of the loneliness which, in their various ways, all the Romantic poets felt. To Wordsworth, Chatterton was

> the marvellous boy,
> The sleepless soul that perished in his pride,

and Coleridge and Keats joined in the work of building a towering monument of praise to the Bristol genius both directly, by writing poems on the subject of his fate, and indirectly, by showing the influence of his work on their own. It was left to Shelley to raise the Chatterton symbol to its highest point of effectiveness in *Adonais*:

> Chatterton
> Rose pale,—his solemn agony had not
> Yet faded from him;

—and, coupling his name with those of Sidney and Lucan, to graft on the figures of Keats and himself to this structure of literary martyrdom.

Thus at one blow the myth was forged, complete and well-nigh indestructible. It was so neat, attractive, and final: Lucan took his life after being condemned to death by Nero, Sidney perished on the field of battle, Chatterton poisoned himself when reduced to destitution, and now it was the turn of Keats ("the curse of Cain Light on his head who pierced thy innocent breast, And scared the angel soul that was its earthly guest!") and of Shelley himself, who

> came the last, neglected and apart;
> A herd-abandoned deer struck by the hunter's dart.

In our own time, with the rise of a more exact, if less picturesque, approach to literary history, and the disappearance of the view of the poet as an outcast, necessarily at odds with society, the legend of Keats's murder has crumbled. Professors White and Marsh, after drawing up an exhaustive list of every review of Keats's work to appear in his lifetime, reached this sober conclusion:

> The *Quarterly*, *Blackwood's*, and the *British Critic*, which assailed Keats, were all powerful publications, but they were outnumbered seven or eight to one by periodicals that were either friendly or tolerant, among them such widely read journals of opinion as the *Examiner* and the *Champion*, and such influential magazines as the *Edinburgh Review* and the *London Magazine*.

And, in fact, arithmetic reveals that

> Only fifteen of more than eighty items are definitely hostile; except for twelve that are neutral or otherwise doubtful, the rest are favourable to Keats.

Nevertheless, it is certainly true that Keats took at least two very hard knocks from contemporary critics. In some ways the least self-sufficient of the major Romantics, painfully avid for celebrity and success (*vide* his cherished ambition of writing a tragedy in which Kean should play the lead), he was wide open to the blows of such knock-down critics as Croker and the merry ruffians of *Blackwood's*.

It was from this latter quarter that the first attack came. In August 1818 appeared the fourth of *Blackwood's* series of articles "On the Cockney school of poetry," the only one of the series to be devoted entirely to Keats. These "Cockney school" articles merit a slight digression, for ever since the first of the series (October 1817) Keats must have been uneasily aware of the forces ranged against him. Not only was it obvious that he would be attacked sooner or later, as one of Hunt's disciples, but that first article was headed by some ludicrous enough lines chosen from Cornelius Webb, another of Hunt's admirers, in which Keats is mentioned as "the Muse's son of promise." The article is reprinted below, although it has no direct bearing on Keats, as being the most complete description of that 'Cockney' spirit which *Blackwood's* found rife among all Hunt's associates.

As we have space here for no more than a few extracts, a complete list of the "Cockney school" articles is in order. They are to be found in the following numbers of "Maga": No. 1, vol. ii, No. 7 (October 1817); No. 2, vol. ii, No. 8 (November 1817); next come two letters from "Z" to Leigh Hunt as "King of the Cockneys," vol. ii, No. 10 (January 1818), and vol. iii, No. 14 (May 1818); then the articles resume their unbroken series, No. 3 in vol. iii, No. 16 (July 1818); No. 4, vol. iii, No. 17 (August 1818); No. 5, vol. v, No. 25 (April 1819); No. 6, vol. vi, No. 31 (October 1819); No. 7, vol. xii, No. 71 (December 1822), and No. 8, vol. xviii, No. 103 (August 1825).

As for the authorship of the series, it has never proved possible to sort out the precise amount of responsibility to be assigned to any individual writer. The signature throughout is "Z," which was certainly associated with the work of John Gibson Lockhart. On the other hand, some of Lockhart's many pseudonyms (which included William Wastle, Dr Ulrick Sternstare, Philip Kemp Lerhausen, Baron von Lauerwinkel, Peter Morris, James Scott, Timothy Tickler, and Dr Mullion) were intended to be group names, at the service of any contributor who felt inclined to use them; and there is small doubt that "Z" was of this kind. The particularly brutal tone of personal insult that runs through the series certainly suggests "the Scorpion," but it is reasonable to suppose that the series was a corporate undertaking. The savagery of the assault on Leigh Hunt indicates a combination of literary and political rancour typical of "Maga" at its most ferocious. In the first letter of "Z" to Leigh Hunt, the standpoint of the critic, or critics, is made clear.

> The charges which I have brought against your literary life and conversation are these; 1. The want and the pretence of scholarship; 2. A vulgar style in writing; 3. A want of respect for the Christian religion; 4. A contempt for kingly power, and an indecent mode of attacking the government of your country; 5. Extravagant admiration of yourself, the Round Table, and your own poems; 6. Affectation; 7. A partiality for indecent subjects, and an immoral manner of writing concerning the crime of incest, in your poem of Rimini; 8. I have asserted, that you are a poet vastly inferior to Wordsworth, Byron, and Moore! . . . I mean to handle each of these topics in turn, and now and then to relieve my main attack upon you, by a diversion against some of your younger and less important auxiliaries, the Keatses, the Shellys [*sic*], and the Webbes.

In the second letter, "Z" goes on to provide a good example of that least effective, least becoming, and least dignified of emotions, righteous indignation.

> You alone, of all the writers in verse of the present day, of any pretensions, real or imaginary, to the character of poet, have been the secret and invidious foe of virtue. No woman who has not either lost her chastity, or is desirous of losing it, ever read *The Story of Rimini* without the flushings of shame and self-reproach. A brother would tear it indignantly from a sister's hand, and the husband who saw his wife's eyes resting on it with any other expression than of contempt or disgust, would have reason to look with perplexing agony on the countenances of his children.

This passage must have sent many a reader springing to the pages of *The Story of Rimini* to see what the fuss was about. It is hard to imagine that its mild voluptuousness could ever have been blamed, even by implication, for an increase in the illegitimacy rates. But such things were the commonplaces of scandalized abuse at that time. (Have they altered since?) "The publication of this novel by a member of Parliament," said T. J. Mathias, later librarian of Buckingham Palace, of M. G. Lewis's *The Monk* (1795), "is in itself so serious an offence to the public that I know not how the author can repair this breach of the public decency."

Now, Keats, notwithstanding his almost complete lack of interest in practical politics, was firmly linked, in the eyes of a Tory observer, with Hunt's Radicalism as well as his literary Cockneyism. As a matter of fact, not only was he indifferent, or almost indifferent, to Hunt's politics; he had been for some time vigorously struggling against the Master's influence on his poetry. Hunt, it appears from a letter to Bailey (October 8, 1817), had tried to dissuade him from writing so long a poem as *Endymion*, and had congratulated himself on having at least kept its length within bounds.

> When he met Reynolds in the Theatre John told him that I was getting on to the completion of 4000 lines. "Ah!" says Hunt, "had it not been for me they would have been 7000!" If he will say this to Reynolds what would he to other People?

And Keats goes on to give his reasons for rejecting Hunt's advice, finally summing up in a spirit of considerable annoyance:

> You see Baily how independent my writing has been—Hunt's dissuasion was of no avail—I refused to visit Shelley, that I might have my own unfettered Scope—and after all I shall have the Reputation of Hunt's eleve [*sic*].

This forecast was soon shown to have been accurate. In the eyes of a Tory reviewer, Keats's connexion with Hunt was not only literary but political, as is indicated by the fact that "Z", when he turned his polite attention to Keats, took the trouble to quote the sonnets to Hunt and Haydon. A month later (for the *Quarterly Review* for April 1818 was not in fact issued until September), came another Tory criticism which followed the lead of *Blackwood's* in treating Keats as the "simple neophyte" of Hunt. Croker's article, however, is of a much higher standard than the work of "Z"; he has paid careful attention to the style of the poem and the dangerously vague standards that governed its writing. It is no more than the truth to say that the story is difficult to follow, the writing loosely associative—one word suggesting the next—and the diction eccentric and often strained. And if it be thought that the great promise of the poem should be held to outweigh these faults, let us remember that this promise is more apparent to the modern reader who travels backwards, approaching *Endymion* from the direction of the great odes. Not that Croker was blind to what he calls the "powers of language, rays of fancy, and gleams of genius" discernible even in "such a rhapsody."

Meanwhile the *Edinburgh* hung fire. "The cowardliness of the *Edinburgh* is worse than the abuse of the *Quarterly*," Keats wrote to his brother George in September 1819; and it was not until August 1820, when the poet had for some months known himself to be dying of tuberculosis, that Jeffrey's excellent criticism appeared. His article is one of the rare examples of a contemporary assessment good enough to hold up its head among the more considered judgments of posterity; if it were more widely read and heeded to-day, it would go far to counteract the more extravagant claims made for Keats by those who see him as a poet to set beside Shakespeare. Jeffrey was, in fact, well to the fore of contemporary literary taste in his recognition of Keats, whose reputation grew very slowly. The idea that Jeffrey had stood in the poet's path would have seemed an absurdity to (for instance) so devout a Keatsian as Richard Monckton Milnes, who in 1848 dedicated his *Life and Letters of John Keats* to Jeffrey, thanking him for having championed Keats at a time "when such views were hazardous even to a critical reputation so well-founded as your own."

But, after all, in fairness to Keats it must be stressed that it was not he who started the legend: it was not he who whined that the Reviews had killed him. His own comment, as one might expect of so fine a character, is firm, self-contained and true. On October 9, 1818, he wrote to James Hessey:

Praise or blame has but a momentary effect on the man whose love of beauty in the abstract makes him a severe critic on his own Works. My own domestic criticism has given me pain without comparison beyond what Blackwood or the Quarterly could possibly inflict, and also when I feel that I am right, no external praise can give me such a glow as my own solitary reperception and ratification of what is fine.

Blackwood's, October 1817

On the Cockney School of Poetry, No. 1

Our talk shall be (a theme we never tire on)
Of Chaucer, Spenser, Shakespeare, Milton, Byron,
(Our England's Dante)—Wordsworth—HUNT, and KEATS,
The Muses' son of promise; and of what feats
He yet may do.
Cornelius Webb.

WHILE the whole critical world is occupied with balancing the merits, whether in theory or in execution, of what is commonly called *The Lake School*, it is strange that no one seems to think it at all necessary to say a single word about another new school of poetry which has of late sprung up among us. This school has not, I believe, as yet received any name; but if I may be permitted to have the honour of christening it, it may henceforth be referred to by the designation of *The Cockney School*. Its chief Doctor and Professor is Mr Leigh Hunt, a man certainly of some talents, of extravagant pretensions both in wit, poetry, and politics, and withal of exquisitely bad taste, and extremely vulgar modes of thinking and manners in all respects. He is a man of little education. He knows absolutely nothing of Greek, almost nothing of Latin, and his knowledge of Italian literature is confined to a few of the most popular of Petrarch's sonnets, and an imperfect acquaintance with Ariosto, through the medium of Mr Hoole. As to the French poets, he dismisses them in the mass as a set of prim, precise, unnatural pretenders. The truth is, he is in a state of happy ignorance about them and all that they have done. He has never read Zaire nor Phedre. To those great German poets who have illuminated the last fifty years with a splendour to which this country has, for a long time, seen nothing comparable, Mr Hunt is an absolute stranger. Of Spanish books he has read Don Quixote (in the translation of Motteux), and some poems of Lope de Vega in the imitations of my Lord Holland. Of all the great critical writers, either of ancient or of modern times, he is utterly ignorant, excepting only Mr Jeffrey among ourselves.

With this stock of knowledge, Mr Hunt presumes to become the founder of a new school of poetry, and throws away entirely the chance which he might have had of gaining true poetical fame, had he been less lofty in his pretensions. The story of Rimini is not wholly undeserving of praise. It possesses some tolerable passages, which are all quoted in the Edinburgh Reviewer's account of the poem, and not one of which is quoted in the very illiberal attack upon it in the *Quarterly*. But such is the wretched taste in which the greater part of the work is executed, that most certainly no man who reads it once will ever be able to prevail upon himself to read it again. One feels the same disgust at the idea of opening *Rimini*, that impresses itself on the mind of a man of fashion, when he is invited to enter, for a second time, the gilded drawing-room of a little mincing boarding school mistress, who would fain have an *At Home* in her house. Every thing is pretence, affectation, finery, and gaudiness. The beaux are attorney's apprentices, with chapeau bras and Limerick gloves—fiddlers, harp-teachers, and clerks of genius: the belles are faded fan-twinkling spinsters, prurient vulgar misses from school, and enormous citizens' wives. The company are entertained with lukewarm negus, and the sounds of a paltry piano-forte.

All the great poets of our country have been men of some rank in society, and there is no vulgarity in any of their writings; but Mr Hunt cannot utter a dedication, or even a note, without betraying the *Shibboleth* of low birth and low habits. He is the ideal of a Cockney Poet. He raves perpetually about "green fields," "jaunty streams," and "o'er-arching leafiness," exactly as a Cheapside shop-keeper does about the beauties of his box on the Camberwell road. Mr Hunt is altogether unacquainted with the face of nature in her magnificent scenes; he has never seen any mountain higher than Highgate-hill, nor reclined by any stream more pastoral than the Serpentine River. But he is determined to be a poet eminently rural, and he rings the changes—till one is sick of him, on the beauties of different "high views" which he has taken of God and nature, in the course of some Sunday dinner parties, at which he has assisted in the neighbourhood of London. His books are indeed not known in the country; his fame as a poet (and I might also say, as a politician too,) is entirely confined to the young attorneys and embryo-barristers about town. In the opinion of these competent judges, London is the world—and Hunt is a Homer . . . .

The poetry of Mr Hunt is such as might be expected from the personal character and habits of its author. As a vulgar man is perpetually labouring to be genteel—in like manner, the poetry of this man is always on the stretch to be grand. He has been allowed to look for a moment from the antichamber into the saloon, and mistaken the waving of feathers and the painted floor for the *sine qua non's* of elegant society. He would fain be always tripping and waltzing, and is sorry he cannot be allowed to walk about in the morning with yellow breeches and flesh-coloured silk stockings. He sticks an artificial rose-bud in his button hole in the midst of winter. He wears no neckcloth, and cuts his hair in imitation of the Prints of Petrarch. In his verses he is always desirous of being airy, graceful, easy, courtly, and *Italian*. If he had the smallest acquaintance with the great demi-gods of Italian poetry, he could never fancy that the style in which he writes, bears any, even the most remote, resemblance to the severe and simple manner of Dante—the tender stillness of the lover of Laura—or the sprightly and good-natured unconscious elegance of the inimitable Ariosto. He has gone into a strange delusion about himself, and is just as absurd in supposing that he resembles the Italian Poets, as a greater Quack still (Mr Coleridge) is, in imagining that he is a Philosopher after the manner of Kant or Mendelshon—and that "the eye of Lessing bears a remarkable likeness to *mine*," *i.e.*, the eye of Mr Samuel Coleridge.[1]

The extreme moral depravity of the Cockney School is another thing which is for ever thrusting itself upon the public attention, and convincing every man of sense who looks into

---

[1] Mr Wordsworth (meaning, we presume, to pay Mr Coleridge a compliment) makes him look very absurdly "*A noticeable man, with large grey eyes.*"

their productions, that they who sport such sentiments can never be great poets. How could any man of high original genius ever stoop publicly, at the present day, to dip his fingers in the least of those glittering and rancid obscenities which float on the surface of Mr Hunt's Hippocrene? His poetry resembles that of a man who has kept company with kept-mistresses. His muse talks indelicately like a tea-sipping milliner girl. Some excuse for him there might have been, had she been hurried away by imagination or passion; but with her, indecency seems a disease, she appears to speak unclean things from perfect inanition. Surely they who are connected with Mr Hunt by the tender relations of society, have good reason to complain this his muse should have been so prostituted. In Rimini a deadly wound is aimed at the dearest confidences of domestic bliss. The author has voluntarily chosen—a subject not of simple seduction alone—one in which his mind seems absolutely to gloat over all the details of adultery and incest.

The unhealthy and jaundiced medium through which the Founder of the Cockney School views every thing like moral truth, is apparent, not only from his obscenity, but also from his want of respect for all that numerous class of plain upright men, and unpretending women, in which the real worth and excellence of human society consists. Every man is, according to Mr Hunt, a dull potato-eating blockhead—of no greater value to God or man than any ox or dray-horse—who is not an admirer of Voltaire's *romans*, a worshipper of Lord Holland and Mr Haydon, and a quoter of John Buncle and Chaucer's *Flower and Leaf*. Every woman is useful only as a breeding machine, unless she is fond of reading *Launcelot of the Lake*, in an antique summer-house.

How such an indelicate writer as Mr Hunt can pretend to be an admirer of Mr Wordsworth, is to us a thing altogether inexplicable. One great charm of Wordsworth's noble compositions consists in the dignified purity of thought, and the patriarchal simplicity of feeling, with which they are throughout penetrated and imbued. We can conceive a vicious man admiring with distant awe the spectacle of virtue and purity;

but if he does so sincerely, he must also do so with the profoundest feeling of the error of his own ways, and the resolution to amend them. His admiration must be humble and silent, not pert and loquacious. Mr Hunt praises the purity of Wordsworth as if he himself were pure, his dignity as if he also were dignified. He is always like the ball of Dung in the fable, pleasing himself, and amusing bye-standers with his *nos poma natamus*. For the person who writes *Rimini*, to admire the *Excursion*, is just as impossible as it would be for a Chinese polisher of cherry-stones, or a gilder of tea-cups, to burst into tears at the sight of the Theseus or the Torso.

The shallow and impotent pretensions, tenets, and attempts, of this man—and the success with which his influence seems to be extending itself among a pretty numerous, though certainly a very paltry and pitiful, set of readers—have for the last two or three years been considered by us with the most sickening aversion. The very culpable manner in which his chief poem was reviewed in the *Edinburgh Review* (we believe it is no secret, at his own impatient and feverish request, by his partner at the Round Table) was matter of concern to more readers than ourselves. The masterly pen which inflicted such signal chastisement on the early licentiousness of Moore, should not have been idle on that occasion. Mr Jeffrey does ill, when he delegates his important functions into such hands as those of Mr Hazlitt. It was chiefly in consequence of that gentleman's allowing Leigh Hunt to pass unpunished through a scene of slaughter, which his execution might so highly have graced, that we came to the resolution of laying before our readers a series of essays on *the Cockney School*—of which here terminates the first.

Blackwood's, August 1818

From "The Cockney School of Poetry," No. IV

... and Keats
The muse's son of promise, and of what feats
He yet may do, *etc.*

Cornelius Webb

OF all the manias of this mad age, the most incurable, as well as the most common, seems to be no other than the *Metromania.* The just celebrity of Robert Burns and Miss Baillie has had the melancholy effect of turning the heads of we know not how many farm-servants and unmarried ladies; our very footmen compose tragedies, and there is scarcely a superannuated governess in the island that does not have a roll of lyrics behind her in her band-box. To witness the disease of any human understanding, however feeble, is distressing; but the spectacle of an able mind reduced to a state of insanity is of course ten times more afflicting. It is with such sorrow as this that we have contemplated the case of Mr John Keats. This young man appears to have received from nature talents of an excellent, perhaps even of a superior order—talents which, devoted to the purposes of any useful profession, must have rendered him a respectable, if not an eminent citizen. His friends, we understand, destined him to the career of medicine, and he was bound apprentice some years ago to a worthy apothecary in town. But all has been undone by a sudden attack of the malady to which we have alluded. Whether Mr John had been sent home with a diuretic or composing draught to some patient far gone in the poetical mania, we have not heard. This much is certain, that he has caught the infection, and that thoroughly. For some time we were in hopes, that he might get off with a violent fit or two; but of late the symptoms are terrible. The phrenzy of the *Poems* was bad enough in its way; but it did not alarm us half so seriously as the calm, settled, imperturbable drivelling of *Endymion.* We hope, however, that in so young a person, and with a constitution originally so good, even now the disease is not utterly incurable. Time, firm treatment, and rational restraint, do much for many apparently hopeless invalids; and if Mr Keats should happen, at some interval of reason, to cast his eye upon our pages, he may perhaps be convinced of the existence of his malady, which, in such cases, is often all that is necessary to put the patient in a fair way of being cured.

The readers of the *Examiner* newspaper were informed, some time ago, by a solemn paragraph, in Mr Hunt's best style, of the appearance of two new stars of glorious magnitude and splendour in the poetical horizon of the land of Cockaigne. One of these turned out, by and by, to be no other than Mr John Keats. This precocious adulation confirmed the wavering apprentice in his desire to quit the gallipots, and at the same time excited in his too susceptible kind a fatal admiration for the character and talents of the most worthless and affected of all the versifiers of our time. One of his first productions was the following sonnet, "*written on the day when Mr Leigh Hunt left prison.*" It will be recollected that the cause of Hunt's confinement was a series of libels against his sovereign, and that its fruit was the odious and incestuous *Story of Rimini.*

> What though, for shewing truth to flattered state,
> *Kind Hunt* was shut in prison, yet has he,
>   In his immortal spirit, been as free
> As the sky-searching lark, and as elate.
> Minion of grandeur! think you he did wait?
>   Think you he nought but prison walls did see,
>   Till, so unwilling, thou unturn'dst the key?
> Ah, no! far happier, nobler was his fate!
> *In Spencer's halls!* he strayed, and bowers fair,
>   Culling enchanted flowers; and he flew
> *With daring Milton!* through the fields of air;
>   To regions of his own his genius true
> Took happy flights. Who shall his fame impair
>   When thou art dead, and all thy wretched crew?

The absurdity of the thought in this sonnet is, however, if possible, surpassed in another, "*addressed to Haydon*" the painter, that clever, but most affected artist, who as little resembles Raphael in genius as he does in person, notwithstanding the foppery of having his hair curled over his shoulders in the old Italian fashion. In this exquisite piece it will be observed, that Mr Keats classes together *Wordsworth*, *Hunt* and *Haydon*, as the three greatest spirits of the age, and that he alludes to himself, and some others of the rising brood of Cockneys, as likely to attain hereafter an equally honourable elevation. Wordsworth and Hunt! what a juxta-position! The purest, the loftiest, and, we do not fear to say, the most classical of living English poets, joined together in the same compliment with the meanest, the filthiest, and the most vulgar of Cockney poetasters. No wonder that he who could be guilty of this should class Haydon with Raphael, and himself with Spenser.

> Great spirits now on earth are sojourning;
> He of the cloud, the cataract, the lake,
> Who on Helvellyn's summit, wide awake,
> Catches his freshness from Archangel's wing:
> *He of the rose, the violet, the spring,*
> *The social smile, the chain for Freedom's sake:*
> And lo!—whose stedfastness would never take
> A meaner sound than Raphael's whispering.
> And other spirits there are standing apart
> Upon the forehead of the age to come:
> These, these will give the world another heart,
> And other pulses. *Hear ye not the hum*
> *Of mighty workings?* . . .
> *Listen awhile ye nations, and be dumb.*

The nations are to listen and be dumb! and why, good Johnny Keats? because Leigh Hunt is editor of the *Examiner*, and Haydon has painted the judgment of Solomon, and you and Cornelius Webb, and a few more city sparks, are pleased to look upon yourselves as so many Shakespeares and Miltons! The world has really some reason to look to its foundations! Here is a *tempestas in matula* with a vengeance. At the period when these sonnets were published, Mr Keats had no hesitation in saying, that he looked on himself as "*not yet* a glorious denizen of the wide heaven of poetry," but he had many fine soothing visions of coming greatness, and many rare plans of study to prepare for it. The following we think is very pretty raving.

Why so sad a moan?
Life is the rose's hope while yet unblown;
The reading of an ever-changing tale;
The light uplifting of a maiden's veil;
A pigeon tumbling in clear summer air;
A laughing school-boy, without grief or care,
Riding the springing branches of an elm.

O for ten years, that I may overwhelm
Myself in poesy; so I may do the deed
That my own soul has to itself decreed.
Then will I pass the countries that I see
In long perspective, and continually
Taste their pure fountains. First the realm I'll pass
Of Flora, and old Pan: sleep in the grass,
Feed upon apples red, and strawberries,
And choose each pleasure that my fancy sees.

Catch the white-handed nymphs in shady places,
To woo sweet kisses from averted faces,
Play with their fingers, touch their shoulders white
Into a pretty shrinking with a bite
As hard as lips can make it: till agreed,
A lovely tale of human life we'll read.
And one will teach a tame dove how it best
May fan the cool air gently o'er my rest;
Another, bending o'er her nimbler tread,
Will set a green robe floating round her head,
And still will dance with ever varied ease,
Smiling upon the flowers and the trees:
Another will entice me on, and on
Through almond blossoms and rich cinnamon;
Till in the bosom of a leafy world
We rest in silence, like two gems upcurl'd
In the recesses of a pearly shell.

Having cooled a little from this "fine passion," our youthful
poet passes very naturally into a long strain of foaming abuse
against a certain class of English Poets, whom, with Pope at
their head, it is much the fashion with the ignorant unsettled
pretenders of the present time to undervalue. Begging these
gentlemen's pardon, although Pope was not a poet of the same
high order with some who are now living, yet, to deny his
genius, is just about as absurd as to dispute that of Worsdworth,

or to believe in that of Hunt. Above all things, it is most pitiably ridiculous to hear men, of whom their country will always have reason to be proud, reviled by uneducated and flimsy striplings, who are not capable of understanding either their merits, or those of any other *men of power*—fanciful dreaming tea-drinkers, who, without logic enough to form one original image, or learning enough to distinguish between the written language of Englishmen and the spoken jargon of Cockneys, presume to talk with contempt of some of the most exquisite spirits the world ever produced, merely because they did not happen to exert their faculties in laborious affected descriptions of flowers seen in window-pots, or cascades heard at Vauxhall; in short, because they chose to be wits, philosophers, patriots, and poets, rather than to found the Cockney school of versification, morality, and politics, a century before its time. After blaspheming himself into a fury against Boileau etc., Mr Keats comforts himself and his readers with a view of the present more promising aspects of affairs; above all, with the ripened glories of the poet of *Rimini*. Addressing the manes of the departed chiefs of English poetry, he informs them, in the following clear and touching manner, of the existence of "him of the Rose," etc.

> From a thick brake,
> Nested and quiet in a valley mild,
> Bubbles a pipe; fine sounds are floating wild
> About the earth. Happy are ye and glad.

From this he diverges into a view of "things in general." We smile when we think to ourselves how little most of our readers will understand of what follows.

> Yet I rejoice: a myrtle fairer than
> E'er grew in Paphos, from the bitter weeds
> Lifts its sweet head into the air, and feeds
> A silent space with ever sprouting green.
> All tenderest birds there find a pleasant screen,
> Creep through the shade with jaunty fluttering,
> Nibble the little cupped flowers and sing.
> Then let us clear away the choking *thorns*
> From round its gentle stem; let the young *fawns*,

Yeaned in after times, when we are flown,
Find a fresh sward beneath it, overgrown
With simple flowers: let there nothing be
More boisterous than a lover's bended knee;
Nought more ungentle than the placid look
Of one who leans upon a closed book;
Nought more untranquil than the grassy slopes
Between two hills. All hail delightful hopes!

As she was wont the'imagination
Into most lovely labyrinths will be gone,
And they shall be accounted poet kings
Who simply tell the most heart-easing things.
O may these joys be ripe before I die.
Will not some say that I presumptuously
Have spoken? that from hastening disgrace
'Twere better far to hide my foolish face?
That whining boyhood should with reverence bow
Ere the dread thunderbolt could reach? How!
If I do hide myself, it sure shall be
In the very fane, the light of poesy.

From some verses addressed to various amiable individuals of the other sex, it appears, notwithstanding all this gossamer-work, that Johnny's affections are not entirely confined to objects purely ethereal. Take, by way of specimen, the following prurient and vulgar lines, evidently meant for some young lady east of Temple-bar.

> Add too, the sweetness
> Of thy honied voice; the neatness
> Of thine ankle lightly turn'd:
> With those beauties, scarce discern'd,
> Kept with such sweet privacy,
> That they seldom meet the eye
> Of the little loves that fly
> Round about with eager pry.
> Saving when, with freshening lave,
> Thou dipp'st them in the taintless wave;
> Like twin water lilies, born
> In the coolness of the morn.
> O, if thou hadst breathen then,
> Now the Muses had been ten.
> Couldst thou wish for lineage *higher*
> Than twin sister of *Thalia?*
> At last for ever, evermore,
> Will I call the Graces four.

N

Who will dispute that our poet, to use his own phrase (and rhyme),

> Can mingle music fit for the soft *ear*
> Of Lady *Cytherea*.

So much for the opening bud; now for the expanded flower. It is time to pass from the juvenile *Poems*, to the mature and elaborate *Endymion, a Poetic Romance*. The old story of the moon falling in love with a shepherd, so prettily told by a Roman Classic, and so exquisitely enlarged and adorned by one of the most elegant of German poets, has been seized upon by Mr John Keats, to be done with as might seem good unto the sickly fancy of one who never read a single line either of Ovid or of Wieland. If the quantity, not the quality, of the verses dedicated to the story is to be taken into account, there can be no doubt that Mr John Keats may now claim Endymion entirely to himself. To say the truth, we do not suppose either the Latin or the German poet would be very anxious to dispute about the property of the hero of the "Poetic Romance." Mr Keats has thoroughly appropriated the character, if not the name. His Endymion is not a Greek shepherd, loved by a Grecian goddess; he is merely a young Cockney rhymester, dreaming a phantastic dream at the full of the moon. Costume, were it worth while to notice such a trifle, is violated in every page of this goodly octavo. From his prototype Hunt, John Keats has acquired a sort of vague idea that the Greeks were a most tasteful people, and that no mythology can be so finely adapted for the purposes of poetry as theirs. It is amusing to see what a hand the two Cockneys make of this mythology; the one confesses that he never read the Greek Tragedians, and the other knows Homer only from Chapman, and both of them write about Apollo, Pan, Nymphs, Muses, and Mysteries, as might be expected from persons of their education. We shall not, however, enlarge at present upon this subject, as we mean to dedicate an entire paper to the classical attainments and attempts of the Cockney poets. As for Mr Keats' *Endymion*, it has just as much to do with Greece as it has with "old Tartary the fierce"; no man, whose mind has ever been imbued

with the smallest knowledge or feeling of classical poetry or
classical history, could have stooped to profane and vulgarise
every association in the manner which has been adopted by this
"son of promise." Before giving any extracts, we must inform
our readers, that this romance is meant to be written in English
heroic rhyme. To those who have read any of Hunt's poems,
this hint might indeed be needless. Mr Keats has adopted the
loose, nerveless versification, and Cockney rhymes of the poet
of *Rimini*; but in fairness to that gentleman, we must add, that
the defects of the system are tenfold more conspicuous in his
disciple's work than in his own. Mr Hunt is a small poet, but
he is a clever man. Mr Keats is a still smaller poet, and he is
only a boy of pretty abilities, which he has done everything
in his power to spoil.

Quarterly Review, April 1818

Endymion: A Poetic Romance. By John Keats. London, 1818. pp.
207.

. . .This author is a copyist of Mr Hunt; but he is more unin-
telligible, almost as rugged, twice as diffuse, and ten times more
tiresome and absurd than his prototype, who, though he
impudently presumed to seat himself in the chair of criticism,
and to measure his own poetry by his own standard, yet gener-
ally had a meaning. But Mr Keats had advanced no dogmas
which he was bound to support by examples; his nonsense
therefore is quite gratuitous; he writes it for its own sake, and,
being bitten by Mr Leigh Hunt's insane criticism, more than
rivals the insanity of his poetry.

Mr Keats' preface hints that his poem was produced under
peculiar circumstances.

> Knowing within myself [he says] the manner in which this Poem has
> been produced, it is not without a feeling of regret that I made it pub-
> lic. What manner I mean, will be *quite clear* to the reader, who must
> soon perceive great inexperience, immaturity, and every error denoting
> a feverish attempt, rather than a deed accomplished.
>
> Preface, p. v.ii

We humbly beg his pardon, but this does not appear to us to be *quite so clear*—we really do not know what he means—but the next passage is more intelligible.

> The two first books, and indeed the two last, I feel sensible are not of such completion as to warrant their passing the press.
> Preface, p. vii.

Thus "the two first books" are, even in his own judgment, unfit to appear, and "the two last" are, it seems, in the same condition—and as two and two make four, and as that is the whole number of books, we have a clear and, we believe, a very just estimate of the entire work.

Mr Keats, however, deprecates criticism on this "immature and ferverish work" in terms which are themselves sufficiently feverish; and we confess that we should have abstained from inflicting upon him any of the tortures of the "fierce hell" of criticism, which terrify his imagination, if he had not begged to be spared in order that he might write more; if we had not observed in him a certain degree of talent which deserves to be put in the right way, or which, at least, ought to be warned of the wrong; and if, finally, he had not told us that he is of an age and temper which imperiously require mental discipline.

Of the story we have been able to make out but little; it seems to be mythological, and probably relates to the loves of Diana and Endymion; but of this, as the scope of the work has altogether escaped us, we cannot speak with any degree of certainty; and must therefore content ourselves with giving some instances of its diction and versification: and here again we are perplexed and puzzled. At first it appeared to us, that Mr Keats had been amusing himself and wearying his readers with an immeasurable game at *bouts-rimes*; but, if we recollect rightly, it is an indispensable condition at this play, that the rhymes when filled up shall have a meaning; and our author, as we have already hinted, has no meaning. He seems to us to write a line at random, and then he follows not the thought excited by this line, but that suggested by the *rhyme* with which it concludes. There is hardly a complete couplet inclosing a complete idea in the whole book. He wanders from one subject to

another, from the association, not of ideas but of sounds, and
the work is composed of hemistichs which, it is quite evident,
have forced themselves upon the author by the mere force of
the catchwords on which they turn.

We shall select, not as the most striking instance, but as that
least liable to suspicion, a passage from the opening of the poem:

> . . . Such the sun, the moon,
> Trees old and young, sprouting a shady boon
> For simple sheep; and such are daffodils
> With the green world they live in; and clear rills
> That for themselves a cooling covert make
> 'Gainst the hot season: the mid forest brake,
> Rich with a sprinkling of fair musk-rose blooms:
> And such too is the grandeur of the dooms
> We have imagined for the mighty dead; *etc., etc.,*
>
> (pp. 3-4).

Here it is clear that the word, and not the idea, *moon* produces
the simple sheep and their shady *boon*, and that "the *dooms* of
the mighty dead" would never have intruded themselves but
for the "*fair musk-rose blooms.*"

Again:

> For 'twas the morn: Apollo's upward fire
> Made every eastern cloud a silvery pyre
> Of brightness so unsullied, that therein
> A melancholy spirit well might win
> Oblivion, and melt out his essence fine
> Into the winds: rain-scented eglantine
> Gave temperate sweets to that well-wooing sun;
> The lark was lost in him; cold springs had run
> To warm their chilliest bubbles in the grass;
> Man's voice was on the mountains; and the mass
> Of nature's lives and wonders puls'd tenfold,
> To feel this sun-rise and its glories old. (p. 8).

Here Apollo's *fire* produces a *pyre*, a silvery pyre of clouds,
wherein a spirit might *win* oblivion and melt his essence *fine*,
and scented *eglantine* gives sweets to the *sun*, and cold springs
had *run* into the *grass*, and then the pulse of the *mass* pulsed *ten-
fold* to feel the glories *old* of the new-born day, etc.

One example more:

> Be still the unimaginable lodge
> For solitary thinkings; such as dodge
> Conception to the very bourne of heaven,
> Then leave the naked brain: be still the leaven,
> That spreading in this dull and clodded earth.
> Gives it a touch ethereal—a new birth. (p. 17).

Lodge, dodge—heaven, leaven—earth, birth; such, in six words, is the sum and substance of six lines.

We come now to the author's taste in versification. He cannot indeed write a sentence, but perhaps he may be able to spin a line. Let us see. The following are specimens of his prosodial notions of our English heroic metre.

> Dear as the temple's self, so does the moon,
> The passion poesy, glories infinite. (p. 4).

> So plenteously all weed-hidden roots. (p. 6).

> Of some strange history, potent to send. (p. 18).

> Before the deep intoxication. (p. 27).

> Her scarf into a fluttering pavilion. (p. 33)

> The stubborn canvass for my voyage prepared. (p. 39)

> Endymion! the cave is secreter
> Than the isle of Delos. Echo hence shall stir
> No sighs but sigh-warm kisses, or light noise
> Of thy combing hand, the while it travelling cloys
> And trembles through my labyrinthine hair. (p. 48).

By this time our readers must be pretty well satisfied as to the meaning of his sentences and the structure of his lines: we now present them with some of the new words, with which, in imitation of Mr Leigh Hunt, he adorns our language.

We are told that "turtles *passion* their voices," (p. 15); that "an arbour was *nested*," (p. 23); and a lady's locks "*gordian'd* up," (p. 32); and to supply the place of the nouns thus verbalized Mr Keats, with great fecundity, spawns new ones; such as "men-slugs and human *serpentry*," (p. 41); the "*honeyfeel* of bliss," (p. 45); "wives prepare *needments*," (p. 13)—and so forth.

Then he has formed new verbs by the process of cutting off their natural tails, the adverbs, and affixing them to their foreheads; thus, "the wine out-sparkled," (p, 10); the "multitude up-followed," (p. 11); and "night up-took," (p. 29). "The wind up-blows," (p. 32); and the "hours are down-sunken," (p. 36).

But if he sinks some adverbs in the verbs he compensates the language with adverbs and adjectives which he separates from the parent stock. Thus, a lady "whispers *pantingly* and close," makes "*hushing* signs," and steers her skiff into a "*ripply* cove," (p. 23); a shower falls "refreshfully," (p. 45); and a vulture has a "*spreaded* tail," (p. 44).

But enough of Mr Leigh Hunt and his simple neophyte. If any one should be bold enough to purchase this "Poetic Romance," and so much more patient, than ourselves, as to get beyond the first book, and so much more fortunate as to find a meaning, we entreat him to make us acquainted with his success; we shall then return to the task we now abandon with despair, and endeavour to make all due amends to Mr Keats and to our readers.

Jeffrey in *Edinburgh Review*, August 1820

1. *Endymion: a Poetic Romance.* By JOHN KEATS. 8vo. pp. 207. London: 1818.
2. *Lamia, Isabella, The Eve of St Agnes, and other Poems.* By JOHN KEATS, author of *Endymion*. 12mo. pp. 200. London: 1820.

We had never happened to see either of these volumes till very lately—and have been exceedingly struck with the genius they display, and the spirit of poetry which breathes through all their extravagance. That imitation of our old writers, and especially of our older dramatists, to which we cannot help flattering ourselves that we have somewhat contributed, has brought on, as it were, a second spring in our poetry; and few of its blossoms are either more profuse of sweetness, or richer in promise, than this which is now before us. Mr Keats, we understand, is still a very young man; and his whole works, indeed, bear evidence enough of the fact. They are full of extravagance and irregularity, rash attempts at originality, interminable wanderings, and excessive obscurity. They manifestly require, therefore, all the indulgence that can be claimed for a first attempt: but we think it no less plain that they deserve it: for they are flushed all over with the rich lights of fancy; and so coloured and bestrewn with the flowers of poetry, that even while perplexed and bewildered in their labyrinths, it is impossible to resist the intoxication of their sweetness, or to shut our hearts to the enchantments they so lavishly present. The models upon which he has formed himself, in the *Endymion*, the earliest and by much the most considerable of his poems, are obviously *The Faithful Shepherdess* of Fletcher, and *The Sad Shepherd* of Ben Jonson; the exquisite metres and inspired diction of which he has copied with great boldness and fidelity—and, like his great originals, has also contrived to impart to the whole piece that true rural and poetic air—which breathes only in them, and in Theocritus—which is at once homely and majestic, luxurious and rude, and sets before us the genuine sights and sounds and smells of the country, with all the magic and grace of Elysium. His subject has the disadvantage of being Mythological; and in this respect, as well as on account of the raised and rapturous tone it consequently assumes, his poem, it may be thought, would be better compared to the *Comus* and the *Arcades* of Milton, of which, also, there are many traces of imitation. The great distinction, however, between him and these divine authors, is, that imagination in them is subordinate to reason and judgment, while, with him, it is paramount and supreme—that their ornaments and images are employed to embellish and recommend just sentiments, engaging incidents, and natural characters, while his are poured out without measure or restraint, and with no apparent design but to unburden the breast of the author, and give vent to the overflowing vein of his fancy. The thin and scanty tissue of his story is merely the light framework on which his florid wreaths are suspended; and while his imaginations go rambling and entangling themselves every where, like wild honeysuckles, all idea of sober reason, and plan, and consistency, is utterly forgotten, and "strangled in their waste fertility." A great part of the work, indeed, is written in the strangest and most fantastical manner that can be imagined. It seems as if the author had ventured every thing that occurred to him in the shape of a glittering image or striking expression—taken the first word that presented itself to make up a rhyme, and then made that word the germ of a new cluster of images—a hint for a new excursion of the fancy—and so wandered on, equally forgetful whence he came, and heedless whither he was going, till he had covered his pages with an interminable arabesque of connected and incongruous figures, that multiplied as they extended, and were only harmonized by the brightness of their tints, and the graces of their forms. In this rash and headlong career he has of course many lapses and failures. There is no work, accordingly, from which a malicious critic could cull more matter for ridicule, or select more obscure, unnatural, or absurd passages. But we do not take *that* to be our office;— and must beg leave, on the contrary, to say, that any one who, on this account, would represent the whole poem as despicable, must either have no notion of poetry, or no regard to truth.

It is, in truth, at least as full of genius as of absurdity; and he who does not find a great deal in it to admire and to give delight, cannot in his heart see much beauty in the two exquisite dramas to which we have already alluded; or find any great pleasure in some of the finest creations of Milton and Shakspeare. There are very many such persons, we verily believe, even among the reading and judicious part of the community— correct scholars, we have no doubt, many of them, and, it may be, very classical composers in prose and in verse—but utterly ignorant, on our view of the matter, of the true genius of English poetry, and incapable of estimating its appropriate and most exquisite beauties. With that spirit we have no hesitation in saying that Mr Keats is deeply imbued—and of those beauties he has presented us with many striking examples. We are very much inclined indeed to add, that we do not know any book which we would sooner employ as a test to ascertain whether any one had in him a native relish for poetry, and a genuine sensibility to its intrinsic charm. The greater and more distinguished poets of our country have so much in them, to gratify other tastes and propensities, that they are pretty sure to captivate and amuse those to whom their poetry may be but an hindrance and obstruction, as well as those to whom it constitutes their chief attraction. The interest of the stories they tell—the vivacity of the characters they delineate—the weight and force of the maxims and sentiments in which they abound —the very pathos, and wit and humour they display, which may all and each of them exist apart from their poetry, and independent of it, are quite sufficient to account for their popularity, without referring much to that still higher gift, by which they subdue to their enchantments those whose souls are truly attuned to the finer impulses of poetry. It is only, therefore, where those other recommendations are wanting, or exist in a weaker degree, that the true force of the attraction, exercised by the pure poetry with which they are so often combined, can be fairly appreciated: where, without much incident or many characters, and with little wit, wisdom, or arrangement, a number of bright pictures are presented to the imagination, and a fine feeling expressed of those mysterious relations by which visible external things are assimilated with inward thoughts and emotions, and become the images and exponents of all passions and affections. To an unpoetical reader, such passages will generally appear mere raving and absurdity—and to this censure a very great part of the volumes before us will certainly be exposed, with this class of readers. Even in the judgment of a fitter audience, however, it must, we fear, be admitted, that, besides the riot and extravagance of his fancy, the scope and substance of Mr Keats's poetry is rather too dreamy and abstracted to excite the strongest interest, or to sustain the attention through a work of any great compass or extent. He deals too much with shadowy and incomprehensible beings, and is too constantly rapt into an extramundane Elysium, to command a lasting interest with ordinary mortals—and must employ the agency of more varied and coarser emotions, if he wishes to take rank with the enduring poets of this, or of former generations. There is something very curious, too, we think, in the way in which he, and Mr Barry Cornwall also, have dealt with the Pagan mythology, of which they have made so much use in their poetry. Instead of presenting its imaginary persons under the trite and vulgar traits that belong to them in the ordinary systems, little more is borrowed from these than the general conception of their condition and relations; and an original character and distinct individuality is then bestowed upon them, which has all the merit of invention, and all the grace and attraction of the fictions on which it is engrafted.

. . . . . .

There is a fragment of a projected Epic, entitled *Hyperion*, on the expulsion of Saturn and the Titanian deities by Jupiter and his younger adherents, of which we cannot advise the completion: for, though there are passages of some force and grandeur, it is sufficiently obvious, from the specimen before us, that the subject is too far removed from all the sources of human interest, to be successfully treated by any modern author. Mr Keats has unquestionably a very beautiful imagination, a perfect ear for harmony, and a great familiarity with the finest diction of English poetry; but he must learn not to misuse or misapply these advantages; and neither to waste the good gifts of Nature and study on intractable themes, nor to luxuriate too recklessly on such as are more suitable.

TENNYSON

So much of "Lawn" Tennyson's life and development lie out-
side the scope of this volume that it is impossible to make the
attempt to show what the contemporary reception of his work
was like and how it affected him. But the two ill-famed reviews
with which Wilson and Lockhart assailed him during his
melancholy and difficult youth are too celebrated to be left out.
Wilson was, at any rate to begin with, a far from hostile critic:
his chief complaint seems to have been not against Tennyson
but against the friends who were (in his, Wilson's, opinion)
unduly flattering him and inflating his reputation. In the in-
stalment of *Noctes Ambrosianæ* published in February 1832,
Wilson, as North, had declared, "I admire Alfred—and hope—
nay trust—that one day he will prove himself a poet," although
"the cockneys are doing what they may to spoil him." But the
real onslaught was reserved for the May issue; Arthur Hallam's
favourable review of the *Poems, Chiefly Lyrical* in the *English-
man's Magazine* (1831) seemed to have infuriated Wilson against
poet and reviewer alike. After the insulting tone of the opening
section of the article, even the generous praise of its later pages
could hardly hope to soothe Tennyson's wounded feelings.
It was perhaps natural that he should relieve these feelings by
writing a (rather laboured) satiric poem on Wilson, but clearly
a great mistake for him to insist that Moxon, his publisher,
should include this piece in his next book, the *Poems* of Decem-
ber 1832. This publication, ignored by "Maga," was dealt
with in the *Quarterly* for April 1833. Whether the article was by
Croker or Lockhart is not certainly established, but in any case
both these men were well disposed towards Wilson, a col-
league of many years' standing, and the review shows an
obvious determination to put Tennyson in his place. It is
therefore all the more surprising to learn that this criticism was
actually of practical value to the poet; much as he resented the

treatment his critics gave him, he profited by their vigilance. As a result of Wilson's review, the *Poems Chiefly Lyrical* was shorn of twenty-four of its fifty-six poems; as a result of the *Quarterly's* review *Poems* of 1832 lost seven of their number, while, says Miss Hildyard, "almost every line with which the critic found fault was either omitted or re-written."

In conclusion, the student of Tennyson would do well to consult the remarkable review by W. E. Gladstone in the *Quarterly* for October 1859, most of which is reprinted in R. Brimley Johnson's *Famous Reviews* (1914).

Wilson in *Blackwood's*, May 1832

Poems, chiefly Lyrical, by Alfred Tennyson. London, Effingham Wilson, 1830. Vol. xxxi. No. CXCIV.

One of the saddest misfortunes that can befall a young poet, is to be the Pet of a Coterie; and the very saddest of all, if in Cockneydom. Such has been the unlucky lot of Alfred Tennyson. He has been elevated to the throne of Little Britain, and sonnets were showered over his coronation from the more remote regions of his empire, even from Hampstead Hill. Eulogies more elaborate than the architecture of the costliest gingerbread, have been built up into panegyrical piles, in commemoration of the Birth-day; and 'twould be a pity indeed with one's crutch to smash the gilt battlements, white too with sugar as with frost, and begemmed with comfits. The besetting sin of all periodical criticism, and now-a-days there is no other, is boundless extravagance of praise; but none splash it on like the trowelmen who have been bedaubing Mr Tennyson. There is something wrong, however, with the compost. It won't stick; unseemly cracks deform the surface; it falls off piece by piece ere it has dried in the sun, or it hardens into blotches; and the worshippers have but discoloured and disfigured their Idol. The worst of it is, that they make the Bespattered not only feel, but look ridiculous; he seems as absurd as an Image in a tea-garden; and bedizened with faded and fantastic garlands, the public cough on being told he is a Poet, for he has much more the appearance of a Post.

The Englishman's Magazine ought not to have died; for it threatened to be a very pleasant periodical. An Essay " on the Genius of Alfred Tennyson," sent it to the grave. The super-human—nay, supernatural—pomposity of that one paper, incapacitated the whole work for living one day longer in this unceremonious world. The solemnity with which the critic approached the object of his adoration, and the sanctity with which he laid his offerings on the shrine, were too much for our irreligious age. The Essay " on the genius of Alfred Tenny-son," awoke a general guffaw, and it expired in convulsions. Yet the Essay was exceedingly well-written—as well as if it had been " on the Genius of Sir Isaac Newton." Therein lay the mistake. Sir Isaac discovered the law of gravitation; Alfred had but written some pretty verses, and mankind were not prepared to set him among the stars. But that he has genius is proved by his being at this moment alive; for had he not, he must have breathed his last under that critique. The spirit of life must indeed be strong within him; for he has outlived a narcotic dose administered to him by a crazy charlatan in the *Westminster*, and after that he may sleep in safety with a pan of charcoal.

But the Old Man must see justice done to his ingenious lad, and save him from his worst enemies, his friends. Never are we so happy—nay, 'tis now almost our only happiness—as when scattering flowers in the sunshine that falls from the yet unclouded sky on the green path prepared by gracious Nature for the feet of enthusiastic youth. Yet we scatter them not in too lavish profusion; and we take care that the young poet shall see, along with the shadow of the spirit that cheers him on, that, too, of the accompanying crutch. Were we not afraid that our style might be thought to wax too figurative, we should say that Alfred is a promising plant; and that the day may come when, beneath sun and shower, his genius may grow up and expand into a stately tree, embowering a solemn shade within its wide circumference, while the daylight lies gorgeously on its crest, seen from afar in glory—itself a grove.

But that day will never come, if he hearken not to our advice, and, as far as his own nature will permit, regulate by it the movements of his genius. This may perhaps appear, at first sight or hearing, not a little unreasonable on our part; but not so, if Alfred will but lay our words to heart, and meditate on their spirit. We desire to see him prosper; and we predict fame as the fruit of obedience. If he disobey, he assuredly goes to oblivion.

At present he has small power over the common feelings and thoughts of men. His feebleness is distressing at all times when he makes an appeal to their ordinary sympathies. And the reason is, that he fears to look such sympathies boldly in the face—and will be—metaphysical. What all the human race see and feel, he seems to think cannot be poetical; he is not aware of the transcendant and external grandeur of common-place and all-time truths, which are the staple of all poetry. All human beings see the same light in heaven and in woman's eyes; and the great poets put it into language which rather records than reveals, spiritualizing while it embodies. They shun not the sights of common earth—witness Wordsworth. But beneath the magic of their eyes the celandine grows a star or a sun. What beauty is breathed over the daisy by lovingly bless-ing it because it is so common! "Sweet flower! whose home is everywhere!" In like manner, Scott, when eulogizing our love of our native land, uses the simplest language, and gives vent to the simplest feelings—

> Lives there the man with soul so dead,
> Who never to himself hath said,
> This is my own, my native land?

What less—what more, could any man say? Yet translate these three lines—not omitting others that accompany them equally touching—into any language, living or dead—and they will instantly be felt by all hearts, savage or civilized, to be the most exquisite poetry. Of such power, conscious, as it kindles, of its dominion over men, because of their common humanity, would that there were finer and more frequent examples in the compositions—otherwise often exquisite—of this young poet.

.   .   .   .   .   .

Our critique is near its conclusion; and in correcting it for press, we see that its whole merit, which is great, consists in the extracts, which are "beautiful exceedingly." Perhaps, in the first part of our article, we may have exaggerated Mr Tennyson's not unfrequent silliness, for we are apt to be carried away by the whim of the moment, and in our humourous moods, many things wear a queer look to our aged eyes, which fill young pupils with tears; but we feel assured that in the second part we have not exaggerated his strength—that we have done no more than justice to his fine faculties—and that the millions who delight in Maga will, with one voice, confirm our judgment—that Alfred Tennyson is a poet.

But, though it might be a mistake of ours, were we to say that he has much to learn, it can be no mistake to say that he has not a little to unlearn, and more to bring into practice, before his genius can achieve its destined triumphs. A puerile partiality for particular forms of expression, nay, modes of spelling and of pronunciation, may be easily over-looked in one whom *we* must look on as yet a mere boy; but if he carry it with him, and indulge it in manhood, why it will make him seem silly as his sheep; and should he continue to bleat so when his head and beard are as grey as ours, he will be truly a laughable old ram, and the ewes will care no more for him than if he were a wether.

Farther, he must consider that all the fancies that fleet across the imagination, like shadows on the grass or the tree-tops, are not entitled to be made small separate poems of—about the length of one's little finger; that many, nay, most of them, should be suffered to pass away with a silent "God bless ye," like butterflies, single or in shoals, each family with its own hereditary character mottled on its wings; and that though thousands of those grave brown, and gay golden images will be blown back in showers, as if upon balmy breezes changing suddenly and softly to the *airt* whence inspiration at the moment breathes, yet not one in a thousand is worth being caught and pinned down on paper into poetry, "gently as if you loved him"—only the few that are bright with the "beauty still more beauteous"—and a few such belong to all

the orders—from the little silly moth that extinguishes herself
in your taper, up to the mighty Emperor of Morocco at meri-
dian wavering his burnished downage in the unconsuming
sun who glorifies the wondrous stranger.

Now, Mr Tennyson does not seem to know this; or if he
do, he is self-willed and perverse in his sometimes almost infan-
tile vanity; (and how vain are most beautiful children!) and
thinks that any Thought of Feeling or Fancy that has had the
honour and the happiness to pass through *his* mind, must by
that very act be worthy of everlasting commemoration.
Heaven pity the poor world, were we to put into stanzas, and
publish upon it, all our thoughts, thick as motes in the sun, or a
summer evening atmosphere of midges!

Finally, Nature is mighty, and poets should deal with her on
a grand scale. She lavishes her glorious gifts before their path
in such profusion, that Genius—reverent as he is of the mysteri-
ous mother, and meeting her at sunrise on the mountains with
grateful orisons—with grateful orisons bidding her farewell
among the long shadows that stretch across the glens when sun-
set sinks into the sea—is yet privileged to tread with a seeming
scorn in the midst of imagery that to common eyes would be as
a revelation of wonders from another world. Familiar to him
are they as the grass below his feet. In lowlier moods he looks
at them—and in his love they grow beautiful. So did Burns
beautify the daisy—"wee modest crimson-tipped flower!"
But in loftier moods, the "violet by the mossy stone," is not
"half-hidden to the eye"—it is left unthought of to its own
sweet existence. The poet then ranges wide and high, like
Thomson, in his *Hymn to the Seasons*, which he had so gloriously
sung, seeing in all the changes of the rolling year "but the
varied god,"—like Wordsworth, in his *Excursion*, communing
too with the spirit "whose dwelling is the light of setting suns."

Those great men are indeed among the "Lights of the world
and demigods of fame"; but all poets, ere they gain a bright
name, must thus celebrate the worship of nature. So it is, too,
with painters. They do well, even the greatest of them, to
trace up the brooks to their source in stone-basin or mossy well,
in the glen-head, where greensward glades among the heather

o

seem the birthplace of the Silent People—the Fairies. But in their immortal works they must shew us how "red comes the river down"; castle of rock or of cloud—long withdrawing vales, where midway between the flowery foreground, and in the distance of blue mountain ranges, some great city lifts up its dim-seen spires through the misty smoke beneath which imagination hears the hum of life—"peaceful as some immeasurable plain," the breast of old ocean sleeping in the sunshine—or as if an earthquake shook the pillars of his caverned depths, tumbling the foam of his breakers, mast-high, if mast be there, till the canvass ceases to be silent, and the gazer hears him howling over his prey—See—see!—the foundering wreck of a three-decker going down head-foremost to eternity.

With such admonition, we bid Alfred Tennyson farewell.

Quarterly Review, April 1833

Poems, by Alfred Tennyson. pp. 163. London. 12mo. 1833.

This is, as some of his marginal notes intimate, Mr Tennyson's second appearance. By some strange chance we have never seen his first publication, which, if it at all resembles its younger brother, must be by this time so popular that any notice of it on our part would seem idle and presumptuous; but we gladly seize this opportunity of repairing an unintentional neglect, and of introducing to the admiration of our more sequestered readers a new prodigy of genius—another and a brighter star of that galaxy or *milky way* of poetry of which the lamented Keats was the harbinger; and let us take this occasion to sing our palinode on the subject of *Endymion*. We certainly did not discover in that poem the same degree of merit that its more clear-sighted and prophetic admirers did. We did not foresee the unbounded popularity which has carried it through we know not how many editions; which has placed it on every table; and, what is still more unequivocal, familiarized it in every mouth. All this splendour of fame, however, though we had not the sagacity to anticipate, we have the candour to acknowledge; and we request that the publisher of the new and beautiful edition of Keats's work now in the press, with graphic illustrations by Calcott and Turner, will do us the favour and the justice to notice our conversion in his prolegomena.

Warned by our former mishap, wiser by experience, and improved, as we hope, in taste, we have to offer Mr Tennyson our tribute of unmingled approbation, and it is very agreeable to us, as well as to our readers, that our present task will be little more than the selection, for their delight, of a few specimens of Mr Tennyson's singular genius, and the venturing to point out, now and then, the peculiar brilliancy of some of the gems that irradiate his poetical crown.

A prefatory sonnet opens to the reader the aspirations of the young author, in which, after the manner of sundry poets, by wishing himself to be something that he is not. The amorous Catullus aspired to be a sparrow; the tuneful and convivial Anacreon (for we totally reject the supposition that attributes the 'Ειθε λύρη καλή γενοίμην to Alcæus) wished to be a lyre and a great drinking cup; a crowd of more modern sentimentalists have desired to approach their mistresses as flowers, tunicks, sandals, birds, breezes and butterflies;—all poor conceits of narrow-minded poetasters! Mr Tennyson (though he, too, would, as far as his true-love is concerned, not unwillingly be "an earring," "a girdle," and "a necklace," (p. 45) in the more serious and solemn exordium of his works ambitions a bolder metamorphosis—he wishes to be—*a river*!

Sonnet

Mine be the strength of spirit fierce and free,
Like some broad river rushing down *alone*—

rivers that travel in company are too common for his taste—

With the self-same impulse wherewith he was thrown—

a beautiful and harmonious line—

From his loud fount upon the echoing lea—
Which, with *increasing* might, doth *forward flee*—

Every word of this line is valuable—the natural progress of

'human' ambition is here strongly characterized—two lines ago he would have been satisfied with the *self-same* impulse—but now he must have *increasing* might; and indeed he would require all his might to accomplish his object of *fleeing forward*, that is, going backwards and forwards at the same time. Perhaps he uses the word *flee* for *flow*; which latter he could not well employ in *this* place, it being, as we shall see, essentially necessary to rhyme to *Mexico* towards the end of the sonnet—as an equivalent to *flow* he has, therefore, with great taste and ingenuity, hit on the combination of *forward flee*—

> . . . doth forward flee
> By town, and tower, and hill, and cape, and isle,
> And in the middle of the green *salt* sea
> Keeps his blue waters fresh for many a mile.

A noble wish, beautifully expressed, that he may not be confounded with the deluge of ordinary poets, but, amidst their discoloured and briny ocean, still preserve his own bright tints and sweet savor. He may be at ease on this point—he never can be mistaken for any one else. We have but too late become acquainted with him, yet we assure ourselves that if a thousand anonymous specimens were presented to us, we should unerringly distinguish his by the total absence of any particle of *salt*. But again, his thoughts take another turn, and he reverts to the insatiability of human ambition: we have seen him just now content to be a river, but as he *flees forward*, his desires expand into sublimity, and he wishes to become the great Gulf-stream of the Atlantic.

> Mine be the power which ever to its sway
> Will win *the wise at once*—

We, for once, are wise, and he has won *us*—

> Will win the wise at once; and by degrees
> May into uncongenial spirits flow,
> Even as the great gulphstream of Flo*ri*da
> Floats far away into the Northern seas
> The lavish growths of southern Me*xi*co! (p. 1).

And so concludes the sonnet.

The next piece is a kind of testamentary paper, addressed

"To———," a friend, we presume, containing his wishes as to what his friend should do for him when he (the poet) shall be dead—not, as we shall see, that he quite thinks that such a poet can die outright.

> Shake hands, my friend, across the brink
>   Of that deep grave to which I go.
> Shake hands once more; I cannot sink
>   So far—far down, but I shall know
>   Thy voice, and answer from below!

Horace said "non omnius moriar," meaning that his fame should survive—Mr Tennyson is still more vivacious, "non *omnino* moriar," —"It will not die at all; my body shall be as immortal as my verse, and however *low I may go*, I warrant you I shall keep all my wits about me—therefore"

> When, in the darkness over me,
>   The four-handed mole shall scrape,
> Plant thou no dusky cypress tree,
>   Nor wreath thy cap with doleful crape,
>   But pledge me in the flowing grape.

Observe how all ages become present to the mind of a great poet; and admire how naturally he combines the funeral cypress of classical antiquity with the crape hatband of the modern undertaker.

He proceeds:

> And when the sappy field and wood
>   Grow green beneath the *showery gray*,
> And rugged barks begin to bud,
>   And through damp holts, newflushed with May,
>   Ring sudden *laughters* of the jay!

Laughter, the philosopher tell us, is the peculiar attributes of man—but as Shakespeare found "tongues in trees and sermons in stones," this true poet endows all nature not merely with human sensibilities but with human functions—the jay *laughs*, and we find, indeed, a little further on, that the woodpecker *laughs* also; but to mark the distinction between their merriment and that of men, both jays and woodpeckers laugh upon melancholy occasions. We are glad, moreover, to observe, that Mr Tennyson is prepared for, and therefore will not be disturbed by, human laughter, if any silly reader should catch the infection from the woodpeckers and jays.

> Then let wise Nature work her will,
> And on my clay her darnels grow,
> Come only when the days are still,
> And at my head-stone whisper low,
> And tell me—

Now, what would an ordinary bard wish to be told under such circumstances?—why, perhaps, how his sweetheart was, or his child, or his family, or how the Reform Bill worked, or whether the last edition of the poems had been sold—papæ! our genuine poet's first wish is

> And tell me—*if the woodbines blow!*

When, indeed, he shall have been thus satisfied as to the *woodbines* (of the blowing of which in their due season he may, we think, feel pretty secure) he turns a passing thought to his friend—

> If *thou* art blest, my *mother's* smile
> Undimmed . . .

but such inquiries, short as they are, seem too commonplace, and he immediately glides back into his curiosity as to the state of the weather and the forwardness of the spring—

> If thou art blessed—my mother's smile
> Undimmed—*if bees are on the wing?*

No, we believe the whole circle of poetry does not furnish such another instance of enthusiasm for the sights and sounds of the vernal season!— The sorrows of a bereaved mother rank *after* the blossoms of the *woodbine*, and just before the hummings of the *bee*; and this is *all* that he has any curiosity about; for he proceeds:

> Then cease, my friend, a little while
> That I may . . .

'send my love to my mother,' or 'give you some hints about

bees, which I have picked up from Aristæus, in the Elysian
Fields,' or 'tell you how I am situated as to my own personal
comforts in the world below'?—oh no—

> That I may—hear the *throstle sing*
> His bridal song—the boast of spring.
> Sweet as the noise, in parched plains,
>   Of bubbling wells that fret the stones,
> (*If any sense in me remains*)
> Thy word will be—thy cheerful tones
> As welcome to—my *crumbling bones*! (p. 4.)

"*If any sense in me remains*!" This doubt is inconsistent with
the opening stanza of the piece, and, in fact, too modest; we take
upon ourselves to re-assure Mr Tennyson, that, even after he
shall be dead and buried, as much "*sense*" will still remain as
he has now the good fortune to possess.

.   .   .   .   .   .

But we must hasten on; and to tranquillize the reader's mind
after the last affecting scene, shall notice the only pieces of a
lighter strain which the volume affords. The first is elegant
and playful; it is a description of the author's study, which he
affectionately calls his *Darling Room*.

> O darling room, my heart's delight;
> Dear room, the apple of my sight;
> With thy two couches, soft and white,
> There is no room so exqui*site*;
> No little room so warm and bright,
> Wherein to read, wherein to write.

We entreat our readers to note how, even in this little trifle,
the singular taste and genius of Mr Tennyson break forth. In
such a dear *little* room a narrow-minded scribbler would have
been content with *one* sofa, and that one he would probably
have covered with black mohair, or red cloth, or a good striped
chintz; how infinitely more characteristic is white dimity!—
'tis as it were a type of the purity of the poet's mind. He pro-
ceeds—

> For I the Nonnerwerth have seen,
> And Oberwinter's vineyards green,
> Musical Lurlei; and between
> The hills to Bingen I have been,
> Bingen in Darnstadt, where the Rhene
> Curves towards Mentz, a woody scene.
>
> Yet never did there meet my sight,
> In any town, to left or right,
> A little room so exqui*site*,
> With *two* such couches soft and white;
> Not any room was so warm and bright,
> Wherein to read, wherein to write. (p. 153).

A common poet would have said that he had been in London or in Paris—in the loveliest villa on the banks of the Thames, or the most gorgeous chateau of the Loire—that he had reclined in Madame de Staël's boudoir, and mused in Mr Rogers's comfortable study; but the *darling room* of the poet of nature (which we must suppose to be endued with sensibility, or he would not have addressed it) would not be flattered with such commonplace comparisons; no, no, but it is something to have it said that there is no such room in the ruins of the Drachenfels, in the vineyard of Oberwinter, or even in the rapids of the Rhene, under the Lurleyberg. We have ourselves visited all these celebrated spots, and can testify, in corroboration of Mr Tennyson, that we did not see in any of them anything like *this little room so exquis*ITE.

The second of the lighter pieces, and the last with which we shall delight our readers, is a severe retaliation on the editor of the *Edinburgh Magazine*, who, it seems, had not treated the first volume of Mr Tennyson with the same respect that we have, we trust, evinced for the second.

To Christopher North

> You did late review my lays,
>   Crusty Christopher;
> You did mingle blame and praise,
>   Rusty Christopher.

When I learnt from whom it came
I forgave you all the blame,
   Musty Christopher;
I could *not* forgive the praise,
   Fusty Christopher. (p. 153).

Was there ever anything so genteelly turned—so terse—so
sharp—and the point so stinging and *so true*?

I could not forgive the *praise*,
   Fusty Christopher!

[*Article ends with a facetious disquisition on the ingratitude of
authors towards reviewers.*]

APPENDIX I

The Genesis of the *Quarterly*: Scott to Gifford

25th October 1808

Sɪʀ, By a letter from the Lord Advocate of Scotland in conse-
quence of a communication between his Lordship and Mr
Canning on the subject of a new Review to be attempted in
London I have the pleasure to understand that you have con-
sented to become the editor a point which in my opinion goes
no small way to insure success to the undertaking. In offering
a few observations on the details of such a plan I only obey the
commands of our distinguished friends without having the
vanity to hope I can point out any thing of consequence which
must not have readily occurred to a person of Mr Gifford's
literary experience and eminence. The task having been so
imposed on me I beg permission to offer my sentiments in the
miscellaneous way in which they occur to me.

The extensive reputation and circulation of the *Edinburgh
Review* is chiefly owing to two circumstances. First that it is
entirely uninfluenced by the Booksellers who have contrived
to make most of the other reviews mere vehicles for advertising
and puffing off their own publications or running down those
of their rivals. Secondly the very handsome recompense
which the Editor not only holds forth to his regular assistants
but actually forces upon those whose rank and fortune make it
a matter of indifference to them. The Editor to my knowledge
acts on the principle that even Czar Peter working in the
trenches must accept the pay of a common soldier. This general
rule removes all scruple of delicacy and fixes in his service a
number of contributors who might otherwise have felt reluc-
tance to accept of compensation for their labours even the more
because that compensation was a matter of convenience to

them. There are many young men of talent and enterprize who are extremely glad of a handsome apology to work for fifteen or twenty guineas, upon whose gratuitous contributions no reliance could be placed and who nevertheless would not degrade themselves by being paid labourers in a work where others wrote for honour alone. From this I deduce two points of doctrine, first, that the projected work must be considered as independent of all bookselling influence, secondly, that the contributors must be handsomely recompensed and that it be a rule that each shall accept of the price of his labour. Mr John Murray of Fleet Street a young bookseller of capital and enterprize and who has more good sense and propriety of sentiment than fall to the share of most of his brethren paid me a visit some time ago at Ashestiel and as I found he had held some communication with Mr Canning (altho indirectly) I did not hesitate to give him my sentiments on these points of the plan and I found his ideas most liberal and satisfactory.

The office of Editor supposing all preliminaries arranged is of such consequence that had you not been pleased to undertake it I fear the project might have fallen wholly to the ground. He must be invested with the unlimited power of control for the purpose of selecting curtailing and correcting the contributions; and as the person immediately responsible to the Public and to the Bookseller that each Number shall be published in its due time it will be the Editors duty to consider and settle the articles of which it shall consist and to take early measures for procuring them from the persons best qualified to write upon the several subjects of criticism. And this you will find so difficult if entirely entrusted to auxiliaries that I foresee with pleasure you will be soon compelled to appear yourself (occasionally at least) in the field. At the same time if you think my services worth acceptance as a sort of Jackal or Lions provider I will do all in my power to assist in this troublesome department of Editorial duty. But there is another point of consequence besides the task of providing and arranging materials for each number. One very successful expedient of the Edinr. Editor and on which his popularity has in some measure risen is the art of giving life and interest even to the fuller articles of the Review. He receives for example a criticism upon a work of deep research from a person who has studied the book and understands the subject and if it happens to be written which may often be the case in a tone of stupifying mediocrity he renders it palatable by a few lively paragraphs or entertaining illustrations of his own or perhaps by generalising and systematising the knowledge which it contains. By this sort of *finessing* he converts without loss of time or hindrance of business an unmarketable commodity into one which from its general effect and spirit is not likely to disgrace those among which it is placed. Such exertions on the part of an Editor are indispensable to a well conducted review for those who possess the knowledge necessary to review books of research or of abstract disquisition are sometimes unable to put those criticisms however just into a readable far less a pleasant or captivating shape and as their science cannot be obtained "for the nonce" by one capable of writing well the only remedy is that a man of talent for composition should revise their lucubrations. And I should hope many friends and wellwishers to the undertaking would be disposed to assist in this part of the task and altho they might not have leisure to write themselves might yet revise and correct such articles.

Permit me to add that you Sir possess in a peculiar degree a facility of the greatest consequence to the undertaking in having access to the best sources of political information. It would not certainly be advisable that the work should at its outset assume exclusively a political character. On the contrary the articles upon science and miscellaneous literature ought to be such as may challenge comparison with the best of contemporary reviews. But as the real reason of instituting the publication is the disgusting and deleterious doctrine with which the most popular of these periodical works disgraces its pages it is essential to consider how opposite and sounder principles can be most advantageously brought forward. On this ground I hope it is not too much to expect from those who have the power of befriending us in this respect that they should upon topics of national interest furnish the Reviewer confidentially and through the medium of the Editor with accurate views of points of fact so far as they are fit to be made public. This is the most delicate yet most essential part of our scheme. On the one hand it is certainly not to be understood that we are to be tied down to advocate upon all occasions and as a matter of course the cause of administration. Such indiscriminate support and dereliction of independence would prejudice both ourselves and our cause in the eye of the public. On the other hand the work will obtain a decided ascendance over all competition so soon as the public shall learn (not from any vaunt of the conductors but from their own observation) that upon political subjects the new critics are possessed of early and of accurate information. The opposition have regularly furnished the *Edinburgh Review* with this command of facts so far as they themselves possessed them. And surely you my dear Sir enjoying the confidence of Mr Canning and other persons in power and in defence of whose principles we are buckling our armour may safely expect to be intrusted with the political information necessary to give credit to the work and with the task of communicating it to those whom you may chuse to employ in laying it before the public.

. . . The first No. of our proposed Review if it can be compiled without the plan taking wind and if executed with the talent which may reasonably be expected will burst among the Whigs (as they call themselves) like a bomb. From the little observation I have made I think they suffer peculiarly under cool sarcastic ridicule accompanied by dispassionate argument. Having long had a sort of exclusive occupation of the press owing to the negligence of all literary assistance on the part of those who thought their good cause should fight its own battle they seem to feel with great acuteness any appeal to the reading public like champions who having been long accustomed to push have lost the art of parrying. Now suppose that upon a foe of this humour our projected work steals out only drawing the attention of the public by the accuracy of its facts and the stile of its execution without giving them the satisfaction of bidding a public defiance I conceive that their indignation expressed probably through the *Edinr. Review* will soon give us an opportunity of coming to close quarters with that publication should it be thought advisable and that with a much better grace than were we to announce a previous determination of hostility. In the mean while I am for gliding into a state of hostility without a formal declaration of war and if our forces for one or two numbers be composed of volunteers and amateurs we will find it easy when our arms have acquired reputation to hire troops of condottieri and to raise and discipline regular forces of the line. You are a much better judge than I can be who are fit to be put into the van of the battle—You have the Ellis's the Roses (cum plurimis aliis) we have lost a host in Mr Frere and can only hope he is serving the common cause more effectually in another capacity. You can never want scholars while Oxford stands where it did. Richard Heber was with me during Murrays visit and knowing his zeal for the good cause I availd myself of his advice: his brother Reginald would be a most excellent coadjutor and I doubt not to get his assistance. I believe I can command some respectable assistance here but I rely much on that of Mr William Erskine the Advocates brother in law and my most intimate friend. I think we can get you both some scientific articles and some Scotch metaphysics which you know are fashionable however deservedly or otherwise. My own studies have been rather limited but I understand in some sort literary antiquities and history and have been reckoned a respectable tirailleur in the quizzing department of the *Edinr. Review* in which I wrote occasionally untill these last two years when its tone of politics became so violent; I only mention this lest you should either estimate my talents by my zeal (which would occasion great disappointment) or think me like many good folks more ready to offer advice than assistance. Mr Murray seems to count upon Malthus for the department of political economy and if you approve I could when I come to town sound Malthus whose study of foreign classics has been proceeding extensively. It [is certain some] push must be made at first for if we fail we shall disgrace ourselves and do great injury to our cause. I would not willingly be like my namesake, Walter the penniless, at the head of a crusade consisting of a disorderly rabble and I judge of your feelings by my own. But "screw your courage

to the sticking place and we'll *not fail.*" Supposing the work
conducted with spirit the only ground from which it can be
assaild with a prospect of success would be a charge of its
being conducted intirely under ministerial influence. But this
may be parried first by labouring the literary articles with as
much pains as the political and so giving to the review a
decided character independent of the latter department further
the respect of the public may be maintained by the impartiality
of our criticism.

[*The letter breaks off in this place.*]

[Text from The Letters of Sir Walter Scott, edited by Sir
Herbert Grierson (Constable, 1932), vol. ii, pp. 100–109.]

APPENDIX II

The Chaldee Manuscript

We have seen (*Introduction*, p. 25) that William Blackwood's plan for a monthly magazine was almost strangled at birth by the poor quality of the first six numbers. Owing, largely, to the investigations of Professor Alan Lang Strout, we have a clear and fascinating picture of what exactly happened. Blackwood's two original editors were James Cleghorn and Thomas Pringle, both bucolic characters (Cleghorn edited the *Farmer's Magazine* for Constable from 1800 to 1825) and, incidentally, both lame. For six months the magazine dragged on, offering its readers nothing more exciting than the traditional content of the "magazine"—a farrago of miscellaneous information, much of it local. There was, for instance, a "chronicle section" devoted to news of births, marriages, deaths, promotions, bankruptcies, and the like. (Not that even the boldest magazine editor could venture to dispense altogether with "chronicles"; it was, in fact, not until 1831 that this kind of material finally ceased to appear in *Blackwood's*.) Nevertheless, the publisher was not satisfied, and on August 20 we find him writing plaintively to Sir Walter Scott:

> You will probably have heard that I have been under the disagreeable necessity of giving notice to the Editors of my Magazine that our connection is to be at an end on the publication of the sixth number. I found myself obliged to do this, as they did little or nothing themselves, though by our agreement they were to provide the whole of the materials, and for this to receive the half of the profits.

It was necessary, therefore, that the first issue of the reconstituted and renamed magazine (October 1817) should contain arresting, even inflammatory, material. And if John Wilson's assault on Coleridge's *Biographia Literaria* ("he seems to consider the mighty universe itself as nothing better than a mirror

in which, with a grinning and idiot self-complacency, he may
contemplate the Physiognomy of Samuel Taylor Coleridge")
and the first of Lockhart's maulings of the "Cockney School"
("The very concubine of so impure a wretch as Leigh Hunt
would be to be pitied") — if these two were not enough, there
was James Hogg's contribution of what he described, in the
high-spirited accompanying letter, as "this beautiful allegory of
mine."

The allegory was a comic description, amusingly sustained
in a fair imitation of the language of the Authorized Version,
of the events of the past few months; the incompetence of
Cleghorn and Pringle and the rivalry between Blackwood and
Constable. Lockhart and Wilson were, evidently, delighted
by the joke, and fell with more relish than discretion on the task
of continuing and expanding it. "The history of it is this,"
wrote Lockhart to Christie (January 27, 1818):

> Hogg, the Ettrick Shepherd, sent up an attack on Constable, the book-
> seller, respecting some private dealings of his with Blackwood. Wilson
> and I liked the idea of introducing the whole panorama of the town in
> that sort of dialect. We drank punch one night from eight till eight in
> the morning, Blackwood being by with anecdotes, and the result is
> before you.

The last two chapters, which contain a gallery of satiric por-
traits of Constable's associates, are almost entirely the work of
the bibulous collaborators, Hogg contributing only a few
verses not of a satiric nature. The savagery of their banter can
be gathered from a few specimens: Charles Kirkpatrick Sharpe,
the caricaturist and minor poet, is described thus:

> But, behold, while they were yet speaking, they heard a voice of one
> screeching at the gate, and the voice was a sharp voice even like the
> voice of the unclean bird which buildeth its nest in the corner of the
> temple, and defileth the holy places. (ii, 62)

And here is John Playfair, Professor of Natural Philosophy in
the University of Edinburgh (the point of the jest is that he was
originally intended for the church, but why he has a number
on his forehead I do not know):

> And the second was a little blind spirit, which hath a number upon his
> forehead; and he walketh to and fro continually, and is the chief of the

P

heathen which are the worshippers of fire. He also is of the seed of the prophets, and ministered in the temple while he was yet young; but he went out, and became one of the scoffers. (iii, 22)

By far the most vicious attack, however, was on John Graham Dalyell, a lifelong cripple. The verses that describe him (iii, 36–44) are omitted from the most widely-used reprint of the Chaldee MS.—that of J. F. Ferrier in his edition of *Noctes Ambrosianæ*, 1868—so it may help to explain the furore that followed if I give them here:

36. Now the other beast was a beast which he loved not. A beast of burden which he had in his courts to hew wood and carry water, and to do all manner of unclean things. His face was like unto the face of an ape, and he chattered continually, and his nether parts were uncomely. Nevertheless his thighs were hairy, and the hair was as the shining of a sattin raiment, and he skipped with the branch of a tree in his hand, and he chewed a snail between his teeth.

37. Then said the man, Verily this beast is altogether unprofitable, and whatsoever I have given him to do, that hath he spoiled: he is a sinful thing, and speaketh abominably, his doings are impure, and all people are astonied that he abideth so long within my gates.

38. But if thou lookest upon him and observest his ways, behold he was born of his mother before yet the months were fulfilled, and the substance of a living thing is not in him, and his bones are like the potsherd which is broken against any stone.

39. Therefore my heart pitieth him, and I wish not that he be utterly famished; and I give unto him a little bread and wine that his soul may not faint; and I send him messages unto the towns and villages which are round about; and I give him such work as is meet for him.

40. But if we go forth to the battle, let him not go with us.

41. For behold the griffin hath heretofore wounded him, and the scorpion hath stung him sorely in the hips and the thighs, and also in the face.

42. Moreover the eagle of heaven also is his dread, and he is terrified for the flapping of his huge wings, and for his cry, which is like the voice of an unknown tongue, also his talons, which are sharper than any two edged sword.

43. And if it cometh to pass that he sees them in the battle, he will not stand, but surely turn back and flee.

44. Therefore let us not take him with us, lest he be for an ensample unto the simple ones.

The storm that blew up over the Chaldee Manuscript astonished its originator. "For the love of God open not your mouth about the Chaldee MS," he wrote to a friend who knew his secret. "Deny all knowledge else they say I am ruined if it can by any means be attached--Let all be silence."

Fifteen years later, in the "Memoir" that prefaced his *Altrive Tales* in 1832, Hogg even sought to disclaim any intention of publishing; he had merely, he explained, sent it to Blackwood as a *jeu d'esprit*.

> On first reading it, he never thought of publishing it; but some of the rascals to whom he showed it, after laughing at it, by their own accounts till they were sick, persuaded him, nay almost forced him, to insert it.

Unfortunately, this convenient story can be shown to be untrue. Blackwood must, indeed, often have wished that he had rejected this most notorious of all contributions to "Maga": a general obloquy descended on him, which the anonymous authors escaped, and Dalyell announced his intention of going to law to sue for £5,000 damages. (In the end he was, wisely, satisfied to accept £230 out of court.) So painful was Blackwood's anxiety that, in issuing Volume II (October 1817—March 1818) as a bound volume, he inserted a statement in which he appealed to the public to spare him any further displeasure, and to pay no heed to his opponents:

> The Publisher is aware, that every effort has been used to represent the admission into his Magazine of an article entitled, "A Translation of a Chaldee Manuscript," as an offence worthy of being visited with a punishment that would involve in it his ruin as a Bookseller and Publisher. He is confident, however, that his conduct will not be thought by the Public to merit such a punishment, and to them accordingly he appeals.

The Chaldee Manuscript is now forgotten. Very few, even among professional scholars, have so much as heard of it. And yet it was once capable of setting a great city in an uproar, and of guaranteeing the success of a brilliant magazine. Here, as a specimen, is Hogg's original opening, the first 37 verses of Chapter I, together with the fake 'scholarly' note which introduced it. The marginalia are the work of Wilson's son-in-law, Professor Ferrier.

Translation from an Ancient Chaldee Manuscript: *Blackwood's*, October 1817

THE present age seems destined to witness the recovery of many admirable pieces of writing, which had been supposed to be lost for ever. The Eruditi of Milan are not the only persons who have to boast of being the instruments of these resuscitations. We have been favoured with the following translation of a Chaldee MS. which is preserved in the great Library of Paris (Salle 2d., No. 53, B.A.M.M.), by a gentleman whose attainments in Oriental Learning are well known to the public. It is said that the celebrated Silvester de Sacy is at present occupied with a publication of the original. It will be prefaced by an Inquiry into the Age when it was written, and the name of the writer.

1. And I saw in my dream and behold one like the messenger of a King came toward me from the east, and he took me up and carried me into the midst of the great city that looketh toward the north and toward the east, and ruleth over every people, and kindred, and tongue, that handle the pen of the writer.

1. The city of Edinburgh.

2. And he said unto me, Take heed what thou seest, for great things shall come of it; the moving of a straw shall be as the whirlwind, and the shaking of a reed as the great tempest.

3. And I looked, and behold a man clothed in plain apparel stood in the door of his house: and I saw his name, and the number of his name; and his name was as it had been the colour of ebony, and his number was the number of a maiden, when the days of the years of her virginity have expired.

3. Mr William Blackwood of No. 17 Princes Street.

4. And I turned mine eyes, and behold two beasts came from the land of the borders of the South; and when I saw them I wondered with great admiration.

4. The editors of the first six numbers of *Blackwood's Magazine*.

5. The one beast was like unto a lamb and the other unto a bear; and they had wings on their heads; their faces also like the faces of men, the joints of their legs like the polished cedars of Lebanon, and their feet like the feet of horses preparing to go forth to battle: and they arose and they came onward over the face of the earth, and they touched not the ground as they went.

5. The address of one, the Lamb, was mild and soft; that of the other, the Bear, was quite the reverse. They were both very lame, and went upon crutches.

6. And they came unto the man who was clothed in plain apparel, and stood in the door of his house.

7. And they said unto him, Give us of thy wealth, that we may eat and live, and thou shalt enjoy the fruits of our labours for a time, times, or half a time.

8. And he answered and said unto them, What will you unto me whereunto I may employ you?

9. And the one said, I will teach the people of thy land to till and to sow; to reap the harvest and gather the sheaves into the barn; to feed their flocks, and enrich themselves with the wool.

9. The Bear, who was a great agriculturist, and editor of the *Farmer's Magazine*.

10. And the other said, I will teach the children of thy people to know and discern betwixt right and wrong, the good and the evil, and in all things that relate to learning, and knowledge, and understanding.

10. The Lamb.

11. And they proffered unto him a Book; and they said unto him, Take thou this, and give us a piece of money, that we may eat and drink that our souls may live.

11. They propose to edit a magazine for Mr Blackwood.

12. And we will put words into the Book that shall astonish the children of thy people; and it shall be a light unto thy feet, and a lamp unto thy path; it shall also bring bread to thy household, and a portion to thy maidens.

13. And the man hearkened to their voice, and he took the Book and gave them a piece of money, and they went away rejoicing in heart. And I heard a great noise of many chariots, and of horsemen horsing upon their horses.

13. Who closes with their offer, and their crutches clatter with joy as they retire.

14. But after many days they put no words into the Book; and the man was astonied and waxed wroth, and he said unto them, What is this that you have done unto me, and how shall I answer those to whom I am engaged? And they said, What is this unto us? see thou to that.

14. They belie their promise, and turn out to be a couple of incapables.

15. And the man wist not what for to do; and he called together the friends of his youth, and all those whose heart was as his heart, and he entreated them, and they put words into the Book, and it went forth abroad, and all the world wondered after the Book, and after the two beasts that had put such amazing words into the Book.

15. Mr Blackwood, therefore, gets assistance from more competent friends.

16. Now, in those days there lived also a man who was crafty in counsel, and cunning in all manner of working:

16. Mr Constable, publisher of the *Edinburgh Review*, and the old *Scots Magazine*.

17. And I beheld the man, and he was comely and well-favoured, and he had a notable horn in his forehead wherewith he ruled the nations.

17. The *Edinburgh Review*.

18. And I saw the horn, that it had eyes, and a mouth speaking great things, and it magnified itself even to the Prince of the Host, and it cast down the truth to the ground, and it grew and prospered.

19. And when this man saw the Book, and beheld the things that were in the Book, he was troubled in spirit, and much cast down.

19. Constable's consternation on the appearance of *Blackwood's Magazine*.

20. And he said unto himself, Why stand I idle here, and why do I not bestir myself? Lo! this Book shall become a devouring sword in the hand of mine adversary, and with it will he root up or loosen the horn that is in my forehead, and the hope of my gains shall perish from the face of the earth.

21. And he hated the Book, and the two beasts that had put words into the Book, for he judged according to the reports of men; nevertheless, the man was crafty in counsel, and more cunning than his fellows.

22. And he said unto the two beasts, Come ye and put your trust under the shadow of my wings, and we will destroy the man whose name is as ebony, and his Book.

22. Constable invites the two beasts to come over to his camp.

23. And I will tear it to pieces, and cast it out like dung upon the face of the earth.

24. And we will tread him down as the dust of the streets, and trample him under our feet; and we will break him to pieces, and grind him to powder, and cast him into the brook Kedron.

25. And I will make of you a great name; and I will place you next to the horn that is in my forehead, and it shall be a shelter to you in the day of great adversity; and it shall defend you from the horn of the unicorn, and from the might of the Bulls of Bashan.

25. And to become the editors of his magazine.

26. And you shall be watchers and a guard unto it from the emmet and the spider, and the toad after his kind.

27. And from the mole that walketh in darkness, and from the blow-fly after his kind, and the canker-worm after his kind, and the maggot after his kind.

28. And by these means you shall wax very great, for the things that are low shall be exalted.

29. And the two beasts gave ear unto him; and they came over unto him, and bowed down before him with their faces to the earth.

29. They hearken to his voice.

30. But when the tidings of these things came to the man who was clothed in plain apparel, he was sore dismayed, and his countenance fell.

30. Blackwood is, at first, disheartened.

31. And it repented him that he had taken the Book, or sent it forth abroad: and he said, I have been sore deceived and betrayed; but I will of myself yield up the Book, and burn it with fire, and give its ashes to the winds of heaven.

32. But certain that were there present said unto him, Why art thou dismayed? and why is thy countenance fallen? Go to now; gird up thy loins like a man, and call unto thee thy friends, and the men of thine household, and thou shalt behold and see that they that are for thee are more and mightier than those that be against thee.

32. His friends cheer him up.

33. And when the man whose name was as ebony, and whose number was the number of a maiden, when the days of the years of her virginity have expired, heard this saying, he turned about.

34. And he took from under his girdle a gem of curious workmanship of silver, made by the hand of a cunning artificer, and overlaid within with pure gold; and he took from thence something in colour like unto the dust of the earth, or the ashes that remain of a furnace, and he snuffed it up like the east wind, and returned the gem again into its place.

34. He takes a pinch of snuff.

35. Whereupon he opened his mouth, and he said unto them, As thou hast spoken, so shall it be done.

35. And rallies.

36. Woe unto all them that take part with the man who is crafty in counsel, and with the two beasts!

37. For I will arise and increase my strength, and come upon them like the locust of the desert, to abolish and overwhelm, and to destroy, and to pass over.

[Text from Ferrier's edition of Wilson's "*Works*" (1865), vol. iv, p. 296.]

NOTES

p. 41. *O'Doherty*. A frequent pen-name of Maginn's, and the name under which he figures in the *Noctes Ambrosianæ*.

p. 41. *Balaam-Box*. 'Balaam' was printer's slang for material kept in type in newspaper offices to fill up spaces that were found at the last minutes to be vacant. This material usually concerned freaks of Nature, etc. Ultimately the reference is scriptural (Numbers xxii, xxviii).

p. 46. *Dr Phillpotts*. Henry Phillpotts (1778–1869), who became Bishop of Exeter in 1831, was an acrimonious controversialist on the Tory and anti-Catholic side, who had written a pamphlet defending the action of the government in the Peterloo affair.

p. 47. *Procter*. Procter (1787–1874), a barrister who wrote verse and did a large amount of miscellaneous literary work: a friend of Leigh Hunt, Lamb, and Dickens.

p. 55. *has drawn him inimitably*. The works referred to are Shenstone's *Schoolmistress* (1742) and Goldsmith's *Deserted Village* (1770), ll. 193–216.

p. 61. *Master Silence*. A rustic dotard in Shakespeare's *Henry IV*, Part 2.

p. 61. *Castalian cups*. Castalia, daughter of the river-god Achelous, threw herself into a spring on Mount Parnassus, whose waters were thenceforward supposed to impart poetic inspiration.

p. 61. *Hippocrene*. Another sacred, inspiration-giving spring, struck by the foot of Pegasus from the slopes of Mount Helicon.

p. 71. *Mr Shoemaker Gifford*. Gifford, the son of a glazier, was for a time apprenticed to a shoemaker.

p. 75. *a Pindaric poet of the seventeenth century*. The so-called 'Pindarique' ode was a popular form in the hands of late seventeenth-century poets such as Cowley and Dryden. It owed, in fact, nothing to Pindar (as Congreve pointed out in his *Discourse on the Pindarique Ode* in 1786), but consisted of an arbitrary arrangement of long and short lines, easily leading to bombastic and extravagant writing. It is characteristic of Jeffrey that he condemns the fashion *en bloc*.

p. 88. *Dryden's Ode*. Probably *Alexander's Feast; or, The Power of Musique. An Ode in Honour of St Cecilia's Day* (1697).

p. 92. *Joanna Southcote.* A fanatical self-styled prophetess, who declared in 1802 that she was about to give birth to a spiritual man, Shiloh.

p. 101. *Gardyloo. I.e.* 'gardez l'eau,' the cry of Edinburgh housewives when emptying slops from upper windows.

p. 101. *Dilletanto* [*sic* for *Dillentante*] *Society.* An association of amateurs of the fine arts, founded in 1733 or 1734.

p. 106. *Sir James Mackintosh* (1765–1832). Philosopher and author of many influential works, notably *Dissertation on the Progress of Ethical Philosophy,* 1830.

p. 106. *Mr Gurney.* Joseph Gurney (1804–79), shorthand writer and Biblical scholar, was reporter to the Houses of Parliament from 1849 to 1872.

p. 111. *Vico or Wolfe.* Giovanni Battista Vico (1668–1744) had said about Homer, among other things, that the records of his personal existence were largely mythical; F. A. Wolf (1759–1824) had inaugurated, in his *Prolegomena to Homer* (1795) the controversy as to the multiple authorship of the Homeric poems; the writer, in explaining that it is *not* in deference to them that he calls Homer a disembodied voice, provides a good example of the stylistic vice of useless reference.

p. 132. *the grot of Egeria.* The grove of the Muses, near Rome, where King Numa consulted the nymph Egeria, who was regarded as the goddess of prophecy.

p. 132. *the Palatine.* The chief of the Seven Hills of Rome.

p. 135. *Tales of the Genii* (1764). A celebrated collection of Eastern stories, purporting to be a faithful translation from Persian manuscript sources by "Sir Charles Morell, at one time ambassador from the British settlements in India to the great Mogul," actually the work of James Ridley (1736–65).

p. 136. *"labours and the words move slow."* See Pope, *Essay on Criticism,* ll. 370–371.

p. 163. *Aldrich.* Henry Aldrich (1647–1710), whose short treatise on logic, *Artis Logicae Compendium* (1691), remained a standard textbook until well into the nineteenth century.

p. 165. *Political Justice.* The work of anarchistic political philosophy by William Godwin, 1793. The writer means that the old sage in the poem is probably a portrait of Godwin: actually the chief model was Dr Lind, a physician of Windsor.

p. 171. Δεσμώτης. Prisoner; (as adj.) bound; *i.e.,* the *Prometheus Bound* of Æschylus.

p. 172. *Mῦθος*. Anything delivered by word of mouth, hence 'speech,' etc., but here used in its derived English sense of 'myth.'

p. 183. *Cornelius Webb*. Published a volume of poems, *Lyric Leaves*, in 1832. Keats, writing to Bailey on November 3, 1817, describes him as "Poetaster—who unfortunately was of our Party occasionally at Hampstead and took it into his head to write the following—something about, 'We'll talk on Words-worth Byron—a theme we never tire on;' and so forth till he comes to Hunt and Keats."

p. 185. *Mendelsohn* [*sic* for Mendelssohn]. Moses Mendelssohn (1729–86), Jewish philosopher, friend and collaborator of Lessing.

p. 186. *John Buncle*. A work of that name by Thomas Amory (2 vols., 1756–66), the imaginary autobiography of a man who had seven wives in succession.

p. 186. *The Flower and the Leaf* was an allegorical poem included by error in the earlier editions of Chaucer. The point is that both these are examples of slightly libertine writings on sexual love.

p. 187. *the ball of Dung in the fable*. See Swift, *Brother Protestants* (1733), opening lines:

> An Inundation, says the Fable,
> O'erflow'd a Farmer's Barn and Stable;
> Whole Ricks of Hay and Stacks of Corn,
> Were down the sudden Current born;
> While Things of heterogeneous Kind
> Together float with Tide and Wind;
> The generous Wheat forgot its Pride,
> And sail'd with Litter Side by Side;
> Uniting all, to shew their Amity,
> As in a general Calamity.
> A Ball of new-dropt Horse's Dung,
> Mingling with Apples in the Throng,
> Said to the Pippin, plump, and prim,
> *See, Brother, how we Apples swim.*

The origin of the fable is obscure, but it has been traced back as far as Friedrich Dedekind's *Grobianus* (1549).

p. 187. *the Theseus* [*sic* for *Theseum*]. A Doric temple to the north of the Acropolis at Athens, traditionally supposed to be the shrine of Theseus.

p. 187. *the Torso* (of the Belvedere). A huge fragment of antique statuary, closely studied by Michelangelo, who described himself as a "pupil of the Torso."

p. 188. *Miss Baillie.* Joanna Baillie (1762–1851), a prolific Scottish poetess.

p. 189. *Land of Cockaigne.* A fabulous land of luxury and idleness; the pun on 'Cockney' is the main point of its introduction here.

p. 208. *"gently as if you loved him."* A submerged joke. The reference is to Izaak Walton's instructions (*Compleat Angler*, cap. viii) on how to use a frog for bait.

Put your hook into his mouth . . . and out at his gills, and then with a fine needle and silk sow the upper part of his legg with onely one stitch to the arming wire of your hook, or tie the frogs leg above the upper joynt to the armed wire, and in so doing, use him as though you loved him, that is, harm him as little as you may possibly, that he may live the longer.

p. 211. 'Ειθε λύρη καλή γενοίμην. 'Would that I might become a beautiful lyre.' On the controversy, evidently raging at the time, as to whether this line was written by Anacreon or Alcæus, I cannot comment.

p. 215. *Aristæus.* Son of Apollo and Cyrene, a god or hero regarded as the protector of cattle and fruit-trees. Virgil in the *Georgics* tells of how Aristæus, incurring the wrath of the nymphs, was punished by the death of his bees, and of how he made good the loss.

p. 222. *condottieri.* Mercenary soldiers.

p. 222. *the Ellis's and the Roses.* George Ellis (1753–1815), founded the *Anti-Jacobin* with Canning. He shared Scott's antiquarian interests, publishing in 1805 *Specimens of Early English Romances in Metre.* William Stewart Rose, a minor poet and friend of Scott, is faintly remembered as having translated Ariosto into English verse.

p. 222. *Mr Frere.* John Hookham Frere (1769–1846), a very active satiric author and successful diplomat, was 'lost,' presumably, because at the time the letter was written he was British Minister with the Junta.

A SELECTION OF BOOKS AND
ARTICLES FOR FURTHER READING

Place of publication, unless otherwise stated, is London.

Abbreviations

JEGP: *Journal of English and Germanic Philology.*
MP: *Modern Philology.*
PMLA: *Publications of the Modern Language Association of America.*
PQ: *Philological Quarterly.*
TLS: *Times Literary Supplement.*

General

SAINTSBURY, GEORGE: *A History of Nineteenth Century Literature* (1896) (edition of 1910 consulted).
The Cambridge History of English Literature (1915), vol. xii, chap. vi.
GRAHAM, WALTER: *English Literary Periodicals* (New York, 1930).
COX, R. G.: "The Great Reviews," *Scrutiny,* vol. vi (1937), pp. 2–20, 155–175.
JOYCE, MICHAEL: *Edinburgh, the Golden Age* (1951).

On Specific Periodicals

Edinburgh Review
COPINGER, W. A.: *The Authorship of the First Hundred Numbers of the Edinburgh Review* (Manchester, 1895).

Quarterly Review
SMILES, SAMUEL: *Memoir and correspondence of John Murray* (1891), 2 vols.
Centenary articles in issues for April and July 1909, Nos 419 and 420.
GRAHAM, WALTER: *Tory Criticism in the Quarterly Review, 1809–1853* (1921).

Other Periodicals
ZEITLIN, JACOB: "The Editor of the *London Magazine*," *JEGP,* xx (1921), pp. 328–354.
BLUNDEN, EDMUND (ed.): *Leigh Hunt's 'Examiner' Examined* (1928).
NESBITT, G. L.: *Benthamite Reviewing: Twelve Years of the Westminster Review, 1824–1836* (1934).
THRALL, M. M. H.: *Rebellious Fraser's* (1934).

Individual Critics

Jeffrey
SMITH, D. NICHOL (ed.): *Jeffrey's Literary Criticism* (Oxford, 1910).

GRIEG, J. Y. T.: *Francis Jeffrey of the Edinburgh Review* (Edinburgh, 1948). See also Lockhart's *Life of Scott* (1837–38), Froude's *Life of Carlyle* (1882–84), and Harriet Martineau's *Autobiography* (1877).

Smith
Works (1839–40), 3 vols.
HESELTINE, G. C. (ed.): *The Letters of Peter Plymley, with other selected writings, sermons, and speeches* (1929).
There are a number of semi-popular biographies of Sydney Smith, most of which may be read with profit.

Wilson
Noctes Ambrosianæ, ed. R. S. Mackenzie (1854), 5 vols. (Excludes those contributions which have been identified as not by Wilson.)
Works, ed. J. F. Ferrier (1855–58), 12 vols.
Poetical Works (Edinburgh 1891).
STROUT, ALAN LANG: "John Wilson, 'champion' of Wordsworth," *MP*, xxxi (1934), pp. 383–394.

Lockhart
LANG, ANDREW: *The Life and Letters of John Gibson Lockhart* (1897) 2 vols.
HILDYARD, M. C. (ed.): *Lockhart's Literary Criticism* (Oxford, 1931).

Gifford
LONGAKER, J.: *The Della Cruscans and William Gifford* (Philadelphia, 1924).
CLARK, R. B.: *William Gifford, Tory Satirist, Critic and Editor* (New York, 1930).

Croker
JENNINGS, L. J. (ed.): *The Croker Papers* (1884), 2 vols.
BRIGHTFIELD, M. F.: *John Wilson Croker* (Berkeley, 1940).

Articles Summarizing Useful Information

GRAHAM, WALTER: "Robert Southey as Tory Reviewer," *PQ*, ii (1923), pp. 97–111.
"Contemporary Critics of Coleridge, the Poet," *PMLA*, xxxviii (1923), pp. 278–289.
"Shelley and Leigh Hunt," *PMLA*, xl (1925), pp. 185–192.
WHITE, N. I., and MARSH, G. L.: "Keats and the Periodicals of his time," *MP*, xxxii, 1 (1934), pp. 37–53.
STROUT, ALAN LANG: "James Hogg and 'Maga,'" *TLS*, December 14, 1935, p. 859.
"James Hogg's 'Chaldee Manuscript,'" *PMLA*, lxv (1950), pp. 695–718.